THE BIOLOGY
OF
MUSIC MAKING

Proceedings
of the
1984 Denver Conference

Edited by

Franz L. Roehmann
Frank R. Wilson

THE BIOLOGY
OF MUSIC MAKING

PROCEEDINGS OF THE
1984 DENVER CONFERENCE

Edited by Franz L. Roehmann and Frank R. Wilson

ISBN 0-918812-51-8

TABLE OF CONTENTS

Section IV: In Praise of Musical Instruments

Section V: Panel Discussion

Epilogue 84/Prologue 87

Editors' Preface

An emergent regard for multidisciplinary studies is one of the most significant new forces in higher education, and the phenomenon should surprise no one. From academic planners to the casual observer, it is clear that the life of an advanced society cannot be described, let alone understood, in the terminology of any single, traditionally defined scholarly discipline. Established paradigms which have long served to define and organize formalized thought seem less and less responsive to contemporary intellectual and social problems; the necessary rethinking of traditional academic and administrative structures has not only been acknowledged, but is well underway.

Multidisciplinary inquiry, besides enriching the possibilities for applied problem solving, expands our capacity to ask the right questions. One might even go so far as to suggest that it allows for the formulation of questions different in kind from those generated within the bounds of disciplinary thought. The role of music in human life seems to us an especially appealing candidate for study according to the multidisciplinary paradigm. Where would one find, for example, contemporary, similarly credentialed scientists actively investigating the effects of musical experience on the human nervous system? What existing research institute would commit its resources to a study of the power of music to expand, focus, or otherwise influence human capability? And what of the investigation of musical experience "in the small" — why do humans hear certain musical counterpoints as inversions of the notated original? Do dyslexics process musical information in a way that might help account for their naming and reading difficulties? Where is the single individual or institution sufficiently motivated, qualified, and equipped to undertake studies of such questions? The multidisciplinary paradigm for music not only generates its own questions, but informs and accelerates the process of seeking answers by anticipating the need for artistic, pedagogic, biologic, medical, psychologic, philosophic and sociologic specialists in the planning and conduct of research.

The 1984 Biology of Music Making Conference was conceived and organized to test the notion that music, medicine, and the behavioral and biological sciences are ready to forge a research and educational partnership in order to articulate and confront a set of questions of mutual concern. For five full days, from nine in the morning until well after nine at night, nearly 300 people gathered in Denver to share their thoughts, their work, and their ideas for future collaboration. Nurses, music therapists, high school band teachers, psychiatrists, and dancers found themselves in the same room with neurophysiolgists, chemical and biomechanical engineers, voice coaches, pianists, neurologists, orthopedists — it was a remarkably diverse assemblage. Initially wary of one another, and of the proceedings, the group became so quickly self-amazed and delighted that any doubts about a working relationship, and a long range agenda, were quickly put to rest.

Events in the nearly four years since our first conference have borne out this assessment. A journal, *Medical Problems of Performing Artists* has been founded and has a substantial readership; an annual symposium at the Aspen Music Festival on Medical Problems of Musicians and Dancers will convene for its sixth session this summer; at least ten cities now boast specialty medical programs for performing artists (Boston, New York, Philadelphia, Chicago, Louisville, Houston, Cleveland, Indianapolis, San Francisco and Denver being the most prominent at this writing); the International Arts-Medicine Association, based in Philadelphia, has a large and growing membership; tentatively, at the university level, support grows for multidisciplinary studies involving music. In several cities (Rochester, NY and San Francisco, for example) there are concerted efforts underway to find effective ways for educators, performers, researchers and physicians to plan, finance and conduct projects together. There is reason to be encouraged.

Although the 1988 publication of the proceedings of a 1984 conference might seem to some so tardy as to be pointless, we hold a different view. Having lived at close quarters with much of the activity described above, we are increasingly impressed with the quality and undiminished relevance of the material an exceptional international faculty brought to this conference. These reports remain fresh and important, and we are satisfied that they will add substantially and durably to the dialogue that was in its fledgling stages in July, 1984. All of the contributors have had the opportunity to revise and update their presentations during the past year, and the suggested modifications have been made.

Regrettably, we are unable to produce a complete written record of the conference. A number of the presentations simply did not lend themselves to a document of this kind: cellists Margaret Rowell and Irene Sharp demonstrated their work with two students from the San Francisco Conservatory of Music; Eloise Ristad made stage fright come alive as a force for bringing audience and performer closer together; Milton Babbitt and Roy Pritts played early electronic music from their own archives; Howard Mel, Charles Tobias, Don Lewis and Kurt Rodarmer played for us, and Nancy Spanier's superb dance company danced for us.

Readers of the Proceedings who attended the conference will notice that we have not strictly followed the order of the conference presentations. The explanation for this change is simple: the conference was a conference, and it turns out that the book is a book. We believe the rearrangement creates a stimulating new perspective on this material — it imparts its own *spin*, as it were. It will also be noticed that masses of illustrative material have been omitted. Again, there is a simple explanation: a budget is a budget.

As it stands, this volume contains a only a small fraction of the visual illustrations that were presented, and none of the sound illustrations. Presentations whose clarity was dependent on such material could not be included here. And, for a variety of reasons, other equally worthy presentations had to be omitted. For anyone seriously interested in the unedited record, a complete conference archive exists on both audiocassette and videotape and can be reviewed by special arrangement with The Biology of Music Making, Inc.

The 1984 conference was the first of a planned series of three such gatherings. The second conference, *Music and Child Development*, was held in July, 1987, and a written proceedings is in the editing stage as we go to press with our first volume. The third conference in the series, *Music and Aging*, is planned for the summer of 1990.

Franz L. Roehmann
Golden, Colorado

Frank R. Wilson
Danville, California

June 1, 1988

The Biology of Music Making, Inc., is a non-profix, tax-exempt educational corporation established in 1984 for the purpose of organizing and conducting symposia concerning physical processes in music making. For information concerning programs and publications, contact:

The Biology of Music Making, Inc.
c/o College of Music
University of Colorado at Denver
1200 Larimer Street, Box 162
Denver, CO 80204

Acknowledgments

It is impossible not only to thank individually all those who contributed materially to the success of the 1984 Conference on the Biology of Music Making, but to distinguish clearly those contributions made on behalf of the conference from those made to support publication of these Proceedings. Still, if distinctions are blurred, or if some memories have faded, our sense of gratitude remains strong and clear. We continue to remember with affection and gratitude the many friends who turned Denver into the top of the world in July, 1984. Most especially we thank: Gene M. Nordby and Glendon F. Drake, each of whom, as Chancellor of the University of Colorado, Denver, offered continuing assistance to The Biology of Music Making, and support for publication of the proceedings; Donald R. Seawell, Chairman of the Board, The Denver Center for the Performing Arts, for his great generosity in offering this exceptional facility as host for the conference; Wilbur James Gould, M.D., Director of the Recording and Research Center at the DCPA, for his great kindness in bringing this conference to the Denver Center; Martin J. Wilson, who acted imaginatively, energetically and effectively as the administrative director of the conference; the Henry J. Kaiser Family Foundation and the Yamaha International Corporation (now Yamaha Music Corporation, USA) for substantial financial grants in support of the conference; the IBM Fund for Community Service for grants to support publication of the proceedings; Broadcast Music, Inc., The Selmer Company, and a host of other individual and corporate donors, for additional financial support; the American Music Conference (and especially Tari Marshall, now with the National Association of Parents and Teachers) for invaluable advice and assistance in promotion of the conference; our many friends within the leadership of the Music Teachers National Association and the Music Educators National Conference, for their valued counsel and continuing support; the entire faculty of the conference, who contributed their time and energy both to the conference and to the completion of the proceedings; Bob L. Berschauer and Suzanna Wilson for untold hours of labor and desktop publishing consulting services; and, finally, Pat Wilson, who, though an unofficial editor, is the *official* workhorse and heroine of the publication project.

THE BIOLOGY OF MUSIC MAKING

1984 Conference Faculty

Milton Babbitt
Professor of Music
Princeton University
> *The Electronic Medium, Perception, and Other Mysteries*
> *Composition in the Electronic Medium*

Margaret Ballonoff
Myotherapist
Englewood, CO
> *Panel, Alternative Methods in Performance Problems*

Florence B. Blager, Ph.D.
Associate Professor of Otolaryngology
University of Colorado Health Sciences Center, Denver
> *Panel on Care of the Professional Voice*

Charles O. Brantigan, M.D.
Assistant Clinical Professor of Cardiovascular Surgery
University of Colorado Health Sciences Center, Denver
> *Panel on Music and Medicine*

Oren L. Brown
Voice Faculty
The Juilliard School
> *Techniques for Training and Remediating Voices*

Karl Bruhn
Senior Vice President
Yamaha Music Corporation, USA
> *The Manufacturer of Musical Instruments in the Electronic Age*

John C. M. Brust, M.D.
Director, Department of Neurology
Harlem Hospital Center, New York City
> *Brain Mechanisms in Auditory Perception (Moderator)*

Luiz De Moura Castro
Chairman, Piano Faculty
Hartt School of Music, Bloomfield, CT
Mechanical Problems of Instrumentalists (Moderator)

Michael Johnson-Chase
Alexander Therapist, Movement Learning Resources
Denver, CO
Panel, Alternative Methods in Performance Problems

Diana Deutsch, Ph.D.
Research Psychologist, Department of Psychology
University of California, San Diego
The Perception of Musical Configurations

Robert Efron, M.D.
Director, Neurophysiology and Biophysics Laboratory
University of California, Davis (VAH Martinez)
Brain Function and Musical Experience

Margret Elson
Director, The Center of Artistic Counseling
Oakland, CA
Panel, Alternative Methods in Performance Problems

Leonard J. Essman, M.D.
Tour Physician, New York Philharmonic and
    National Symphony Orchestras
Mamaroneck, NY
Panel on Music and Medicine

Robert Freeman
Director, Eastman School of Music
University of Rochester
Moderator, Panel on Music and Medicine

Rita M. Fuszek
Professor of Music
California State University, Fullerton
Panel on Applications of Research to Pedagogy

Gary S. Gelber, M.D.
Assistant Clinical Professor of Psychiatry
University of California, San Francisco
The Conservatory Experience and Psychological Development

Edna Golandsky
Associate Music Director
Dorothy Taubman School of Piano
Coordinate Motion in Piano Technique

Wilbur J. Gould, M.D.
Director, Voice Recording and Research Laboratory
Denver Center for the Performing Arts
Moderator, Panel on Medical Treatment and Care of Vocalists

Minoru Hirano, M.D.
Professor and Head, Department of Otolaryngology
School of Medicine, Kurame University, Japan
Control Mechanisms in Vocal Performance

Lorin Hollander
Concert Pianist, Lecturer
New York City
The Price of Stress in Education

Bruce W. Jafek, M.D.
Chairman, Department of Otolaryngology
University of Colorado Health Sciences Center, Denver
Panel on Care of the Professional Voice

Leonard B. Jansen, M. Ed.
Assistant to the Director, Department of Computer Services
United States Olympic Committee, Colorado Springs
Moderator: After the Musician with Computer and Camera

Tedd Judd, Ph.D.
Neuropsychologist
Pacific Medical Center, Seattle
A Neuropsychologist Looks at Musical Behavior

Michael Kasha, Ph.D.
Director, Institute of Molecular Biophysics
Florida State University, Talahassee
Science, Art, and a Box with the Sound You Dream About

Paul Lehrer, Ph.D.
Associate Professor of Psychiatry
University of Medicine and Dentistry of New Jersey
Research on the Causes and Cures of Performance Anxiety: A Review

William R. LeVine, M.D.
Professor of Psychiatry
The University of Kansas School of Medicine, Wichita
Biofeedback in Violin and Viola Pedagogy
The Treatment of Severe Muscle Spasms with Biofeedback

Don Lewis
Electronic Musical Instrument Design Consultant
Pleasanton, CA
The Musician in the World of Electronics (Synthesizer Performance)

Elizabeth Jones
Director of Instruction, Music Education Divison
Yamaha Music Corporation, USA
Panel on Applications of Research to Pedagogy

John C. Mazziotta, M.D., Ph.D.
Assistant Professor of Neurology
UCLA School of Medicine
Positron Emission Tomography: Brain Metabolism in Auditory
and Automatic Motor Behavior

Frank F. McGinnis
Professor of Music
California State University, Northridge
Panel on Alternative Approaches to Performance Problems

Howard Mel, Ph.D.
Professor of Biophysics
University of California, Berkeley
Unraveling the French Horn and Shrinking the Violin

Robert F. Miller, Ph.D.
Associate Professor of Music Education
University of Connecticut
Panel on Applications of Research to Pedagogy

Robert Moog, Ph.D.
Electronic Instrument Designer and Engineer
Leicester, N.C.
The Instrument Designer in Electronic Music

George P. Moore, Ph.D.
Professor of Biomedical Engineering
University of Southern California
The Study of Skilled Performance in Musicians

Helen Myers, Ph.D.
Associate Editor for Ethnomusicology
The New Grove Dictionary, London
In Praise of Musical Instruments

Jonathan Newmark, M.D.
Neurologist and Director, Performing Arts Medicine
University of Louisville
Hand Difficulties Among Musicians: The MGH Experience

Peter F. Ostwald, M.D.
Professor of Psychiatry
University of California, San Francisco
Robert Schumann and His Doctors: A Case Study of Music and Medicine

H. David Prensky, D.D.S.
Consultant on Dentistry for Musicians
West Palm Beach, FL
The Other Set of Ivories: A Dentist Looks at Musicians

Roy A. Pritts
Associate Professor and Acting Dean, College of Music
University of Colorado, Denver
Music and Musicians in a Technologic World (Introduction)

Rudolph A. Pyka, M.D.
Orthopedic and Hand Surgery
Redlands, CA
    Panel on Music and Medicine

Lorraine A. Ramig, Ph.D.
Assistant Professor, Communication Disorders and Speech Science
University of Colorado, Boulder
    Vocal Aspects of Neurologic Disorders

Bonnie Raphael, Ph.D.
Research Associate
Denver Center for the Performing Arts
    Panel on Care of the Professional Voice

Mark Reese
Feldenkrais Therapist
Encinitas, CA
    Panel, Alternative Methods in Performance Problems

Joel Revzen
Dean
St. Louis Conservatory of Music
    Moderator: The Human Side of the Musical Career

Eloise Ristad (Deceased)
Author, *A Soprano on Her Head*
    The Performer Within: Diary of a Workshop

Joseph Robinson
Principal Oboe
New York Philharmonic Orchestra
    The Oboe is a Wind Instrument

Kurt Rodarmer
Guitarist
Woodstock, NY
    Performer (Demonstration of the Kasha Guitar)

Franz L. Roehmann, Ph.D.
Professor of Music
University of Colorado, Denver
Panel on Alternative Methods to Performance Problems

David B. Roos, M.D.
Vascular and Thoracic Surgery
Denver, Colorado
Anatomy of the Upper Extremity

Elliott D. Ross, M.D.
Associate Professor of Neurology and Psychiatry
The University of Texas Health Science Center at Dallas
Music and the Neurology of Language and Emotions

Margaret Rowell
Lecturer, Department of Music
University of California, Berkeley
Playing From The Inside Out

Ronald Scherer, Ph.D.
Research Scientist, Recording and Research Center
Denver Center for the Performing Arts
Panel on Care of the Professional Voice

Stuart A. Schneck, M.D.
Professor of Neurology
University of Colorado School of Medicine
Music and the Brain: The Neurology of Musical Behavior (Introduction)

Gerald I. Shapiro, D.M.D.
Consultant on Dentistry for Musicians
Delray, FL
Panel on Music and Medicine

Irene Sharp
Instructor in Cello
San Francisco Conservatory of Music
Playing from the Inside Out

Donald J. Shetler, Ed.D.
Professor of Music Education, Eastman School of Music
University of Rochester
Panel, Research Goals and Methodology in Music Performance

Ivan A. Shulman, M.D.
Tour Physician
Los Angeles Philharmonic Orchestra
On the Road with the LA Phil: Rigors of the Musical Career

Nancy Spanier
Artistic Director
Nancy Spanier Dance Theatre of Colorado
Movement in Song and Dance

Dorothy Taubman
Founder
Dorothy Taubman Institute of Piano
A Teacher's Perspective on Musicians' Injuries

Frederick Tims, Ph.D., R.M.T.
Past President
National Association for Music Therapy
Panel on Music and Medicine

Ingo R. Titze, Ph.D.
Associate Professor, Speech Pathology and Audiology
University of Iowa
Biomechanics of Vocal Performance

Charles Tobias, Ph.D.
Professor of Chemical Engineering
University of California, Berkeley
Unraveling the French Horn and Shrinking the Violin

Bo Tomlyn
Music Clinician
Yamaha Music Corporation, USA
The Musician in the World of Electronics (Synthesizer performance)

Ernest M. Urvater, Ph.D.
President, JTJ Films
Amherst, MA
Science, Art and Pedagogy: The Work of Dorothy Taubman

Dr. Christoph Wagner
Professor of Physiology of Music, Hochschule für Musik und Theater,
  Hannover, West Germany
Success and Failure in Music: Biomechanics of the Hand

Frank R. Wilson, M.D.
Assistant Clinical Professor of Neurology
University of California, San Franciso
Brain Mechanisms in Highly Skilled Movements

Dr. Helga Ulsamer Winold
Associate Professor of Music
Indiana University
High-Speed Photography of Cello Playing

Raymond P. Wood II, M.D.
Vice Chairman, Department of Otolaryngology
University of Colorado Health Sciences Center, Denver
Panel on Care of the Professional Voice

Dolores Zupan
President
Music Teachers National Association
Moderator, Panel on Applications of Research to Pedagogy

Section I

The Human Side
of the Musical Career

THE HUMAN SIDE OF THE MUSICAL CAREER

Moderator: Joel Revzen
Dean, St. Louis Conservatory of Music[1]

Good afternoon. It is really quite an honor to have been invited to preside as moderator for this afternoon's session, "The Human Side of the Musical Career." Having graduated from the Juilliard School, taught at New York State University and the Aspen Music Festival, and now as Dean of the St. Louis Conservatory of Music, I have become increasingly aware of the critical need for a healthy psychologic environment at the institutions which train our future musical artists. I have seen in many students an inability to separate success in music performance from their self-concept as human beings, particularly among students who achieved high parental recognition and praise for their musical skill during their formative years. It is no small wonder that, as many of these children grew up and the standards of music performance grew increasingly more difficult for them, there developed a fusion between self-concept and performance which resulted in considerable anxiety. I believe, therefore, that it is imperative that our nation's conservatories nurture and train the talented artists of the future while simultaneously maintaining understanding, compassion, and care for those often anxious human beings who come to us for help in realizing their dreams.

Music is an intensely human experience, as well as an aural art. It is, therefore, most appropriate for physicians who deal with the physiologic aspects of man and psychiatrists who deal with the psychologic aspects of man, to concern themselves with musicians who call upon both physiologic and psychologic strength to bring a resonating beauty into the world. We gather at this conference to share and explore greater means of bringing the physical, psychologic, and musical spirit into closer working harmony.

With us today is Dr. Gary Gelber, who will speak about the conservatory experience and its associated psychologic development. Dr. Gelber practices adult and child psychiatry in San Francisco and teaches at the University of California School of Medicine. Prior to receiving a Bachelors degree at Yale,

---

1.   Mr. Revzen is now Assistant Conductor of the St. Paul Chamber Orchestra — *Eds.*

he studied clarinet at both Peabody and Juilliard. Dr. Gelber has been a soloist with the Atlanta Symphony and has performed in chamber music concerts at the Tanglewood Festival.

The second speaker this afternoon will be Dr. Peter Ostwald. He will discuss the positive and negative interactions between musicians and doctors using as a case study the composer, Robert Schumann, about whom he has written a book. Dr. Ostwald is Professor of Psychiatry and director of a specialty clinic at the University of California Medical Center, San Francisco, for the treatment of musicians and other performing artists. He has written several books on the relationship of emotion and sound, and has dealt extensively with the medical problems of musicians. Dr. Ostwald continues to involve himself in his own music making as a violinist.

Our third speaker will be Dr. Ivan Shulman. He will speak about the need for greater awareness of the special medical needs of musicians based on his experience as tour physician of the Los Angeles Philharmonic. Dr. Shulman is an oboist who has performed with the Los Angeles Philharmonic, at the Aspen Festival, and with the Los Angeles Doctor's Symphony Orchestra, of which, I believe, he is the Chairman of the Board.

Following our break this afternoon, Dr. Paul Lehrer, Associate Professor of Psychiatry at Rutgers Medical School and a founding member of the International Society for the Study of Tension in Performance, will speak about the literature which describes the causes and cures of performance anxiety.

Our final speaker this afternoon is the world-renowned concert pianist, Lorin Hollander. Mr. Hollander began his career at the age of eleven, and has appeared with virtually every major orchestra in the world, as well as on television and radio. He has recently been lecturing on the interrelationship of musical, psychologic, and creative processes. Today he will focus on the price of stress in education. I think it significant that all of these musicians and physicians gather to share a common concern for the stress in music performance among today's artists.

PSYCHOLOGICAL DEVELOPMENT OF THE CONSERVATORY STUDENT

Gary S. Gelber
Assistant Clinical Professor of Psychiatry
University of California, San Francisco

I would like to discuss today certain aspects of psychological development during some of the formative stages of a musical career. First, I will comment on the pre-conservatory period and the relationship between the music student and his or her parents. Next I will discuss some of the challenges of conservatory life and the student's complex reactions to the major instrument teacher. Then I will speak about the musician's desire to play technically perfect concerts. I will close my discussion with a few remarks about musical workaholism.

A musical career is not just any career. Becoming a musician differs from the ways students enter most other careers in the United States. The British philosopher and mathematician, Alfred North Whitehead, divided the evolution of careers into three major phases:

1. An inspiration period, which we can call the phase of Romance.

2. A phase of training and hard work.

3. A final stage of wisdom, when a person generalizes and abstracts from his or her years of experience.

Many of the musicians I have seen in treatment, and many of those I have known and played with as a musician, had such an intense interest in music while growing up that they were not inclined to become involved in many other pursuits. Whitehead's Romance phase, in musicians, can be colossal in its dimensions and may continue for many years.

The second phase, the training period, usually occurs earlier in the lives of musicians than in other careers. Training may begin before the fifth or sixth birthday and, at some point, becomes rigorous and time consuming. The music student who wants to have a music career may have fewer hours in his day than many of his peers to devote to academic, athletic, and social interests.

Music has a tremendous power to captivate people. Music students respond to its magnetism by putting enormous amounts of energy into practicing. During adolescence they may have an almost inexhaustable supply of energy to devote to their music. Their playing provides the opportunity to express their emotional strivings and longings. By practicing and gaining mastery over music, the music student develops the feeling that he has control over himself and even over his emotional urges. Thomas Mann captured this sense of control in his story, *The Infant Prodigy*, when he described the prodigy's thoughts as he was about to begin his piano recital: "This was the realm of music that lay before him. It lay spread out like an inviting ocean, where he might plunge in and blissfully swim, where he might let himself be borne and carried away, where he might go under in night and storm, yet keep the mastery and control...." Because music provides an oasis of control during a period when there is a need for control, music becomes even more important for the teenager.

Music seizes the energies of its devotees to a degree which may constrain them in other important areas of development. Music can provide much, yet it can take away, too. Musicians can be relatively unsocial and may be less social than other artists such as writers and painters. The after-five work schedule of symphony musicians may continue to inhibit the development of social relationships throughout a professional career.

Musical training may therefore be different from other fields because its first two phases tend to be precocious and intense. Musical training provides controls, organization, and inspiration and offers the illusion of a safe port in which to sink an anchor. It is so engrossing that it may constrict the adolescent's development and be anything but a safe port.

The Music Student's Relationship with His Parents During Adolescence

During adolescence, many of the intense feelings that would be very difficult to express toward one's parents are expressed through music. I think that music can actually begin to substitute for a person's bond with his parents. It is often too difficult for the adolescent to talk about the true feelings he has for his parents. These feelings are sometimes contradictory or unpleasant because they are critical of the parents. Adolescents also feel the need to suppress feelings of longing and dependency toward parents. Using music, teenagers can play out, and even "listen out" these otherwise forbidden feelings.

Pre-teenagers in particular use music to express unconscious feelings toward parents and siblings. As the young musician grows into the teen years, the emotions expressed through music tend to shift in their unconscious and conscious aims toward people outside the family. The teen dethrones the parents and forms new relationships with musical heroes — for example, relationships with music teachers and relationships from a distance with performing and recording artists. We all know about the crushes that teens may have on rock music stars.

The childhood idealizations of parents may be displaced onto composers. For example, a patient told me that when she was 15 years old, she dreamed that she had met Tchaikovsky. She realized in her dream that she had encountered an "infinitely understanding man, ... a fellow sufferer. He was a truly gifted musician and had all the musical taste which Dad lacked so badly." This young woman, whom I'll call Janet, felt that her father was lacking in many ways. "He did not understand me." But she could easily imagine the profound understanding and solace which Tchaikovsky could provide. She was striving to find a more acceptable man than she felt her father to be, and her musical hero allowed her to imagine that she had found one. Tchaikovsky also gave her hope that she could find such a man in real life, and that he would probably be a musician. Janet had thus displaced important needs from her relationship with her father onto music and, in this instance, onto a composer who was safe and could talk only through the medium of his marvelous musical compositions.

Musical heroes can also provide the adolescent with models for building a sense of identity. When a teen identifies strongly with a composer, the teen often identifies with someone who has suffered a great deal. This identification may be useful in certain instances. It can be a realistic preparation for a life that some musicians will face as adults, especially if they become composers who do not have regular employment.

Music may provide an aesthetic or emotional experience which can displace the parents' central place in the life of a teenager. It can also rescue the teen who is alienated from parents and/or peers. On the other hand, music can constrict the individual inordinately, as occurred with a violist in his fifties who used music as a means of experiencing love and warmth. He felt that he had not been appreciated or loved by his mother when he was a child. He rarely saw his divorced father. Music became the major focus of his childhood strivings. He put little effort into cultivating friendships. In a certain sense, music was too accessible for him, too easy to use as a refuge from life's frustrations. Even though music provided a necessary form of emotional stimulation, expansion, and growth, it also provided an easy escape. He was less motivated to overcome the frustrations of peer interactions and academic challenges. As he grew older, he continued his singular focus on music and remained limited in his social and academic development.

Challenges of Conservatory Life

I would like to discuss some of the special issues that arise when the student leaves home and goes to a conservatory. First, I'd like to compare the experience of the conservatory student with a college student for a moment. When the first year conservatory student arrives at his music school, he will often find himself living on his own in a big city, rather than in a college dormitory. College students, by contrast, often live on a campus, a protected island with its grassy areas and expansive plazas.

Collegiate school spirit, and the self-vaunting rivalries with other schools, show us the extent to which adolescent students need to set themselves apart from their peers at other universities and establish an illusion of supremacy.

The conservatory student is training for a career in a society that generally cares little for musical careers. Therefore, the music student's self-esteem may need even more strengthening than that of a college student, who may be entering a mainstream career. To accomplish this strengthening, conservatories need to maximize student contact with each other (a Juilliard graduate told me that he learned more from fellow students than from the faculty).

Because of the exposure to a variety of subjects in a liberal arts curriculum, college students have a greater range of career choices. Moreover, they make their choices at a later age than conservatory students, when they have a better sense of their own capabilities. If they do decide to change careers, they will often have the background to make the transition more easily. This situation contrasts with the conservatory student who makes his choice early, has little knowledge of the ways of the world, and probably possesses little formal, general education beyond the high school level.

Gary Gelber

Conservatories also differ in another respect. In the two conservatories I attended, there were many more homosexuals than were apparent in any other educational setting in which I have ever been. Not only were there more gay students, but important teaching and administrative positions were occupied by gays. They were an important part of the conservatory's power structure. This situation calls for adaptations on the part of the heterosexual student that are not always necessary in other career choices. Some heterosexuals will flee into an exaggerated machismo that could most easily be seen in the "jazz clique" when I was a student. On the other hand, some heterosexuals are able to deal with homophobic feelings and learn to accept their own inherent and previously warded off identification with the opposite sex.

The Major Instrument Teacher

The music student often arrives at the conservatory after leaving parents, siblings, friends, and former hometown music teachers. If the student quests after parent surrogates at the conservatory, the major instrument teacher is likely to be the first choice.

In my experience, the major instrument teacher is much more personable than professors in a college or university. The one-to-one contact for at least one hour per week is more intense than the contacts a student typically has in college with professors. Significant bonds usually form with the teacher. The teacher's influence on the student may also be greater than most college professors have with their students.

The importance of the major instrument teacher is so great that if the match between teacher and student is not good, the entire conservatory experience may be compromised. The student's reactions to the teacher are based on the teacher's qualities as a musician and artist, but the teacher can also become a transference object for the student. The student transfers or displaces onto the teacher wishes, longings, hopes, disappointments, resentments, and a myriad of other feelings originally felt toward the parents. Some students handle these feelings in ways that don't interfere with progress. Others get so tied in knots that they don't listen, or can't listen, to their teachers.

For example, Lenore was a gifted violinist who had entered a conservatory when she was sixteen. Her violin playing had earned her praise from prominent local violinists as well as a scholarship at the conservatory. She was gifted in areas other than music, having graduated first in her class from a competitive private high school in San Francisco. When she returned to San Francisco during Christmas break of her first year of conservatory work, she came back into therapy briefly and reported that she was having a great deal of difficulty with her violin teacher at the conservatory. He had told her that her previous training was "spotty" and even "incorrect," and he criticized her for not playing with emotion. She and I did not have enough time to explore things any further until summer vacation. By then she was so discouraged that she was thinking about leaving music. What I learned was that her teacher, whom I'll call Mr. Sforzando, was not only a rigorous teacher, but appeared condemnatory. For example, if Lenore played a piece that he found objectionable, he would order her out of the room, thus ending the lesson.

How did Lenore get herself into this situation? There are musical reasons as well as complex psychological reasons. I would like to supply a few of the psychological reasons. On closer study of Lenore's background, it turned out that Sforzando's hypercritical attitudes were already familiar to her. Her father was a very critical, overbearing individual. He had outbreaks of intense anger at Lenore as well as at her mother.

Lenore, like many individuals, had a tendency to repeat the difficulties of her family life in her relationships with people outside her family. She had an automatic, unthinking tendency to attach herself to people, especially men, who had the same stern, exigent characteristics of her father. Therefore, when Lenore arrived at the conservatory, she chose her martinet teacher, even though she knew that he had the reputation of being very severe, and even though she knew that other fine teachers were available. Furthermore, she had the unfortunate characteristic of remaining attached; she felt too guilty to leave Sforzando.

I was on the East Coast that summer and phoned Sforzando. He told me that he felt Lenore was very talented and had an excellent musical ear. He said that she remembered everything like a tape recorder, but that she was too cocky about her capabilities. Her family seemed to have brought her up thinking that she was a genius, and Sforzando felt it necessary to attack this notion. He did this by putting her in her place. He commented, "She doesn't express her emotions when she plays. It's always a power struggle with her. Everything goes through her brain. The only way to get to her is through her ego, by criticizing her. You improve things through criticism, don't you? Even in the best of situations, you can only get her to imitate, but you can never get her to play with her own feelings."

I recommended to Sforzando, as tactfully as I could, that he be less critical and more complimentary to her. We spoke for over an hour, and he said he would. The situation improved the next fall, but then some of the old problems returned. Lenore finally changed to another teacher.

Sforzando may have been correct about Lenore's not bringing enough emotion to her playing. She was a bit stiff and awkward and had difficulty expressing feelings while playing, similar to the difficulty she had expressing her feelings in her psychotherapy. On the other hand, Sforzando had a strong inhibiting effect on her.

Lenore contributed in some measure to the situation by choosing a man such as Sforzando and by not attempting to leave him at the end of her first year. Her father transference onto Sforzando caused her to feel tense and to resist what he did have to offer.

There are, of course, other issues that enter into the complex teacher-student relationship. Janet, the young woman who dreamed she met Tchaikovsky, was a 21 year old pianist who came into treatment on an emergency basis two days before her senior recital. She feared that she would not be able to play because of feelings of panic. I gave her propranolol to help with the acute situation, and after the recital, which went well, we began work.

Janet began studying the piano when she was nine. From the start, her father liked her piano playing very much. He was an engineering consultant who spent almost all of his time working. Janet was able to win his attention during his rare free moments better than her brother, and even better than her mother. He told Janet that she was his only friend. She adored her increasingly long talks with him.

As she advanced in her playing she saw that her father favored sentimental music. He let her know that he wanted her to play waltzes by Johann Strauss and selections of Gershwin's music. She began to realize that his taste in music was lacking and she did not want to play this type of music. As she grew older, the conflict became more pronounced. He did not attend her recitals, apparently because he did not like the music she played. She felt trapped by her father; he wanted her to be his "sweet little girl" of childhood, playing Gershwin, and she felt she could not get out of his trap.

She also felt trapped by her conservatory teacher. Janet had experienced difficulty with her piano teachers at the conservatory and had changed teachers once before beginning therapy. Her piano teacher at this time was a very understanding and flexible person. In fact, she began having trouble with him when he showed her that he was personally concerned about her. When he showed his concern, she stopped working hard for her lessons, a seemingly paradoxical reaction. She began to feel trapped again by music.

Her teacher's well-meaning suggestions were distorted by the channel of her neurosis. His suggestions were warped to the extent that she felt he was pressuring her and, in a sense, luring her into a trap. For example, one day during therapy she told me about a recent dream in which her teacher was hugging her and wanted to seduce her. The fantasies she had in association with the dream suggested that she both desired and feared his seduction. She also revealed that while growing up she both feared and desired to be seduced by her father. It appears that Janet's need to reject her kindly teacher was influenced by her old need to distance herself from her father, with whom her relationship had been too sexually suggestive. The threat of an imagined incestuous closeness with her father contributed to Janet's compulsion to distance herself from her teacher.

It is hard to imagine a teacher finding his way unaided through Janet's defensive labyrinth. There is no formula that applies to all students, because students bring to their studies a great psychological diversity. After two years of psychotherapy, Janet began to function well and is now employed as a musician.

I would like to recommend a few changes to conservatories. Conservatories should try to make mental health facilities available for their students, preferably with therapists who are familiar with musical performance and musical careers. We all know how important it is that a single teacher shape and help students grow musically. Nevertheless, consideration should be given to offering a switch of the major teacher to some students who feel they cannot do well with their teacher. The conservatory's administration is in the best position to evaluate the chemistry of a student-teacher mix, and the violin player I spoke of (Lenore) needed help in making a switch. The recommendation for a change could be made by the teacher, by the chamber music teacher, by the dean, or by the student. The focus of concern, though, must be on the student. Rivalries between teachers should be handled in ways that promote cooperation and student growth. For example, master classes or repertoire classes could involve the combined students of different teachers while having all the teachers present with revolving leadership. The teachers could stay away from touchy issues and focus on elements of style, expression, and interpretation. There are probably more areas of compatibility among the teachers than they might expect. Each teacher has areas of strength and specialization.

Are Some Teachers Truly Unique?

Because the major instrument teacher is so important to the student's conservatory experience, I would like to consider a few additional aspects of the teacher's role. Even when the student is studying with a master teacher, the student, at a certain point in his development, must have freedom in his musical expression. The teacher needs to put limits on the student in order for the student to develop a good technique. But in terms of the musical or expressive style, the outcome should be an extension of the student's emotional and even physiologic makeup.

When I was a conservatory student, I noticed that some of the well known teachers had the attitude that their aproach was the only valid one. The student, who is searching for certainty, may come to believe there is only one path to musical enlightenment.

Rival teachers, in conservatories as well as in other schools and organizations, are sometimes prone to develop a sort of paranoia, in which they overestimate the worth of their own approach and tend to reject the possible contributions of their rivals.

Do some music teachers have something essential or unique to teach? I believe that there are teachers who do have something quite unique to teach. I am most familiar with this phenomenon in teachers who have brought a tradition from elsewhere to a place where that tradition did not formerly exist. For example, earlier in this century, the oboist Marcel Tabuteau and the clarinetist Ralph McLane brought from France unique approaches and artistic ideals to their teaching at the Curtis Institute of Music. Their impact on future generations was profound. The same may be true with other instruments. The influence of the violinists taught by Leopold Auer and other musicians who came out of the Russian school was very great. Joseph Fuchs and Franz Letz helped to spread the Austrian and German influence. *Nul n'est prophete en son pays.* I don't know if these great teachers would have been prophets in their own countries, but they certainly were in the United States. There may still be prophets, those master teachers who have an approach which is truly unique or special.

The Emphasis on Technical Perfection During Performances

As students develop more competence in music, they may strive for technical perfection in their performances. Why do students and some performing musicians feel pressured to attain a perfect performance? Here are a few of my suppositions:

1. An overemphasis on technique may reflect the exuberant tendency of youth to show off. For some students, a flashy technique is the equivalent of physical strength. Flying fingers, pounding hands, death defying leaps, and incredible cadenzas are proof of having what it takes to become an accomplished and brave adult.

2. There may be a wish to recreate the gleam of love from a parent's eyes: "Look Mom, I'm playing 16th note double octaves." Admiration of this sort is displaced from the parents and then sought from the teacher, peers, and later, the audience.

3. As students develop, they may overemphasize technique because it makes them feel protected from criticism. It is difficult for them to protect themselves from both the Apollonians who want the peformance to have a well ordered, rational approach, and at the same time from the Dionysians who want the performance to be very expressive and creative. A perfect technique may create the illusion of protection from this conflict in musical expression.

4. A musician's style of self-discipline is often reminiscent of the parents' method of discipline. If the parents were strict, the musician will often be strict. The parents may have withheld love to push their child to greater efforts. If the music teacher is also very strict, then the parent's pattern is reinforced and the young musician may emphasize technical perfection even more.

5. A strict pattern of discipline is further reinforced by the perfomer thinking that the last one percent of effort

Gary Gelber

spent on refining and polishing a piece can turn a so-so performance into a really good one. The margin of error seems so small in music that a certain amount of perfectionism is mandatory.

6. The desire to emulate great musicians can also motivate students to overemphasize technique. The student may base an imitation on recordings made by musicians he or she admires. But recordings create artificial standards for live musical performance and thus lead to added stress and performance anxiety.

7. Technique is the only aspect of music that can be quantified. For example, fast metronome markings and tempos can be vaunted by the proud student. I've heard young performers bragging about how little time it took them to play a fast movement, somewhat the way a race car driver might boast about how quickly he completed the Indianapolis 500 race. Also, mistakes in a piece can be counted. A student who can play faster, sing higher or lower, and do so with fewer errors may feel he or she has true musical machismo.

8. Teachers and conservatories may believe that their students' technical achievements are proof of their own excellence in the pedagogic enterprise and, therefore, they may push their students inordinately. Students who comply with these expectations may develop even more intense rivalries with other students. Some students enjoy hearing the mistakes of others during lessons and performances.

9. Lastly, musical competitions contribute to the tendency to be a technical pefectionist.

Musical Workaholism

I would like to close by discussing whether conservatory students should be encouraged to become more well-rounded in nonmusical areas. Workaholism can produce individuals in fields other than music who are one dimensional and who lead monotonous lives. Being on a work treadmill can result in reduced creativity and a loss of the ability to enjoy life. Why would workaholism fail to produce the same result in musicians?

The president of one of the best conservatories said that one-third of his student body dropped out before graduation. I think that the drop-out rate from musical careers after graduation is high as well. To prevent this high drop-out rate, it is important that music students receive an education sufficiently broad to allow them to land on their feet if they work outside of music at some point in their lives. They should not have to work as waiters and waitresses after graduation.

Some of the dissatisfaction with musical careers is captured in an anecdote quoted by Tom Hall in a recent issue of *Senza Sordino:* "(A symphony orchestra musician), spotting a young student carrying a violin case down the street, called out, 'Turn back before it's too late!'"

A friend of mine who plays in a major orchestra with one of the best pay scales in the country told me that he estimates that one-half of the musicians in his orchestra are engaged in non-musical work. Why? They do it because they cannot earn all they wish from their orchestra salaries, or because they are frightened about the economic future. Excellent symphony orchestra musicians have told me that they wanted to find work in another field or that they wanted to change careers.

Understandably, the primary role of conservatories is not to educate students for work outside of music. Since it is not unusual for two hundred and fifty musicians to audition for a single vacancy in a symphony orchestra, these musicians must be extremely well prepared by the conservatory. Still, I believe that there is a restrictive process which can begin early in training and may continue at the conservatory. For example, some students at a well known conservatory asked for permission to take some courses at a nearby university. The administration's response was, "Why would you want to take courses there? We have academic courses here." This response reflects a parochial attitude which is all too common. I believe that the conservatory education is too narrow. Students can develop sufficient musical skills even if they study other fields. Artistry derives in some measure from a broad experience of life.

In summary, I have tried to show some of the ways that a musical career is different from other careers. The differences arise because of the relative intensity of the stages of Romance and hard work as outlined by Whitehead. The differences became more apparent in contrasting conservatory life with life on the college campus.

This presentation began with a discussion of how music may function as a vehicle for unspoken passions towards a student's parents during the pre-conservatory years. Identifications with musicians, including identifications with composers, aid the unfolding of relationships away from the parents in later adolescence. Music helps organize the student by providing a sense of control, yet music and music conservatories can contribute to a process of personality and career constriction.

The major teacher in the conservatory is often the object of the student's psychological transferences. Although some of the student's teachers may have unique things to teach, the student should also be encouraged to develop his or her own style. I attempted to explain some of the reasons that musicians strive to play technically perfect performances. Perfectionism can help, but may also compromise, the development of a personal and musical self-concept.

Lastly, musical workaholism constricts the adaptability of the student, and the mature musician, as well.

For some students music is like a golden ladder towards nothingness. If conservatories could provide a better liberal arts curriculum and courses in practical subjects, they might produce more adaptable and happier musicians.

References

Thomas Mann, "The Infant Prodigy." In *Stories of Three Decades*. Translated by H. T. Lowe-Porter, New York: Alfred A. Knopf, 1936.

Senza Sordino, 22(5):June, 1984.

ROBERT SCHUMANN AND HIS DOCTORS:
A CASE STUDY OF MUSIC AND MEDICINE

Peter F. Ostwald
Professor of Psychiatry
University of California, San Francisco

It is a great pleasure and privilege to be here at this unique conference. Unique, I think, in a way that was anticipated by the Greeks who assigned the same god, Apollo, to both music and medicine. It is also a great pleasure to be able to talk about one of my favorite patients, Robert Schumann. I don't have to be afraid of betraying confidentiality, as I would by talking about a patient I'm seeing today, nor do I have to worry about malpractice. In this case all the harm and, of course, the good, too, was done by other physicians.

We think of Schumann as one of the pivotal figures of the 19th Century. Schumann was born in 1810 and died in 1856. He was a man of genius, a contemporary of Mendelssohn, Liszt, and Chopin, who forged a link between the early romanticism of Weber, Beethoven, and Schubert and the late romanticism of Brahms, Wagner, and Richard Strauss. Schumann was also a very influential music critic and, of course, he was the husband of Europe's greatest woman pianist, Clara Schumann. Alas, we also know him as a sick man who spent the last two years of his life in a hospital.

Schumann had many illnesses. Allow me to recall the ones we know or suspect he had. As a child Schumann had an anxiety disorder that interfered with his school adjustment and led to a certain reclusiveness and social withdrawal. When he was a teen-ager, he developed a depressive disorder after his sister committed suicide and his father died. He continued to have depressive episodes for the rest of his life. Schumann also had a number of serious infectious diseases. He came down with malaria in his early twenties, and he may have had malarial meningitis. Tuberculosis was rampant in his family, and he probably was infected with this condition. It has been rumored that Schumann had syphilis, which is a moot point. I've reviewed every scrap of medical information available and find the evidence for syphilis quite unconvincing. However, Schumann did have some embarrassing sexual problems which several of his doctors knew about. He also had what he himself called a hypochondriacal lifestyle, worrying incessantly about his health and making meticulous notes each day about his aches and pains. He had, as you know, a disorder of the right hand which interfered with his success as a pianist. He may have had high blood pressure which kept him out of military service. He probably had migraine attacks and Meniere's disease, leading to headaches, dizziness, and ringing in his ears. He had hemorrhoids and muscle pains. Finally, when in his forties, Schumann had a psychotic tendency which expressed itself in very frightening dissociative states and in a paranoid psychosis with auditory hallucinations. It is this which led to his hospitalization.

One of the first attempts to deal with Schumann scientifically was made by the British psychiatrist, Elliot Slater, who prepared a chart of Schumann's life. It shows two great episodes of creativity. It is interesting to observe how the creative impulse expressed itself in Schumann's life beginning at age nineteen, gradually building up to a great output of musical composition. Then, in his thirties, the creative output began to decline, only to pick up again in his mid to late thirties. Later we see that same sort of enormous peaking and decline. Slater tried to relate this to a kind of biologic process.

One could also take a look at the aesthetic ideals which Schumann was attempting to realize in his composing. The first phase of creativity sees Schumann essentially as an innovator, as a person who wanted very much to be daring and original. His second phase sees him wanting very much more to be conventional. He himself recognized this duality in his make-up. He gave the name of Florestan to the side of him which was the daring, aggressive innovator, and the name Eusebius to his more conventional, quiet, withdrawn side.

One of the interesting things about Schumann is the influence of physicians in his life, starting from his birth. His maternal grandfather, Abraham Schnabel, and his uncle on his mother's side were physicians. There was also a physician on his father's side of the family who was important in that he committed suicide when Schumann was only seven years old.

Schumann grew up in a small town, Zwickow, in Saxony, now East Germany. His early life was very turbulent. His father was a writer and bookseller who had become an invalid early in his career. This meant that Schumann really only knew his father as an ailing man. In fact, many of their symptoms and diseases were the same. Also, the Napoleonic invasion took place when Schumann was a very small child. This event had a devastating affect on his social milieu, bringing a great deal of destructiveness, fear, and disease into the community. Schumann's mother fell ill with a serious infection when the boy was an infant. For three years he was actually separated from his mother, being raised by another woman whom he regarded as his true mother. This situation of having two "mothers" is something one runs across quite frequently in the life histories of geniuses. In Schumann's case it probably contributed to his identity confusion.

It is understandable that Schumann would seek comfort in symbolic, creative expression (he turned to literature as well as music). He read widely in his father's library as well as taking music lessons with the organist of St. Mary's Church. At this time Schumann's teen-age development was again disrupted by medical problems. His sister developed a very severe skin disease. We don't know exactly what it was, but in her twenties, as the disease progressed, she became psychotic and committed suicide by drowning herself. That started a kind of chain reaction in Schumann's thinking; a fear of depression and madness and suicide and a tendency to think of himself as destined to die through suicide.

Shortly after he lost his sister, his father died. It is important to note that his father was the only person in the family who actually supported Schumann's desire to become a musician. "I was hurled into the night without a leader, a teacher, or a father," he wrote in his diary. The loss of a teacher refers to Carl Maria von Weber, with whom he had hoped to study, who died at that same time. So really, during his adolescence, Schumann was faced with three very serious losses: his sister, then his father, and then the teacher, von Weber.

It was at this time of his adolescence that he had his first encounter with a psychiatrist. Dr. Ernst August Carus was at that time a local physician in Saxony, and himself a musician. Carus was married to a singer who needed to have a pianist to accompany her — and she chose Schumann. Dr. Carus, who was at that time the director of a mental hospital, took interest in the young Schumann and gave him a great deal of time, with the result that he became a very important ego ideal in Schumann's life. Schumann's relationship with Dr. Carus also probably added to his long standing fear of mental hospitals. During his vacations Schumann would visit Dr. Carus and his wife in Colditz. If some of you watch late night television, you may remember a British spy thriller, *Escape From Colditz*. In Schumann's day the Colditz castle was an insane asylum. Later it was used by the Germans as a concentration camp and then as a prisoner of war station for RAF prisoners. Of course, Schumann would have numerous contacts with the inmates of the asylum. In fact, there is fairly good evidence that he may have played music there to entertain the inmates.

Peter F. Ostwald

At age eighteen Schumann moved to Leipzig. Dr. Carus' influence on Schumann continued because he, too, had moved to Leipzig to become Professor of Medicine at the medical school there. Schumann enrolled as a law student since his family was opposed to his studying music. Dr. Carus, somewhat in opposition to Schumann's mother, encouraged Schumann to practice his music. It was Dr. Carus who introduced Schumann to Friedrich Wieck, the piano teacher in Leipzig with whom Schumann later studied. That is also how he met Wieck's talented young daughter, Clara. It may have been fortunate that Schumann was directed from early life to two career goals. His family directed him toward literature because they were in the business of publishing and selling books. Dr. Carus and other musicians directed and encouraged him toward music.

It was after this move to Leipzig that Schumann had his first personal experience with what he described in his diaries as madness. This was a brief, confusional episode during a time when he had been spending many hours by himself. During these periods of solitude he used to spend considerable time reading novels by Jean-Paul Richter, a very famous writer of that time. Schumann was reading one of Richter's books in which a man pretended to be dead so that he could avoid getting married. Schumann became obsessed with this imagery and began to believe that he himself was being buried alive. He describes very graphically in his diaries how he could not control his feelings and how his limbs were thrashing about uncontrollably. He used the word, "madness" to characterize this most unpleasant experience. He also fantasized a great deal at this time about having a double personality, an image that he adopted from the romantic literature of the time. The idea of having two personalities was a favorite kind of imagery in the Romantic era, and something that Richter described over and over in his books.

Among other doctors whom Schumann consulted while living in Leipzig was Dr. Christian Glock. They became close friends while Schumann was at the university and Glock was a medical student there. Glock was an excellent cellist, joining Schumann at his apartment in town to play chamber music. It is interesting that some of Schumann's earliest compositions actually included cello. It seems that Glock, not only as a physician but also as a musician, had a very beneficial effect on Schumann. I'd like you to hear just a little bit of the piano quartet Schumann composed at the age of eighteen or nineteen. He would rehearse it with his friend Glock and play it for Dr. Carus and other visitors who came to the apartment. (Excerpt from piano quartet is heard). That's really quite extraordinary for someone who's had practically no composition instruction and only a few piano lessons as a child. Schumann was no child prodigy. Yet his early compositions are quite amazing, and, as this one shows, contradict the view that he began by composing exclusively for the piano.

As you know, Schumann's early career as a pianist came to an unhappy end. At age nineteen he moved to the small college town of Heidelberg where he was suddenly catapulted to fame. In Leipzig he was just a student with much competition from other pianists. But in Heidelberg, where there was no serious competition, he found himself constantly being invited to perform at various salons and parties. He would practice feverishly and probably incorrectly, which led to some pain in his right hand. He tried to treat this by drinking a great deal of wine, not an ideal therapy. Soon he began to have intolerable bouts of stage fright. After returning to Leipzig he also began to use some kind of finger stretcher, hoping that this would help his hand. Well, that was the end of his career as a pianist. Then, panic-stricken and fearful, he began to consult numerous physicians, one of whom was Karl August Kuehl. He recommended a therapy that consisted of going to the butcher shop and putting the ailing hand into the belly of a freshly slaughtered animal. You can imagine the undesirable effects that would have on a very young, sensitive musician who had already developed great preoccupations with and fear of death and dying. Another doctor tried to treat Schumann's hand with electric shock applied to the muscles of the arm. This only made matters worse. Finally, he found a physician, Dr. Franz Hartmann, who used much more conservative methods. Hartmann belonged to the homeopathic school, which was prominent in Leipzig at that time. His approach was to encourage Schumann to stop drinking and smoking, to eat a regular diet, and to get more sleep. He used a great deal of psychotherapy, sensible counseling and reassurance, and a tiny bit of medication. The theory was that by using very small doses of medication one could stimulate the natural recuperative powers of the body.

Dr. Hartmann also treated Schumann when he fell ill with malaria at the age of twenty-three. Schumann lost a great deal of weight at that time, followed by a severe panic reaction to the news of the death of his brother and sister-in-law. Again, he thought he was going to lose his mind and go mad. Finally he attempted suicide. With the help of Dr. Hartmann and several other physicians, Schumann recovered from this psychiatric disorder.

By age twenty-five he had given up playing the piano. He had regained his weight, in fact a little bit too much, and was making his living as a music critic. He was editing his own newspaper in Leipzig called *The New Journal for Music*, which kept him very busy and provided some income. From time to time he would compose, interestingly enough, exclusively for the piano. He

Peter F. Ostwald

wrote extremely difficult works, the sort of compositions he could no longer play himself. Thus he became very dependent on other pianists who would try to perform his music for him. One piece, the *Toccata in C Major,* shows exactly the kind of finger technique that Schumann was no longer able to use himself. He dedicated this piece to his roommate, a very good pianist named Ludwig Schunke. (Excerpt from *Toccata in C Major* is heard). I'm sure the pianists in the audience can appreciate the amount of stress and strain involved in practicing and performing that work.

One of Schumann's favorite physicians in Leipzig was Dr. Emil Reuter. This doctor told Schumann that in order to improve his health he ought to "look for a wife. She will cure you immediately." It was on Dr. Reuter's advice that Schumann decided to marry a young heiress, Ernestine Von Fricken, who was also a pianist. But Schumann's mother disapproved of this woman. Frau Schumann wanted her son to marry Clara Wieck. Schumann was very nervous about the engagement and, in fact, took a doctor along to the engagement party. In any event, the engagement came to an end when Schumann discovered that Ernestine was an illegitimate child and would inherit nothing from her father.

When he was twenty-six, Schumann's mother died. He was left totally bereft and quite confused about his future. Into that void stepped Clara Wieck, who was by now a confident and successful seventeen year old piano virtuoso. Her father did everything in his power to interfere with this relationship. Friedrich Wieck had known Schumann well and was quite aware of his past and continuing problems. But love won out, and after years of struggle and a turbulent engagement, even a legal fight, Schumann and Clara were married. Schumann was thirty, Clara twenty-one.

Only three months after the wedding Clara had to admit in her diary that Schumann "never felt entirely well." He was often morose, angry, and depressed. But he would try to control his violent emotions through creative work. He worked feverishly on his newspaper and also composed numerous songs. This peak in his first creative cycle is made up mostly of songs which he composed one after another in a year and a half. He also composed symphonies and chamber music. In fact, some of his most successful music was written during the first few years of his marriage. An oratorio, *Paradise and Peri,* something we don't hear in this country but is performed in Germany, was also written during this period.

The couple had many children, eight altogether. So many children created problems. And there were other problems as you can imagine in a marriage of two great artists. Clara loved to travel. She wanted to be on the go and to give concerts. It didn't matter if she were pregnant or not. She was an amazing trooper, while Schumann complained. He wanted to stay at home and compose. Essentially, he was a homebody, a quiet man.

Then there was the competition between two artists. Clara couldn't practice while Schumann was composing, and you can imagine what that led to. There was also the problem of upstaging. Schumann bitterly resented all the fame and attention that his wife received. He was very poor at making small talk. At a reception after a concert he would be terrified and humiliated if someone came up to him and said, "Well, are you also a musician?"

The Schumanns made a disastrous trip to Russia where Clara earned a great deal of money and where Robert became severely depressed. Later, after moving to Dresden, where Clara's father was living, there were new problems. Schumann now had to give up his newspaper work which had been such an important creative outlet for him as well as keeping him occupied. He became a semi-invalid, much like his father. He was moody, couldn't sleep, was having crying spells, and became very dependent on his wife. Two physicians in Dresden undertook his treatment. The first was Dr. Karl Gustaf Carus, a distant relative of the earlier mentioned Carus. He was a famous scientist in his day who had written textbooks about anthropology, linguistics, and the epidemiology of mental disease. He was also the personal physician to the King and Queen of Saxony. Dr. Carus advised Schumann to go for long walks in the fresh air, to take some pills, and to consult a hypnotherapist by the name of Dr. Karl Helvig. The long walks seemed to help but the pills made Schumann itch, so he stopped taking them. As for the hypnosis, Schumann rather enjoyed that at first. A great believer in magic, he bought himself an amulet which he wore to keep away evil spirits. But soon, after several hypnotic sessions, he became quite fearful and confused. Nowadays we understand that hypnosis is not an ideal form of treatment for the kind of illness Schumann had. He began to believe that the hypnotist might be trying to poison him. He also became obsessed with the fear of all metallic objects, like keys and knives, probably a negative reaction to the magnet that Dr. Helbig was using.

In the course of the treatment, Dr. Helbig made a suggestion that Schumann tried to follow. He was told to stop composing. This brings up an interesting dilemma which, I think, we will be discussing again in this conference, namely, what sort of advice do you give a workaholic musician? Helbig said, "Now stop this composing." That put Schumann into a terrible conflict. He had just given up his job as a music critic, and, without composing, had nothing to do.

He put off the work he was doing on scenes for Goethe's *Faust*, concentrating instead on counterpoint studies. He became very enamored of Bach's *Well Tempered Clavier* and wanted to write an edition of the work.

Interestingly, while Schumann was convalescing from this depressive illness, he started to compose another symphony, his great *Symphony in C Major*. It contains a beautiful adagio, one of his most eloquent statements, which is reminiscent of the older music of Bach and Handel. It gives evidence that the illness he had just gone through did not affect his creativity in any negative way. There is, I think, no greater or more profound example of the interaction of music and unwellness, and the power of creativity in overcoming a serious life crisis, than is demonstrated in this wonderful work.

When Schumann was forty he moved to Düsseldorf because of a revolution in Saxony. It was an up-and-coming city looking for a very dynamic and aggressive music director to run the local symphony and choral society. Clara was very much in favor of this move, which she thought would enhance her own career and give Schumann a chance to perform his new compositions. But Schumann, thinking he might experience another depression, was not at all sure that he could survive another resettlement. His first year in Düsseldorf did not go badly, but Clara complained about the city. Schumann kept himself very busy composing a great deal of new music and putting on some very impressive concerts. He nevertheless lacked the qualities of a strong leader and a capable conductor. Not a verbal man, he spoke rarely, and not at all to the orchestra. He seldom gave any cues. Orchestral conducting was definitely not Schumann's strong point, nor was he the clever politician or good administrator necessary to run an orchestra. Soon there were dissatisfactions among the board of directors and the orchestra. The newspapers began to complain.

Schumann saw several doctors in Düsseldorf. One of the most important ones was Dr. Wolfgang Mueller Von Konigswinter, who was on the governing board of the music society. Clearly, Dr. Mueller played a very important role, not only in treating Schumann but also in excusing him from some of his duties. Dr. Mueller sent Schumann and his wife to Holland for hydrotherapy. Schumann improved, but Clara had an abortion there which, though very unsettling, may have helped temporarily. Schumann was becoming frantic about the problem of his ever expanding family.

In 1853 Johannes Brahms came to Düsseldorf and captured the hearts of both Robert and Clara. Schumann saw him as a messianic figure, a genius who would soon be Germany's greatest composer. It was kind of a capitulation;

Schumann was ready to give up and turn over to this new young genius the future of musical art in Germany. Clara became pregnant again the same week that Brahms arrived. It occasionally has been rumored that Brahms may have been the father of Clara's last child. I think it is unlikely that they had sexual intercourse, though I do believe that they probably had a fairly passionate love affair later on.

After visiting Brahms in Hanover, Schumann became agitated and fearful. He complained of constant auditory hallucinations and wanted to enter a mental hospital. Clara didn't want to let him go. In panic, Schumann jumped off a bridge and had to be hospitalized.

I might mention at this point that Schumann complained of ear problems all his life. While a teen-ager, and especially during his law studies in Heidelberg, he mentioned the intrusive effects of various noises in his ears, sometimes music and poetry. There were no ear specialists at the time, so we really don't know what the problem was. He never went deaf like Beethoven or Smetana. When he was psychotic, he believed that there were heavenly voices talking to him and that he was being pursued by demons. Often he had hallucinations that would condemn him and criticize him for being an inadequate composer. These voices would tell him that he must die.

He had two psychiatrists in the hospital. The most important was Dr. Franz Richarz, a very experienced clinician who believed that all mental illnesses were primarily the result of disturbances in the heart and blood circulation. He used mostly physical methods to treat Schumann, such as sedation, blood letting with leeches, and hydrotherapy. He made what seemed to be a good recovery, and after several months the friends who visited him in the hospital reported that he seemed to be back to normal. For a time Schumann wrote letters to his wife, friends, and publishers, and analyzed Brahms' new music. He even tried to do some composing in the hospital, but nothing gave him much satisfaction.

It soon was apparent that Schumann was still depressed and suicidal. The doctors would not release him. Clara, in order to pay for the treatment, went on concert tours and gave many recitals, often traveling with Brahms. Brahms, in turn, acted as a kind of go-between, visiting Schumann in the hospital and reporting back to Clara. One of the most touching compositions that Brahms wrote at this time are the *Variations on a Theme by Schumann, Opus 9*, dedicated to Clara.

In a final fit of despair Schumann stopped eating and, despite the efforts of his psychiatrists to force feed him, he lost a great deal of weight. Shortly

Peter F. Ostwald

before his death, Clara visited him for the first time. She tried to feed him. He did accept food and even drank some wine, which is rather persuasive evidence that he didn't have anything which would organically interfere with eating. An autopsy was done by Dr. Richarz, but it does not tell us the cause of Schumann's death.

In conclusion, it is a sad story in a way, but also a very wonderful story of a genius who combated many different illnesses throughout his life. The points I want to emphasize in connection with Schumann's case and the cases of musicians like him are that, first, one is seldom dealing with just a single disorder. Illnesses must be seen in their total complexity. Usually there are patterns of multiple disorders affecting the musician's body, his mind, his work, his family, and his social relationships. Second, the course of a disease is influenced not only by the pathologic process itself, but also by the treatment or mistreatment which the physician prescribes for the patient. There are many unsolved and even unrecognized problems which confront musicians. I think we are on a new frontier of medicine, a kind of specialty, which will require new approaches to diagnosis and treatment. Were Robert Schumann alive today, I'm certain that we could do a better job in treating him and possibly prolonging his life than the doctors of the 19th Century; they were without antibiotics, antidepressants, and any of the basic diagnostic methods we have available today. I would hope that this conference, and others like it in the future, may point the way to better care for musicians, who may represent, especially in our time, an endangered species.

ON THE ROAD WITH THE
LOS ANGELES PHILHARMONIC:
RIGORS OF THE MUSICAL CAREER

Ivan A. Shulman
Tour Physician and Consultant
The Los Angeles Philharmonic Orchestra

The rigors of a musical career are indeed great. When a career is magnified by the collective careers of over one hundred traveling musicians, the undertaking becomes analogous to a military campaign. To be a physician among such a group of people is a unique experience and a unique responsibility. Orchestral musicians on tour are different from run-of-the-mill tourists. Musicians perform. They must be ready to do something unique; that is why they are there. The audience expects a high level of performance. The player expects it, as does the conductor. The task of the tour physician is to see to the physical health of the musicians, allowing them to perform to their greatest potential.

Before going on tour I pass out an introductory letter which covers a few guidelines that I feel are worth reviewing with the orchestra. I encourage musicians to take along their own first aid supplies, that is, something for pain (aspirin or Tylenol), decongestants, antihistamines, something for motion sickness, Band-Aids, and for people who wear contact lenses I recommend they carry a pair of regular glasses in case of corneal abrasion. For almost everyone I recommend sunglasses because the changes in lifestyle may cause some unexpected eye problems. Immunizations are more or less a moot subject today. Smallpox once was a problem but, as you know, the last case of smallpox in the world was reported in Ethiopia in 1978. I might suggest that in the situation of an orchestra going to India, gamma globulin be given for hepatitis protection.

For musicians who are taking medications, I like to know what they are taking in case of adverse reactions or medical problems. I suggest to them that they take their usual supply and double it, placing each supply in a separate suitcase. This way, if the baggage gets lost or separated there is a good chance that the person will still have what they need.

In 1981, prior to a trip to Mexico, I had a long talk with the orchestra about the prevention of *turista*. I gave them a set of suggestions about water supply, ice, salads, fruits, and in general about the types of things to eat. Most large groups traveling in Mexico report a forty percent incidence of *turista*, this based on a self-survey done by the American Gastroenterologic Association. On this trip with the orchestra we reported a twenty-four percent level of incidence; not ideal, but satisfactory.

If you will pardon the pun, I did a quick and dirty survey of *turista* several days after the tour while the orchestra was performing in Ames, Iowa. I made several observations at this time. I suggested to the orchestra that they take a prophylaxis for *turista*. The literature at that time suggested the use of doxycycline, the generic name for Vibramycin®. The capsules come in 100 milligram doses. Two are normally taken on the first day of the trip and one on each of the following days. I compared the various attack rates of *turista* and diarrhea among the groups taking Vibramycin®, Pepto-Bismol®, and, in the case of holistically-inclined members, acidophilus. Other members of the orchestra took nothing. We found a sixteen percent incidence of *turista* among those taking Vibramycin®, eighty percent among those taking Pepto-Bismol® (this finding is skewed because in my data collection I did not differentiate between those who took Pepto-Bismol® for therapy and those who took it for prophylaxis), forty-two percent among those taking acidophilus, and twenty-five percent among those who took nothing. I published these results in the Western Journal of Medicine several years ago. Parenthetically, I just came back from the People's Republic of China where I noticed that several people in the group were very compulsive about what they did and did not eat. Those of us who were less careful ended up healthier than those who worried about it. Nevertheless, I do recommend that some care must be taken.

One of the high points of my experience with the Los Angeles Philharmonic was in 1982, a time when Carlo Maria Guilini was very active with the orchestra. That spring he conducted opera for the first time in twelve to fifteen years. As you may remember, his performance of Verdi's *Falstaff* was quite exceptional. He took a group of people who had never before sung *Falstaff*, and confined everyone to Los Angeles for six weeks, telling them that they were not allowed any other engagements or travel during this period of time. It was a truly remarkable experience, during which I served as the ensemble's physician. I had very little to do, which can largely be attributed to the fact that people were not running off to varying parts of the globe. Mr. Guilini's method of how to go about preparing this opera was, from a medical point of view, really quite effective.

There is always a question about jet lag. It is a ten and one-half hour flight from Los Angeles to Tokyo, non-stop. It is interesting that the orchestra had much less difficulty going from the West coast of the United States to Asia than from the East coast to Europe. Research that supports this observation points to a change in circadian rhythms. I found that the best suggestion for orchestra members was to keep themselves well hydrated during the long flight. I also suggested that they refrain from alcohol because it tends to act as a diuretic and therefore increases the degree of dehydration. We also tried as best we could to maintain a regular dietary schedule.

When I gave my talk prior to leaving for Mexico I thought I might have over-stressed the *turista* matter somewhat, so I downplayed it for the Japan trip. I was rushed onto the stage to give my talk immediately after a rehearsal with Maxim Shostakovich. I got up and began to talk about how *turista* would not be a problem in Japan and Korea. Mr. Shostakovich gently pushed me aside and said to the orchestra, "Listen, you must understand, the water in Korea is much worse than in Mexico."

The general enthusiasm of the Japanese audience for the orchestra, particularly for Mr. Guilini, was extraordinary. There were huge ovations, and huge crowds backstage. Everyone was really quite upbeat. I mentioned this about ten days before we were to return to the United States, and it was at about that time that people began to become ill. This phenomenon then is consistent with the Shulman theory of disease: an orchestra can travel any length of time and members won't get sick until approximately ten days before the end of the trip. I do not know what causes this; maybe our psychiatrist friends can help. I saw some fraying around the edges during the middle of the trip, but it was not until the final ten days that I really began to be busy.

I would like to make a few observations about Mr. Guilini. He is an extraordinary man, who has decided not to be music director of the Philharmonic after the 1984-85 season so that he can spend more time with his wife and pursue more personal activities. He is a very shy, gentle, and introspective man. When he gets on the podium, however, he is very intense. It is almost scary to see him as he leaves the podium after a performance because he is dripping wet and white as a sheet. One literally has to take the baton from him, hold a glass of water for him, and give him a towel before he can go back on stage to take his well deserved bows.

Because of his wife's illness, Maestro Guilini felt that he could not go on the 1983 European tour. Zubin Mehta filled in at the last moment, necessitating some concert cancellations in Vienna, Paris, and London, much to the orchestra's dismay. I think these cancellations put a little edge on the orchestra. Nevertheless, we had a very successful trip to Florence, Milan, Bonn, Copenhagen, and Hamburg. During this trip I felt that jet lag was a serious problem. Turista was not even an issue. It is about an eleven hour flight from Los Angeles to Frankfurt, non-stop. We changed planes in Frankfurt and flew on to Pisa, where we took a bus to Florence. The orchestra was quite exhausted after all this travel, and the exhaustion was beginning to show. I prescribed some sleeping pills for those members who looked about ready to drop. It seemed that everyone awoke at two in the morning, ready to go. There was, of course, nothing to do but go back to sleep. People were sleeping when they were supposed to be awake and awake when they were supposed to be sleeping.

As noted before, going to Europe from the United States can be a problem. In general, I suggest that people stay awake as long as possible and then try to fit into a European time schedule as soon as possible. It is not an easy adjustment to make, taking some orchestra members about a week to reach a sense of normalcy. People were not hungry, yet they should have been eating and taking in fluids. Some people tried alcohol to get to sleep, which I do not recommend. Age did not seem to be a factor in that jet lag effected younger and older musicians equally.

Weather was a problem in that the rain led to some exacerbation of arthritis. We also had a serious urologic problem and some orthopedic problems. The mother of Gidon Kremer, the violinist, had come to hear her son play and while leaving the hall was mugged. I was called upon to act as an intermediary for the Italian physicians and the family.

I would like to summarize what I have learned. One of the most important things that physicians who take care of musicians must understand is how crucial it is that both groups speak the same language. It is not enough when a violinist says that his arm hurts when performing spiccato or that a pianist talks about pain during arpeggios. I think that physicians must observe musicians in a musical setting, to watch how they play. It also would be helpful if musicians learned some basic medical language. Communication is not an easy matter; it takes an open mind to put forth the effort to understand what each is saying to the other. Here I am speaking to the converted, to physicians who have an understanding of musician's problems, and to musicians who understand that there are sympathetic physicians.

While on this subject, I think that we need to involve other people who are not represented here today. I believe there is a role for surgery in specific instances. I certainly would not make a categoric statement that there is no role for surgery in certain kinds of hand problems.

As a tour physician I find that I spend a great deal of time listening to orchestra members who want very much to describe some of their problems to a physician. They may not have had an opportunity to do so before. It could be that they do not have a personal physician or they do not have a satisfactory relationship with their physician. I like to make myself available to the orchestra membership to answer any of their questions, be they obtuse or strange. I should mention that many of these questions are anxiety driven and interpersonal. Several years ago we did have to send someone home who was not so much suffering from culture shock as from homesickness. This person was an experienced traveler under stress due to family problems.

During this conference we have talked a great deal about about anxiety and beta-blockers. Orchestra members are very interested in the drug propranolol. I have taken it and know that it works. But I want to qualify my enthusiasm for its use, especially to limit its use to selected instances only. I believe it has the potential for medical abuse. People, no matter what their age, should probably have an EKG before they start on the drug. This is because there are some latent cases of first and second degree heart block which are completely asymptomatic but may be exposed by the use of the beta-blocker, even if the drug is used for a short duration. I think it would be best if we were to limit this drug to episodic use. The drug is being used by many, many people, whether we like it or not. Someone gives a few pills to someone else, and so it goes. We as physicians need to accept the fact that propranolol and its cohorts are here to stay. Musicians want them and are going to use them whether we like it or not. Our role as physicians must be to temper its use in an appropriate and medically safe manner.

Physicians should also be aware of marijuana and alcohol use and abuse. Both are used extensively in symphony orchestras, and marijuana is frequently taken abroad during tours. While I believe it is primarily used for recreational purposes, we need to recognize the fact that its use is widespread. Smoking, too, is a problem for musicians, especially wind players.

The last subject I would like to touch on briefly is what I take when I go on tour. I bring a large bag which is essentially set up for cardiac arrest. I do not bring endotracheal tubes nor a laryngoscope. I do bring a face mask which gives a good seal around the nose and mouth. With this a patient can be suc-

Ivan A. Shulman

cess fully ventilated. I would like to call attention to the fact that airlines do not help very much. If you get sick on an aircraft, you better hope there is a physician aboard who knows what is going on. Moreover, aircraft do not carry any useful equipment. Perhaps ICSOM can put some pressure on airlines to carry a more adequate first aid kit. I would be very happy to supply them with a list of items to carry.

In summary, it has been an unusual experience for me, a physician, to play on both sides of the stage. Musicians in the orchestra know me both as a physician and as an oboe player. I think they get a great kick whenever I am on their side of the stage. I know I do. It helps to cement a fine relationship between me and the orchestra.

THE CAUSES AND CURES OF PERFORMANCE ANXIETY:

A REVIEW OF THE PSYCHOLOGICAL LITERATURE

Paul Lehrer
Associate Professor of Psychiatry
Rutgers Medical School, New Jersey

Why should scientists be interested in the problem of performance anxiety? Every performer has experienced it and knows exactly what it feels like; and, with better or worse results, all performers and music teachers have devised ways of dealing with it or have resigned themselves to its inevitability. From various quarters, performers are advised to relax unneeded muscles while playing; or to study the Alexander Technique, Yoga, Zen, progressive relaxation, hypnosis, or autogenic training; to be psychoanalyzed; to take a deep breath before walking on stage; to think about the music and forget about the anxiety; to "flow with" the anxiety and to let it make the performance more exciting; or to take drugs to relieve the anxiety or its symptoms; to perform more frequently — or less frequently; to worry deliberately in advance of the performance; or to try to block out all worries.

The problem for the scientist is, do all these techniques work, or are some better than others? Are some more useful than others under particular circumstances or with particular kinds of people? Is it possible that nothing can be done about the problem, or that all these methods are equally useful — or useless?

Another scientific issue is to understand better the nature of performance anxiety. We all know what it feels like, but do we all feel it in the same way? Why do some of us have more of it than others? What, precisely, are its effects on performance? How much tension is adaptive, and how much is too much? What is the relationship between performance anxiety and general physical and psychological health?

In this paper I will discuss scientific strategies for studying these questions. I will review some of the published findings, and will discuss both the promises that science offers for understanding and treating performance anxiety and the limits of these promises.

In order to be believable, techniques for managing performance anxiety must be studied scientifically. Clinical studies are rich in detail and provide important guidelines for scientists and clinicians alike. However, of necessity they can be done only on a small number of cases at a time, and they lack experimental controls. They can suggest and point the way, but they cannot prove. Large scale "parametric" research, on the other hand, can prove the validity of some methods at least statistically, but also has limitations. Methods should not be touted as "scientific" on the basis of only a handful of parametric studies. Finally, not all decisions can be made on the basis of scientifically verified fact. Ethics, artistic values, and personal preferences are all important "non-scientific" factors that play a role in choosing the best anxiety control method for each individual.

Clinical Research

In clinical research we study a few individuals very intensively. We monitor the situations which cause their anxiety, the ways they cope with it, and the ways that their anxiety is related to other important parts of their personalities, such as relationships with family and friends, religious beliefs, value systems, social skills, financial security, physical health, musical abilities and training, etc. In this kind of research we learn to understand and, perhaps, "cure" the problems in particular individuals.

Clinical research completely avoids the problem of treating individuals as statistical averages — which, of course, they never are. Although clinical observation does not sound as "scientific" as the statistical and experimental research methods I will describe later, it is just as scientific and highly useful. Actually, scientific observation *is* primarily careful observation, measurement, and description. Use of the scientific method in research allows others to repeat one's observations by following exactly the same procedures. In the words of my alcoholic high school chemistry teacher, "Shiensh is accurate and shpeshific." The value of science is in the reproducibility of results, which stems from accurate observation. Thus, if the clinician objectively records the performer's words, behaviors, and physiologic responses, and carefully records what is going on in the environment — the setting, the surrounding people, the temperature, what people are doing and saying, etc. — and does this such that other independent observers would make exactly the same observations, then such observations are scientific. It might be helpful, but not necessary, to quantify the observations so that we know how much a person talks, laughs, or sweats. This makes our observations more sensitive, and capable of detecting critical changes or differences.

Clinical observation can be done equally well by the physician, the psychologist, or the music teacher. Without such observations, claims about the usefulness of any method cannot be taken seriously. Without them we have no idea whether the individual actually had a real problem before the treatment, whether the treatment was administered correctly, whether the individual "learned" the method, or whether the method actually worked in live performance. Although the personal, unverified claims of the performer, teacher, and/or clinician are not to be completely ignored, we would do well to regard them all as highly suspect. Fame and fortune are always at stake here. Clearly, the conflict of interest between scientific objectivity and self-promotion is too great to be ignored.

Let me give some examples of clinical research on performance anxiety. Norton, MacLean, and Wachna (1978) treated a female patient with stage fright using a technique called cognitive desensitization. Her symptoms included foot-shaking, memory blanks, and feelings of intense anxiety. In this therapy technique, the woman first mapped out a hierarchy of anxiety provoking scenes related to performing. These started with scenes that bothered her very little, perhaps like singing in a chorus,[1] to scenes that bothered her a great deal, such as having a memory slip during an important concert. She also was taught a muscle relaxation technique. Then, while deeply relaxed, she imagined the scenes, starting with the easiest scene, until she no longer felt anxious while imagining it. She also designed a series of positive self-statements that she could use while practicing and playing the piano. These may have included such statements as, "I am doing as well as I can," "I can control my feelings of anxiety," "I just thought out this passage beautifully," "I am a good and worthwhile person," "Survival is not at stake," etc. Such statements were used as substitutes for negative self-thoughts which were common in this situation. Frequent negative thoughts among performers include: "This is going to be a catastrophe"; "I am going to mess up and no one will love me any more"; "I might die of anxiety right here on stage"; etc.

---

1.   The exact hierarchy of items or positive self-statements were not reported in the Norton, et al, report. These examples are from similar cases treated by the present author.

After doing the desensitization and thinking positive self-statements alone for almost two weeks in daily sessions, the subject of this study practiced giving performances for a few days in front of 5-20 people, deliberately using the relaxation techniques and self-statements she had been taught, while giving the concerts. During her concerts at home and at the university concert theater, the patient reported that she experienced little anxiety, and the memory blanks and foot shaking did not occur. During later performances the anxiety-evoking events were maximized by (a) the presence of a purported symphony musician and (b) a piano with broken pedals. Even under these conditions (she) did not experience anxiety, memory blanks, or foot shaking. Before and during the performance she appeared calm and composed to the therapist and to a member of the audience who was a skilled pianist.

This type of clinical report can easily be done by any music teacher. It simply requires detailed specification of the exact technique that was applied, and of the methods used to assess the results (in this case, the report of the patient and the observation of others during a concert).

I will briefly describe a more complex case that I treated several years ago. This was also of a 20-year old female pianist. Her presenting symptom was not anxiety, but cold hands, which interfered not only with her piano playing, but also with living comfortably through the cold New Jersey winters. Her hands were cold when exposed to stress and to cold. She had been diagnosed as having a disorder called Raynaud's phenomenon, and had been treated with various drugs that dilated the blood vessels in her hands. This treatment had minimal effect. Over the course of three months I administered twice weekly sessions of finger temperature biofeedback, during which she was taught to increase the blood flow and temperature in her fingers and hands. I also taught her autogenic training, a self-hypnotic method that helps people to regulate certain physiologic functions (Schultz and Luthe, 1969). Although she made much progress during the sessions, she made little progress outside. We then began talking about her relations with her parents, whom she saw as pushy and overinvested with her concert career. After she spoke with them repeatedly, honestly, and assertively about their overinvolvement in her studies, they appeared to become less intrusive, and her symptoms completely disappeared. She was still free of symptoms when I saw her a year later. She reported that she still deliberately used the biofeedback, autogenic training, and assertive skills which she had developed during therapy.

Parametric Research

The problem with the clinical approach is that, despite care in taking measures that are "accurate and shpeshific," the results of clinical studies are still too often not reproducible. People are just too different from one another. Hence the need for parametric research, in which we look at a relatively small number of measures on large numbers of people. Though this type of research only yields averages, and can never completely describe the behavior of a given individual, the results of properly conducted parametric research *are* reproducible. Through it we can predict the proportion of people who will, say, be affected by a specific treatment in a given way. But there will always be some margin of error, thus, the need for a clinical *art*.

Most of the research we read about is parametric. Through it we know that a variety of treatments do appear to be effective, at least in the short term, in decreasing performance anxiety; and some, perhaps, even enhance performance.

Note that I have used such qualifying words as "appear to" or "perhaps," because, in truth, different measures of anxiety, and slight differences in therapy procedures and/or subject populations, often produce very different results. Thus, in a study of desensitization, Wardle (1978) found that judges' ratings of performer's anxiety during performance were not affected by desensitization therapy, while Lund (1972) and Appel (1976) did find such an effect. Only when a multitude of parametric studies have been done, each using slightly different methodology from others, and when the preponderance of these yield the same results, can we begin to be confident about what they mean.

Parametric research on anxiety has pointed to a number of factors that contribute to therapeutic effectiveness. We must be cautious in interpreting such results because few of these studies were actually done on performance anxiety per se. Nevertheless, it may give us a useful jumping-off point. I will list some of the factors that this research suggests may be related to success in reducing performance anxiety.

1. **Intensity of the treatment**. Treatment carried out by a therapist or trainer tends to be more effective than treatment carried out by a tape recording or self-help manuals, although the latter procedures do produce measurable therapeutic effects.

Paul Lehrer

2. **Modality of the treatment method and of the outcome measures**. To paraphrase a colleague of mine who spoke on a similar topic, anxiety is not always anxiety is not always anxiety; and relaxation is not always relaxation is not always relaxation (Schwartz, 1978).

Approximately thirty years ago, when psychologists set out to measure anxiety, they thought they had a good idea of what anxiety is. Anxiety, at the very least, included feelings of dread, of not wanting to go on, the physiologic fight or flight reaction (increased adrenalin flow, muscle tension, heart rate, etc.), and avoidance of situations that made the anxiety worse. It was axiomatic that all of these symptoms were different aspects of anxiety, and that all varied together, i.e., when one measure indicated high anxiety, others would also. Thus, when studying anxiety, it did not seem to matter which kind of measure was used.

But people tended to describe anxiety differently, depending on which measure was used, and results were often contradictory. When psychologists began to put cognitive, somatic, and behavioral measures together in a single study, they found that the various measures were only minimally correlated with each other. When studying people who were afraid of snakes, psychologist Peter Lang (1968) found that people who said that they were most afraid of snakes were not necessarily the ones who stayed farthest away from a real snake when they were asked to approach it and play with it; and neither behavioral approach to the snake nor self-report of anxiety was significantly correlated with heart rate or skin sweating when a snake was placed near the person or the person was asked to imagine a snake. So anxiety may not be like the elephant. There may be no one single thing, "anxiety." It may be different at different times, and in different people. Some of the various kinds of anxiety may be problematic and others not, and various individuals may have different problem areas.

3. **Type of anxiety**. For the past several years I have been giving questionnaires to performers in order to find out what kinds of performance anxiety symptoms they have. I found several clusters of symptoms, each of which appears to be unrelated to the others (Lehrer, 1981).

> 1. Anxiety and fear of fear.
>
> 2. Distraction and memory problems.
>
> 3. Fearing disapproval from others.
>
> 4. Concern about performing abilities.

To repeat, none of the four dimensions is statistically related to any other. This suggests, therefore, that treatments for each dimension or "kind" of performance anxiety might be quite specific, and that treatments that help one type may not be as helpful for others.

I have reviewed all the various treatments for anxiety for a recent book on treatment of stress (Woolfolk and Lehrer, 1984), I found that three kinds of anxiety symptoms (somatic, behavioral, and cognitive) tend to respond differently to specific forms of treatment. Somatic symptoms tend to respond best to somatic therapies, cognitive symptoms to cognitive therapies, and behavioral symptoms to behavioral therapies. Somatic therapies (such as beta blockers, biofeedback, muscle relaxation therapies, breathing exercises, and certain self-hypnotic exercises) have their greatest effects on somatic symptoms of anxiety, e.g., palpitations, muscle tension, tremor, nausea, sweating, etc. Cognitive therapies (such as psychoanalytic psychotherapy (Horney, 1962), rational therapy (Ellis and Grieger, 1977), and conditioning or teaching people to stop thinking unwanted thoughts (Rimm and Masters, 1979, pp. 396-398), have their greatest effects on self-report of anxiety and well being. Behavior therapies (such as desensitization, frequent practice performing in front of gradually more imposing audiences, instruction in how to deal with various problems that may arise (e.g., a poor hall, noisy audience, memory slips, tension related difficulties, etc.) tend to produce the most dramatic effects on behavioral measures (e.g., audibility, lack of memory slips, performing techniques, etc.).

The correspondence between treatment and symptom specificity is not absolute. There is some carry-over from cognitive therapies to behavioral and somatic symptoms, and likewise for other combinations. The biggest treatment effects, however, do tend to occur when there is a match between type of symptom and type of therapy.

Parametric research on music performance per se has confirmed the findings of the more general research I just cited, showing that modality-specific treatment is the most consistently effective form of therapy. Brantigan, Brantigan, and Joseph (1979) reported that propranolol has more consistent effects on physiologic symptoms of anxiety than on mental symptoms of anxiety during a performance. Appel (1976) found that teaching people to analyze the music they are playing has more consistent effects on number of errors in a performance than on the experience of anxiety during a performance. Kendrick, Craig, Lawson, and Davidson found that ratings of self-efficacy as a performer improved more with cognitive therapy than with musical analysis training.

Nevertheless, some indirect effects do occur for each type of technique, although they are weaker and less consistent. Thus, several studies (Brantigan, et al., 1979; Neftel, Adler, Kappel, Rossi, Dolder, Kaser, Bruggesser, and Vorkaut, 1982) did find some effects for propranolol on reducing the psychologic experience of anxiety. Lund (1971) found that desensitization, relaxation therapy, and insight therapy all produced decreases in the self-report of performance anxiety. Several investigators found that cognitive therapy and desensitization produced decreases in performance errors as well as in self-report of performance anxiety (Wardle, 1978; Appel, 1976; Sweeney and Horan, 1982; Lund, 1972).

4. **Number of symptoms.** The difficulty in overcoming anxiety symptoms does not appear to be related to one's age or to the length of time that one has experienced the anxiety. It does appear to be related to the number of anxieties, phobias, and other emotional problems that a person has. Simple behavioral techniques appear to be effective with isolated problems, but less so when people have more complex interrelated problems (Marks, 1969; Meichenbaum, Gilmore, and Fedoravicius, 1973).

There is evidence that many people who report being anxious during a concert also tend to be anxious at other times. For them, a rather complex and perhaps long-term therapy may be needed. Psychologists would say that such people are high in "trait anxiety." Trait anxiety is a stable personality characteristic. A person who is high in trait anxiety tends to be anxious in many situations, e.g., at home, at work, alone, with friends, etc. Trait anxiety may involve a biologic, perhaps inborn, predisposition. It is also affected by one's upbringing and early childhood experiences. Trait anxiety is fairly stable in adult life. Under ordinary circumstances, it does not change dramatically from week to week or month to month, although, over time, various forms of psychotherapy and drug therapy are known to produce dramatic decreases in trait anxiety. State anxiety, on the other hand, refers to a kind of anxiety that is present only at a particular point in time. We all experience a high state anxiety at some points in our lives.

In a recent study of mine (Lehrer, 1981), the correlation between state anxiety during a concert and trait anxiety on Spielberger's State-Trait Anxiety Inventory was found to be .61, suggesting that approximately 36%[2] of anxiety

---

2.   These percentage figures are approximate, since some error is contained in any single
      measure of anxiety.

during the performance can be explained by general anxiety. Conversely, approximately 64% of anxiety during the performance does not appear to be related to general anxiety. Thus, although 36% of an individual's performance anxiety may require lengthy and complex treatment, 64% may be amenable to treatment by specific behavioral and pedagogic techniques. The latter may be as easily carried out by the music teacher as by the psychotherapist — perhaps even better so by the teacher, because many of these techniques require working at the instrument.

5. **The "non-specifics" of treatment.** These generally refer to the therapeutic factors that do not seem to have anything to do with the particular technique that is being employed. Although these factors have not been systematically evaluated in studies of treating performance anxiety, we know that they are quite powerful in all forms of psychological treatment. Sometimes these factors are lumped together and called the placebo effect. The placebo effect should not be brushed off. We want to know how to produce it, because it accounts for a consistently large proportion of the therapeutic effects of most psychologic techniques and psychoactive drugs. This does not mean that all psychoactive drugs, psychologic treatment techniques, and teaching techniques are nothing but placebos. Most of the techniques that I am describing have been compared empirically with various placebo treatments in which the "non-specific" factors are all present, but the specific techniques are not. All these therapies are known to be more powerful than placebo conditions alone.

A highly relevant form of comparison treatment, although not exactly a placebo (relevant because it is not only believable, but is widely used by music educators, and can thus ethically be used as an experimental control) is training in musical analysis of the selection being played. The rationale for music analysis training as a treatment of performance anxiety is that a better understanding of the structure of the music will increase the performer's sense of control over the situation, and thereby decrease anxiety during performance. Appel (1976) found the anxiety-reducing techniques of desensitization to produce greater reductions in self-report of anxiety than did music analysis training, or *no* treatment. Music analysis training was, however, better than no treatment at all. Only desensitization produced a significant decrease in heart rate during the performance. Music analysis training produced a decrease in number of errors, indicating that music analysis does have a specific effect, though not on anxiety. More recently, Sweeny and Horan (1982) compared musical analysis training with a relaxation technique called cue-controlled relaxation. They found that relaxation produced greater

decreases in anxiety, in performance errors, and heart rate during a performance than did music analysis training. In their study, music analysis training produced no measurable improvements in any measure, although subjects
"believed in it" as much as they did in the other two techniques.

One of the important nonspecific effects appears to be expectancy (Frank,
1978). The results are always better when therapy is delivered by someone
who is convinced of the technique, and who puts it across in a way that con-
vinces the patient that it will work. The charisma of the teacher or the
therapist may be particularly important here, although the exact personality
characteristics of the trainer that maximize this effect are not well studied.

Not only do the expectations of the client and therapist, or student and
teacher, affect the outcomes of various techniques, but, unfortunately, so do
the expectations of the experimenters. It is well known that all too often experiments yield findings which are consistent with the hypotheses of the experimenters (Rosenthal, 1969). This is only rarely due to intentional fudging
of the data; most often it is caused by unintentional errors and slips, which
cumulatively can sway the results of an entire experiment. This is why *multiple* studies must be done on each question, and that the hypotheses of the experimenters must be reported and taken into account when the data are interpreted.

Another important nonspecific factor probably is the ability of the trainer to
master his or her own stress, and to be a warm individual who gives of him or
herself. Various relaxation procedures are known not to be teachable by per-
sons who are unable to relax themselves; nor can they be taught effectively by
therapists who are cold, distant, and "professional," rather than warm and
friendly (Taub, 1977).

6. **Durability of effects**. Those techniques which have been extensively
evaluated generally have been examined only with respect to their short term
effects. We know, however, that it is the long term rather than the short term
effects of a technique that will make the technique most useful. How helpful
would a technique be if it helped you through a single performance, but then
seemed to lose its effect; or worse still, produced long term side effects that
were worse than the original symptoms?

Let me illustrate this point by describing an interesting study by Lavallee,
Lamontagne, Pinard, Annable, and Tetreault (1977). They compared the widely used minor tranquilizer, Valium, to a technique of voluntary muscle relaxation. They studied anxiety neurotics, i.e., people who suffer from frequent
panic attacks which seem to come as if from nowhere. Volunteers for this

study were assigned randomly either to a group that received Valium, or to a group that received a placebo. The physicians giving the medicine did not know which kind of pill they were administering to each subject, so they could not bias the study by communicating their own expectations to the subjects. Half of the subjects in each drug group were also trained in progressive relaxation. The other half were told to relax regularly, but they received no special training. After eight weeks of treatment, both treatments seemed to work. Those who had been taught to relax had fewer anxiety symptoms than those who had not, and those who were administered Valium had fewer anxiety symptoms than those who had been administered the placebo. Oddly enough, the two treatments did not interact, i.e., those who had been administered both of the active treatments did not do better than those who had been administered only one.

After finishing the eight week experimental treatment, subjects went back to their own physicians and received whatever treatment they or their physicians felt was best for them. They still did not know whether they had been given an active treatment or had been in a control group. Lavallee, et al., found that, after a year, subjects who had received Valium during the eight week study were more anxious than subjects who had received the placebo, that they took more drugs of various sorts in order to combat their anxiety, and that they used their relaxation methods less. Thus, although Valium appeared to help people over the short run, it appeared to hurt them over the long run by making them more drug dependent and less resourceful in using their own non-drug self-control strategies. Might the same be true for treatment of performance anxiety by propranolol or, in fact, by the Alexander technique, by relaxation therapy, by cognitive therapy, or any other technique? We just do not know. The studies have not been done.

Desirability vs. Effectiveness of a Treatment Technique

Science can uncover facts, but it cannot make choices. Such factors as pleasantness of a choice, expense, and ethics may be more critical. Is relaxation preferable to propranolol for controlling performance anxiety? No comparative study has yet been done on these two methods, as far as I know. But suppose that studies found them to be equally effective in reducing performance anxiety. Relaxation therapy is certainly more expensive, as much as ten times more. Does this mean that propranolol is better? What about risks, side effects, or long term effects? What about the psychologic effects of relying on a drug rather than a sense of self-mastery? What about the ethics of large scale reliance on drugs among performers? What about the artistic quality of the performance? James, et al., (1977), presented data showing that artistic quality, as rated by professional musicians in the audience, often improves when an otherwise anxious performer is taking propranolol. But global ratings are notoriously unreliable. Some specific aspects of performance quality, i.e., rhythmic and dynamic intensity, have been found to suffer following ingestion of beta-blockers (Lehrer, Rosen, Kustis, and Greenfield, 1987). Finally, we know that under some circumstances beta blockers have side effects of depression and decreased muscle strength. Although their overall effect on music performance seems to be positive, comparative studies of various medical and psychologic techniques have not yet been done. When and if they are, the complexity of artistic quality must be taken into account. Measuring subtle differences in treatment and results, a formidable problem, is as yet unsolved.

Science cannot, in the end, tell us which method to use. It is not a question for scientists, physicians, psychologists, or other technical experts. It is, rather, a question for each of us as we make value and moral decisions, and for the counselors, priests, rabbis, friends, teachers, coaches, ministers, and ethical philosophers who try to help us make difficult choices.

Conclusion

The promise of science is reproducible results. Scientific work depends on accurate and well described observations. These can easily be made by clinicians and teachers. Any careful, sensitive, trained observer can document changes in tonal quality, or can comment about ease of performance, willingness to perform more, etc. When we use an approach to help or to teach people, it is important that we document how each instruction produces specific effects. Dramatic claims and testimony from famous performers are generally not convincing unless backed up by careful observation. Once a technique has been repeatedly validated by clinical research or parametric research, it then becomes necessary to test the reproducibility of the effect, the size of the effect, and the contribution of "non-specific" or "placebo" factors to the overall effect.

Thus, if we are advocating a technique of differential relaxation at the piano keyboard, or the Alexander Technique, or autogenic training, or slow, deep-breathing, etc., it is incumbent upon us to prove that they actually work. At best, parametric research should be done. Groups of subjects should randomly be assigned either to learn a special technique, or not. Those not taught the technique should receive some other treatment. Multiple measures of performance anxiety and quality of performance should be taken, and long-term effects measured. If this is not practical one should at least record the student's anxiety level (e.g., on a self-rated 0-100 scale), tone quality, frequency of performance, and other aspects. By keeping good records on each student, there is at least some prospect of making choices of technique on the basis of demonstrated merit.

Even after several apparently well done parametric studies have appeared to validate a technique, we still may not be convinced of its effectiveness. Experimenter bias may lurk as a confounding factor. Also, as I have already described, there are many forms of anxiety. A technique may have a beneficial effect on one kind, but no effect on another. Similarly, from study to study, techniques of teaching or therapy tend to vary slightly, as do the populations on whom the methods are tested, and the personalities of the instructors or therapists. Thus, many studies are needed if we hope to know the conditions under which the technique does and does not work, on whom, and administered by whom.

In the whole field of tension in the performance of music, there are now fewer than a dozen published parametric studies. Therefore, beware of people who say that their techniques are "scientific" on the basis of only one or two studies. Science is a process, not a judge or arbiter. On the other hand, we cannot confine our teaching or therapy to those techniques that have been well validated, because, if we did so we would have almost no tools at all, especially at this early stage. Although scientific findings may be helpful as guides to the teacher or therapist, therapy and teaching (and, in fact, the practice of medicine) still are arts. Although scientific technology can provide useful tools, and although all techniques can be validated only by the use of scientific method, science can, nevertheless, be a blinder as well as a boon, unless we see it in its proper place.

REFERENCES

Appel, S.S., "Modifying solo performance anxiety in adult pianists," *Journal of Music Therapy,* Vol. 13, Pp.1-16, 1976.

Brantigan, C.O., Brantigan, T.A., and Neil, J., "The effect of beta blockage on stage fright," *Rocky Mountain Medical Journal*, Vol. 7, Pp .227-232, 1979.

Ellis, A. and Grieger, R., *Handbook of rational-emotive therapy.* New York: Springer, 1977.

Frank, J., "Expectation of therapeutic outcome — The placebo effect and the role of induction interview." In J.D. Frank, R. Hoehn-Saric, S.D. Imber, B.L. Lieberman, and A.E. Stone (editors), *Effective ingredients of successful psychotherapy,* New York: Brunner/Mazel, 1978.

Horney, K., *Are you considering psychoanalysis?* New York: Norton, 1962.

Kendrick, M.J., Craig, K.D., Lawson, D.M., and Davidson, P.O., "Cognitive and behavioral therapy for musical performance anxiety," *Journal of Consulting and Clinical Psychology,* Vol. 50, Pp.353-362, 1982.

Lang, P.J. "Fear reduction and fear behavior: Problems in treating a construct," In J. Shlien (Ed.), *Research in Psychotherapy,* Vol. III, Washington, D.C. American Psychological Association, 1968.

Lavallee, Y.J., Lamontagne, G., Pinard, G., Annable, L., and Tetreault, L., "Effect of EMG biofeedback, diazepam and their combination on chronic anxiety," *Journal of Psychosomatic Research,* Vol. 21, Pp.65-71, 1977.

Lehrer, P.M. "How to relax and not to relax: A re-evaluation of the work of Edmund Jacobson," *Behavior Research and Therapy,* Vol. 20, Pp.417-428, 1982.

Lehrer, P.M. ,"What is performance anxiety? — A psychological study of the responses of musicians to a questionnaire about performance anxiety," In C. Grindea, E. Ho, P.A. Lehrer, and R. Hall (Eds.), *International Conference on Tension in Performance: Publication of Conference Papers,* Kingston Polytechnic, Kingston upon Thames, England, 1981.

Lehrer, P.M., Rosen, R.C., Kostis, J.B., and Greenfield, D. "Treating stage fright in musicians: The use of beta-blockers," *New Jersey Medicine,* Vol. 84, pp.27-33, 1987.

Lund, D.R., A comparative study of three therapeutic techniques in the modification of anxiety behavior in instrumental music performance, Unpublished Ph.D. dissertation, University of Utah, 1972.

Marks, I., *Fears and phobias.* London: Heinemann, 1969.

Meichenbaum, D.H., Gilmore, J.B., and Fedoravicius, A., "Group insight versus group desensitization in treating speech anxiety," In C.M. Franks and

G.T. Wilson (Eds.), *Annual Review of Behavior Therapy, Theory and Practice*. New York: Brunner/Mazel, 1973.

Norton, G.R., MacLean, L., and Wachna, E., "The use of cognitive desensitization and self-directed mastery training for treating stage fright," *Cognitive Therapy and Research*, Vol. 2, Pp. 61-64, 1978.

Rimm, D.C. and Masters, J.C., *Behavior therapy: Techniques and empirical findings*, Second edition. New York: Academic Press, 1979.

Rosenthal, R.R., "Interpersonal expectations: Effects of the experimenter's hypothesis," In R.R. Rosenthal and R.L. Rosnow (Eds.). *Artifact in Behavioral Research*, Academic Press, Pp. 182-277, 1969.

Schultz, J. and Luthe, W. Autogenic Methods, Vol. I of Luthe, W. (Ed.), *Autogenic Therapy*, New York: Grune and Stratton, 1969.

Schwartz, G.E., "Relaxation is not relaxation is not relaxation: Cognitive and somatic patterning in meditation versus exercise," In F.J. McGuigan (Ed.), *Tension control: Proceedings of the fifth annual meeting of the American Association for the Advancement of Tension Control*, Louisville, KY, 1979.

Sweeney. G.A. and Haran, J.J., "Separate and combined effects of cue-controlled relaxation and cognitive restructuring in the treatment of musical performance anxiety," *Journal of Counseling Psychology*, Vol. 29, Pp.486-497, 1982.

Taub, E., "Self-regulation of human tissue temperature," In G.E. Schwartz and J. Beatty (Eds.), *Biofeedback: Theory and Research*, New York: Academic Press, 1977.

Wardle, A., Behavior modification by reciprocal inhibition of instrumental performance anxiety," In C. Madsen, R.D. Greer, and C.H. Madsen (Eds.). *Research in music behavior: Modifying music behavior in the classroom*. New York: Teachers College Press, 1978.

Woolfolk, R.L. and Lehrer, P.M., *Clinical stress management*. New York: Guilford Press, 1984.

THE PRICE OF STRESS IN EDUCATION

Lorin Hollander
Concert pianist and lecturer
New York City

We are living in very remarkable times. These are not only troubled times, but also times of truly unprecedented opportunity. I am speaking on a global level. Before looking specifically at what we are here for, I think we should acknowledge the many crises that are facing humankind at this remarkable point in history, because some of the answers may hinge upon what we discover here. There are so many crises one hardly knows where to begin. One reads that between one-quarter and one-third of the people on the planet are starving. Pollution and the depletion of natural resources are awesome problems. Peter Russell described what seems to be happening as some giant cancer on the surface of the planet, depleting in decades the gifts left to us from millenia of natural evolution.

On the other hand, there are many who see this as a time of a new flowering of human potential. We may be witnessing and be a part of what is called the "new age of consciousness." We may be delving anew into the ancient and profound mysteries of life, a path of enlightenment and mystical experience. There may be, in fact, a global evolution of consciousness happening. We are just beginning to grasp the awesome and wondrous scope of the universe, of our place on this planet, and of the importance of the still unanswered mysteries of the origins of consciousness and our destiny.

There is yet another crisis, perhaps the most serious of all: the crisis in education. It has been about one year since the publication of the United States government's Commission on Excellence in Education. The government's report, *A Nation at Risk,* offered a much quoted statement, that we are drowning in a rising tide of mediocrity that threatens our very existence as a nation and a people. Although this study is primarily concerned with developing basic skills in school, and affirms the importance of art and music in education, it really did not state what, in my opinion, it should have stated, and what many of our cognitive and perceptual sciences are confirming: that the arts, and particularly music, are imperative to the basic education of every human being.

This has been understood in many other societies. Indeed, anthropologists and historians have studied uncounted numbers of societies, those now living and those long gone, noting that virtually every one of them places high among its priorities the teaching of its arts, its music and mystical or religious traditions, to the young.

I think it can be inferred that we are no longer nurturing creativity in our children. We may even be damaging the creativity of our children in the schools.

Interestingly, our discussions today on stage fright and performance anxiety in musicians suggest how we may be hurting young people in the schools. I want to emphasize that this is through no sinister intent on the part of teachers. Teachers are wonderful, sharing people, grossly underpaid and undervalued in our society, who are there because of their commitment to and love of children. But if we explore stage fright and how, in childhood, it may become ingrained, I think we find a clue. I need not go into the details of what is experienced in stage fright. This subject has been lucidly examined by many people today. I can tell you that in my work, hundreds, and now perhaps thousands of music students, have confided in me that they have felt this to be a very serious problem indeed. We dread the upcoming concert, feeling that perhaps we should have never scheduled it, wishing it would go away. One conductor recently told me that he prays before every concert, "Oh dear God, let me get through this one and I promise I'll never do it again."

Sometimes the musician senses that the entire audience has become critical, has recognized a flaw, and is becoming judgmental. Of course, the artist's concentration is lost. This leads to other problems, perhaps another missed note, or a missed passage, or a serious memory slip. Sensing the presence of these people, a performer becomes more concerned with what they are thinking than with the communication of the emotion of the music. We even mis-translate a tension in our bodies and mistake it for the presence, attitude, and disapproval of judges or critical people. This is the very mechanism of the shadow projection. We take our own drive, and instead of feeling it as our drive to communicate, we sense it as a pressure from without. Our own anger we experience as fear.

The tightening in the body is intimately connected with our sense of rhythmic pulse. The experience of undulation in the body, the experience of the dance, is a powerfully important psychologic mechanism. In *Steppenwolf,* Harry

Haller could not proceed along the path of enlightenment until he learned to dance. A musician knows that when things are going well in the practice room or on the stage, there is a sense of pulse, of rhythmic movement, of dance. The body has entered an undulatory experience, a rising and a falling which one can just step away from and the body continues. As with breathing, one can control it or let it happen. When we are relaxed and free, communicative and sharing, it is there. Indeed the rhythm or the dance is there in much of life; it is, in fact, a metaphor for much of life. So much of nature has a rhythmic pulse; the heart beat, the beat of wings, planetary movements, the seasons, electromagnetism, even the big bang, with its explosion and swirling dance of galaxies spiraling to its eventual size, only to collapse and explode once more (a "Big Twang"). We are involved in a powerful, rhythmic, undulatory experience.

Music therapy and music psychology confirm that underneath an emotional struggle is a locking up or a tightening of the experience of the dance. Hurt, resentment, and anger all lead to a tenseness which tightens the sense of pulse. And this happens in the schools. A child turns in a paper and the teacher, possibly just because he or she was too busy, marked it for the spelling or grammatical errors, inadvertently dismissing the content. The child who reached out and shared much of herself or himself so creatively and so daringly, feels hurt, put down, and humiliated, and decides that he or she will never again risk sharing quite so openly. Later the child is speaking in front of a class, or acting in a school play, when suddenly something awful happens. There is a tightening, a clutching in the deep muscle layers, which the child mistranslates as, "I am now sensing the presence and disapproval of authority figures, my teachers, my peers," and then stops. The child becomes more concerned with what others are thinking than with self-expression.

The memory of this experience, and the anguish, do not quickly fade. A public speaker says something that may not be one hundred percent accurate, or overstates something, and someone may comment on it, leading the speaker to sense a "critical other." Writers begin to write, and as they sit down before the word processor or typewriter they experience the thought of some critical person before they have broken through to the experience that is a part of themselves. The lawyer's critical other is the judge; the teacher's critical other is in the supervisor or in the classroom where, on certain days, students can see right through him or her. Scientists describe that what often keeps them from being most daring and most brilliant is the sense of the "scientific authority" which, though consistent with the rigor and integrity of scientific method, still arrests creativity.

I do not advocate the abolition of criticism. I advocate enlightened criticism. There is a Sufi saying: "Look not for the devil in the desert; seek him in the over-critical teacher." Those who have played a musical instrument in a class lesson, or even alone for a teacher, know how it feels when the teacher puts something down, even if the comment is made in the heat of a moment. Those who are on stage and evidence some slight flaw, and start to sense the critical other, might notice that their sense of pulse has become stuck. Next comes the withholding of expression, which we are finding is a part of the description of a creatively stifled, neurotic person. This is what Kubic spoke about in the *Neurotic Distortions of the Creative Process.*

This leads us to a very interesting possibility. One of the ways back, perhaps the most rapid way back to a creative experience, can be accomplished through dance, song, and the expression of emotion. Indeed, it seems that music can be in education a process by which a child rediscovers creative curiosity and joy. Music touches the very mechanisms that become, in their basic structural somatic levels, blocked. Do you realize what this could mean to music education and for musicians in general, at a time when the very survival of humans might hinge on nurturing creativity in children? We are in a very complicated territory because, as it is becoming apparent today, musicians are often as blocked and stifled as anyone, having themselves suffered from a music education that has inadvertently stifled creativity. A great deal of concern has been expressed that we are not nurturing the emotional, joyous, communicative, visionary experiences and expression in our children. Rather, we seem preoccupied with their accuracy and speed. We therefore find professionals whose music is often lacking in soul and warmth, lacking a vision and daring poetic beauty.

An opportunity exists for music teachers, now and in the future. They are, after all, in an ideal position to become, together with the power of music, healers of many of our children's ills. But we must nurture their own humanity, equipping them with the necessary psychologic knowledge and wisdom that will allow them to accomplish this important task. Beauty is found in the fact that as musicians learn to break through their own creative blocks and fears, going through that painful but remarkable process of giving up resentments and fears to reach out to humanity through their music, they may be able to help others break through in a similar way.

Music has always been known to touch the highest reaches of the human soul and spirit. It is shaped upon the crystalline vision of creative wonder and is imbued with the awesome palette of human emotions. Herman Hesse spoke about the immortals — certain people who, in their creative process, poke their heads out and glimpse something he called the "icy ether," something that has been spoken to us so often in the mystic traditions and shown to us so often in great art. Huxley termed this the perennial philosophy. It is what Hofstadter spoke of as the eternal golden braid. It is the experience of Bach's fugues, of the mathematic concepts of Gödel, and of the graphic tessellations of Escher. They grasped one of the oldest truths. The cathedrals are shaped upon its laws, the mosques are decorated with its designs; the implicate order, the sacred geometry.

In our society, music is not understood as a basic among basics, as it has been known since antiquity. Those who do not see music as a basic do not understand that the very gifts of music supply the cognitive skills, intellectual rigor, discipline, and conceptual frameworks that they blindly search for elsewhere. The harmonic, contextual thinking in music touches the very structures of our thinking; it allows us to explore the relations of the mind and body. Music has always been known to hold the answers.

We need more research. We need to bring together, as we have brought together here, musicians and scientists to explore this magnificent human capability. It holds many secrets and supplies many answers. As Kepler sensed, there is a music of the spheres. As Rumi noted, "We have heard these melodies in Paradise; but while we are shrouded by gross earthy veils, how can the tones of the dancing spheres reach us?" Music can be a tremendous healing force in education. I encourage you in this important work.

Section II

Neuropsychologic Issues in Music

MUSIC AND THE BRAIN: THE NEUROLOGY OF MUSICAL BEHAVIOR

INTRODUCTION

Stuart A. Schneck
Professor of Neurology
University of Colorado Health Sciences Center
Denver, Colorado

The session this morning is entitled, "Music and the Brain: The Neurology of Musical Behavior." You will hear presentations concerning anatomic, physiologic, and psychologic correlates of musical experience and activity, concepts that assign a significant role for musical perception and expression to the right cerebral hemisphere. This view is a relatively recent one, for at the end of the last century, amusia, that is, an impaired capacity for musical activity, was thought to be intimately associated with abnormalities of the left hemisphere, similar to those productive of language disturbances in most people.

Many clinical and pathologic studies done on brain injured patients have seemed to support this view. However, particularly since Milner's work in 1962 and subsequent studies using information derived from normal subjects, many now believe that the right hemisphere is predominant for musical behavior. This is particularly thought to be so in terms of emotional experience, expression, and the initial development of general musical ability. Individuals whose left hemisphere has been removed may still sing better than they speak. Also, blocking the function of the right hemisphere with sodium amytal produces amusia with little change in language function.

Most brain events, however, are rarely simple enough to assign exclusively to one hemisphere, or even to one biologic system. There is evidence that learning influences laterality for musical perception. In some tests, musically naive subjects may have right hemisphere dominance, while musical sophistication is associated with left hemisphere predominance, especially as analytic processes for music become enhanced.

Very recent work with birds illustrates the effects of certain hormones, particularly testosterone, on forebrain control of the complex learned behavior of singing. All canaries, for example, have a special anatomic pathway for song. But this is a learned behavior found only in adult male birds. Castration before adult life prevents singing in male canaries, while testosterone given to females allows the development of song. We obviously have much to learn before we understand better the neuro-psycho-physiologic substrata of musical behavior.

One of our speakers will talk about the brain mechanisms utilized by musicians to make highly skilled muscular movements. You undoubtedly have been thrilled, as I have, by the speed and exactmess of the fingers of a virtuoso pianist or violinist. Sir James Paget once studied a pianist playing a presto by Mendelssohn. In the course of this four minute and three second piece an average of seventy-two bi-manual finger movements were made per second. Seventy-two movements in each hand per second. An expert pianist can make ten repetitions of a single note per second. That is only fifty milliseconds for each downstroke. Just how this incredible activity is controlled, and how we may influence it therapeutically for those performers who have motor control problems is very much worth increased attention from researchers, ranging from systems engineers to physiologists.

Finally, there is the question of musical recall. Just where musical memories are stored was given exciting emphasis by Penfield in the 1950's. He found that electrical stimulation of the superior and lateral aspects of the first temporal convolution of the brain, more on the right than on the left, was sometimes productive of musical perceptions in unanesthetized patients. This, however, is a far cry from understanding how Mendelssohn could write out from memory the score of *A Midsummer's Night Dream* overture, when the original was left in a London taxi. Or how Enesco, after a single rehearsal of a work by Ravel, was able to play immediately every note again, from memory! Those of you who watched a recent television presentation of *idiots savants* on *60 Minutes* saw and heard an example of a very similar phenomenon.

A NEUROPSYCHOLOGIST LOOKS AT MUSICAL BEHAVIOR

Tedd Judd
Department of Psychiatry
Pacific Medical Center
Seattle, Washington

INTRODUCTION

Music, the Universal Language — we've heard that phrase many times, and so, presumably, had the 19th Century neurologists who began the neuro-psychological study of music. They therefore assumed that music would be strongly lateralized in the brain as language is, and that there would be, if not universality, at least a fair amount of consistency about its representation from one individual to the next. They were wrong on both counts.

The Lateralization of Music

In 1895, Edgren (Table 1) reviewed 50 cases of amusia, that is, acquired neurologic disorders of musical abilities. He compared amusia to aphasia, that is, acquired disorders of language. He concluded that, while amusia and aphasia did not always coincide, amusia, like aphasia, resulted from left hemisphere damage and that music therefore was a left hemisphere function.

But, in 1898, Ludwig Mann published a case of a singer with a traumatic injury to the posterior inferior part of the right frontal lobe who was left unable to sing or whistle accurately. Four similar cases came out of World War I (Henschen, 1920), tempting some investigators to conclude that music was a right hemisphere function.

Then, in 1920, Henschen reviewed over 300 cases in which music was investigated. Only these five cases just described involved unilateral right hemisphere damage and no aphasia. He concluded that music was a left hemisphere function. Consequently, in 1935, Weisenberg and McBride were able to write, "The older supposition that music depended largely on the right hemisphere . . . has been discarded."

But then, in 1962, Brenda Milner demonstrated an acquired impairment in tonal memory and timbre discrimination in patients undergoing right but not left anterior temporal lobectomy. In 1964, Doreen Kimura found a left ear or presumed right hemisphere advantage in identifying excerpts of Baroque music in a dichotic listening experiment with normals. There followed the widespread belief the music was a right hemisphere function.

Then, in 1974, Bever and Chiarello demonstrated a right ear or presumed left hemisphere advantage on a monotic musical task with trained choirboys. Thus, music once again shuttled across the corpus callosum into the left hemisphere, at least for "musicians."

TABLE 1

A BRIEF HISTORY OF DOCTRINES OF THE LATERALIZATION OF MUSIC IN THE BRAIN

Left	Right
Edgren, 1895	
	Mann, 1898
Henschen, 1920	
	Milner, 1962
Bever & Chiarello, 1974	

Why all this confusion? I think that much of it comes from the false assumptions I noted at the outset — that music is like language and that everybody's brain handles music the same way.

In fact, when you review the literature, it seems that a lesion almost anywhere in the brain can disturb musical abilities in some way.

At the same time, it is impressive how resilient musical abilities are. For example, from Homer to Stevie Wonder it is clear that you can be blind and be a musician. Beethoven, Smetana, Faure, and many others have demonstrated that not only can the deaf compose music, they can also perform music extraordinarily well, including the congenitally deaf (Edwards, 1974; Hood, 1977). In fact, there is a student right now in the British Royal Academy of

Music, a double major in piano and percussion, who is profoundly deaf (Cleall, 1983).

The examples of musical *idiots savants* make it quite clear that one can be quite musical with a very low IQ (Hill, 1978). There are now a number of well-documented cases of musicians who have continued with professional careers in spite of severe aphasias, most notably the Russian composer Shebalin (Luria, Tsvetkova, & Futer, 1965). And in a few minutes I will describe the preservation of many musical skills in a composer with a large right hemisphere stroke. So you can be blind, or deaf, or mentally retarded, or without language skills and still be musical.

Observations like these have lead many of us to adopt a new position: we now feel that the whole brain is involved in music, but that different areas of the brain make their own characteristic contributions to musical behaviors. It should also be clear by now that the metaphor of music as a language is inadequate to serve our needs. We need to look for other ways of describing and understanding musical behaviors. We need new metaphors for music other than language. In short, neuromusicology compels us to improve our psychomusicology.

The Psychology of Musical Abilities

At this point I would like to sketch out an overview of what might be involved in attempting to take a fresh look at the psychology of music. What might a theory of musical behaviors look like that could be of some help in understanding the brain? Figure 1 facetiously presents a gross oversimplification of one corner of such a theory.

To begin with we would want to have a list of behaviors, or at any rate, some sort of description of the domain of interest, of what constitutes musical behaviors. I've listed a few activities at the top of Figure 1 that might fall within that domain to give you a feel for its breadth. Then we would want some sort of catalogue of the underlying skills required to perform those activities, such as the list at the bottom of Figure 1. Of course, these are not likely to fit into discrete boxes like this, but this gives you the idea.

Then we would want to have some idea of the connections between the behaviors and the skills — which of these skills is necessary at what levels of achievement and in what combinations to perform each of these activities. So that, for example, the ability to keep a beat is very important for playing in a marimba band and conducting an orchestra but not so important for composing or writing a review, and so on. Neuro-psychology can be especially helpful

FIGURE 1

WHAT MIGHT A THEORY OF MUSICAL BEHAVIORS LOOK LIKE?

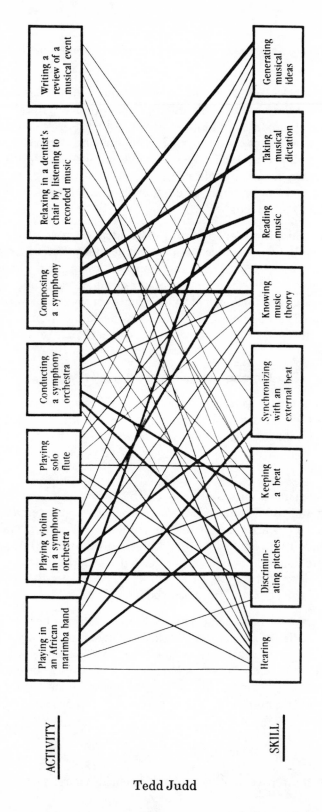

Tedd Judd

in determining the nature of these connections. Eventually we would want some heirarchic or spatial organization of the representation of these skills, since we would want to know, for example, if hearing was a prerequisite for discriminating pitches.

I would like to take a closer look at the first two of these activities to see what the theory might look like in a little more detail (Table 2). Playing orchestral violin is an activity fairly commonly examined in the psychology of music, (since many of the researchers, including myself, have orchestral training) but African marimba playing is not. I have chosen this example because if we

---

TABLE 2

SKILLS INVOLVED IN:

PLAYING LEAD MARIMBA IN AN AFRICAN MARIMBA BAND	PLAYING VIOLIN IN A SYMPHONY ORCHESTRA
Listen to the band and coordinate with it, especially rhythmically	Listen to the orchestra and coordinate with it, especially on intonation and dynamics
Maintain and manipulate tempo	Follow the conductor
Remember and produce the patterns and structure of the piece	Read the music
Plan and play variations	Minimize variations
Alter the piece according to the performance of the other players and the response of the crowd	Ignore audience — accept coordination from conductor and score
Maintain excitement (much facial expression, body movement, whistling shouting, singing)	Maintain decorum — modest body English

---

are truly to study the biology of music making, we have to consider all kinds of music, not just the composed classical music of the upper classes of Europe. Perhaps the notion of music as a universal language has made people feel that what we find with one musical culture will apply to all, so we need not bother to study others. I hope to demonstrate here that this is not so. Had linguists felt that it was adequate to study only European languages and not make a serious search for universals in language, the Chomskian revolution in linguistics probably would have been a long time in coming. The other reason I have chosen this example is because I play in an African style marimba band, specifically playing the music of the Shona people of Zimbabwe.

The music we play comes from an aural tradition. Pieces consist of short repeated phrases with each marimba playing a different part. The lead develops the piece through improvised but stylistically and structually constrained variations on the lead melody and through preestablished musical signals to the rest of the band. The skills involved in playing the lead, then, include listening to the band and coordinating with it, with the emphasis on rhythmic coordination. The violinist must listen and coordinate, too, but here part of the burden of rhythmic coordination is on the conductor. For the violinist, though, there is a greater need for coordination of intonation and dynamics. The marimba player need not worry about intonation in performance, since it is a fixed-pitch instrument. The marimba player must be very sensitive to maintaining and manipulating the tempo of the piece, while in the orchestra the conductor does much of this work. The marimba player must remember and produce the patterns and structure of the piece, while the violinist need not remember so much, but must read music. The marimba player plans and plays variations, responds to the crowd, and is very expressive in extra-musical ways, while the violinist minimizes variations, generally ignores the audience while playing, and maintains decorum.

That's just considering the more or less cognitive skills. There are also differences in the mechanical skills involved due to the differences in the instruments. As we can see, then, two musical activities which appear superficially the same — playing instruments in an ensemble — actually involve markedly different skills because of the musical traditions involved. One of the most striking contrasts is that between an aural and written musical culture, and so I would like to explore these two skills, music reading and musical memory, in some more detail. As we shall see later, this difference can be neuromusicologically significant.

Music Reading

We will start with music reading. Here is a sample of entirely fictitious staff music notation, (Figure 2). Although this system of music notation is widespread, it is only one of many dozens of systems in use around the world, each with their own peculiarities. The first thing we may notice is that staff notation incorporates within it a language writing system (largo, accelerando, etc.). So, if you are going to read music, you have to be able to read language to some extent. In this language writing system there is an arbitrary correspondance between a set of graphic shapes or letters and certain language sounds and/or the speech gestures necessary to produce those sounds. That is, it is a phonetic system. The system also includes some figures which are not phonetic but ideographic, like the Chinese writing system, that is, symbols that stand for words or ideas. These include numbers, and also punctuation. This system becomes even more complex through the use of different languages and abbreviations.

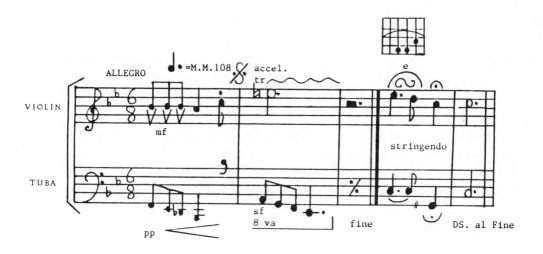

Figure 2

Varieties of Symbolism in Staff Music Notation

Turning to the notes, we see that they are also in some sense phonetic, actually, diastematic, in that there is one note for each sound in a very rough sense.

But whereas duration is represented by the shape of the note, pitch is not (except in the Appalachian shape-note variation of staff music notation). It is represented instead by position on the staff, and even there, it takes on meaning only relative to a host of other symbols, (clef signs, key signatures, accidentals, etc.). Duration is also redundantly represented by position, the space left after a note being roughly proportional to its duration. We also have what we might call ideographs, symbols which refer to a collection of notes, rather than just one note (ornament symbols, bar repeat signs, etc.).

There are also symbols for how one plays the notes, (articulation and bowing symbols). There are symbols which represent loudness, both linguistically and spatially. There are traffic signs that don't refer to sound at all but to the sequence of the reading process, (repeat signs, D.C., etc.). There are other signs that have no representation in sound but refer instead to a way of thinking about the music, (time signatures, bar lines). Many of these symbols have conventional sizes and positions on the page which make them more distinguishable and contribute to their significance. Key and time signatures, for example, are usually at the beginning of the line and a given size, etc. Guitar tablature is a pictographic representation of the fretboard. To summarize, staff notation uses spacing and size more than written English and it has a wider array of things represented and ways of representing them.

With all of this marvelous complexity available, it seems inadequate to say of a brain damaged subject simply that he or she was unable to read music, as is usually the case in the literature. I will describe for you a few cases in which some of these analyses became relevant.

Howard Gardner, Norman Geschwind and I (Judd, Gardner, and Geschwind, 1983) studied a 77 year old composer who suffered a left occipital lobe stroke and a resulting alexia without agraphia, that is, inability to read language with a preserved ability to write. Unlike several previous such cases, he was able to read music fairly well. In language reading he was able to identify individual letters in isolation on the page, but had much more difficulty when they were next to one another as in words, a fairly typical finding for this condition. However, the opposite was true for musical symbols. With randomly scattered symbols he was only able to identify half, but in their proper musical context, he identified almost all of them. He reported that he tended to read the pitch of notes relative to their predecessors rather than relative to their position on the staff, and this was evident in his reading errors. Verbal identification of musical symbols was frequently quite difficult for him, even though he was able to play the music those symbols represented quite easily. So, we can see that the redundancies of size and position are important. So,

Tedd Judd

too, is the nature of the task, the nature of the material represented, and the way it is represented. All affect his ability to read it, and suggest that different skills and different brain areas are involved.

Another relevant case, published by Dr. Brust in 1980, was a young woman who had had a tumor removed from her left parietal lobe, and developed alexia with agraphia, that is, inability to read or write. She showed some preservation of semantic reading sometimes seen in such cases. For example, she might read the word "boat" as "ship." Her music reading was also impaired. I had an opportunity to examine her and found that she was able to read the letter names of chords from the notation in order to play chords on her guitar, yet she was unable to name the letters. So what is represented again makes a difference. She was also able to read the guitar tablature.

Musical Memory

We have talked about music reading, which is critical to written musical cultures. Now let us turn to musical memory, which is so important to aural musical cultures.

A 47 year old man was referred to me for a neuromusicological assessment. He had been a high school music teacher when, at age 35, he had a stroke from a ruptured anterior communicating artery aneurism. He had a mild residual right hemiparesis, that is, weakness on the right. He had been living in a nursing home since then where he often played the piano and went out twice a week to sing in a church choir.

On testing, I found that he was able to sing well and to correct my sight-singing and make suggestions consistent with his teaching background. When I gave him some difficult sight-singing exercises, he made some reasonable errors, corrected himself, and then repeated the exercise correctly. After we had done several of these he said, "Let's do this next." I said, "We already did that one." He said, "No, we didn't," and proceeded to sing correctly an exercise we had already done. He insisted he had not done it. When I saw him the next day he did not remember me or our test session. His stroke had caused in him a severe antereograde amnesia, that is, an inability to learn anything new. In spite of his anmesia, however, he had been able to learn and retain the correct singing of the exercise, even though it seemed unfamiliar to him.

This phenomenon was not entirely new. In 1970, Starr and Phillips described a patient with a profound antereograde amnesia resulting from a surgical lesion who was nevertheless able to learn new pieces on the piano. Like G.M., he denied any knowledge of the piece, but given the opening bars, he played it through without difficulty. Gardner (1975) described a similar case who was also able to learn a simple song with intensive drilling. These last two cases were also shown to have preserved learning of simple motor skills.

These three cases illustrate that music learning is somehow special because it can take place in the face of amnesia. Music learning is part of a cluster of special learning abilities which are spared in the amnesic syndrome.

What are these special learning abilities? They include classical and operant conditioning, motor skills such as mirror writing and rotor pursuit tasks (like trying to keep a pencil on a particular spot on a phonograph record as it goes around), perceptual learning such as identifying incomplete pictures of objects, and complex learning such as musical pieces or mathematical procedures (Parkin, 1982). These special skills have been described as procedural memory, or habit memory, or knowing how to do something, as contrasted with knowing that something is the case.

The medial parts of the temporal lobe are usually damaged in the amnesic syndrome. If these areas of the brain are not critical to this kind of music learning, what other area is? The answer may lie in the frontal lobes. Damage to the frontal cortex of experimental animals produces a variety of related deficits in the regulation and sequencing of responses. In a review of these studies, Nauta (1971) concluded, "It could even be suggested that the 'frontal' animal has suffered a memory impairment after all, even though this loss affects the storage of its action plans rather than that of its external-perceptual images."

Similar conclusions apply to humans. Frontal lobe lesions have long been associated with impairments in planning skills and self-regulation of complex activities. Bancaud and co-workers (1976) found that stimulation of the cingulate cortex in the frontal lobes in humans during surgery for epilepsy produced complex coordinated movements involving especially the hands and mouth. They concluded that cingulate cortex "seems to have a major role in inciting to action and in coordination of highly complex movements."

Faillace and co-workers (1971) studied four patients before and after bilateral cingulotomies for intractable pain. Cingulotomy is essentially a refinement of the frontal lobotomy procedure and involves discrete lesions to the cingulate bundle, a main connection between the cingulate cortex, the hippocampus, and the frontal cortex. The hippocampus is a part of limbic system which has been especially implicated in new learning. All four of the cingulotomy patients showed major post-surgical impairments in learning and performing a complex tapping sequence. The test consisted of tapping four geometrical figures in a row in a specified, demonstrated order (Figure 3). The most complex of these sequences was 1 2 3 4 3 2 1 2 3 4 2 3 1 2 3 4 3 2 1. This sequence quite long but has considerable structure which makes it possible for normals

Tapping Board

Tapping Sequences: A) 1 2 3 2 1 2 3

B) 1 2 3 4 3 2 3 2 1 2 3 4

C) 1 2 3 4 2 3 1 2 3 4 2 3 1 2 3 4

D) 1 2 3 4 3 2 1 2 3 4 2 3 1 2 3 4 3 2 1

Task: For each sequence, instruct by demonstration without verbal labeling of the task until 4 consecutive correct sequences are achieved. Administer 5 trials of 30 seconds each; count the number of fully correct repetitions of the sequences.

Figure 3

Faillace, et. al. (1971) Sequential Tapping Task

to learn it relatively easily. That structure is not unlike many musical structures — one might call it an ABA or theme and variation.

I have had the opportunity to examine a guitar player-folksinger three years after bilateral cingulatomy for pain and depression (Teuber, Corkin, and Twitchell, 1977, Case K.M.). She came to me complaining of difficulty learning, composing, improvising, and performing music. She claimed that component skills were intact, but she had difficulty putting them all together to play and sing a song and maintain the flow of the music. She also complained of difficulty following the logic of a conversation or story, remembering appointments, remembering where she had put things, and playing chess and gin rummy.

In standard neuropsychological testing she was essentially normal except for mild memory impairment. However, she was markedly impaired on my replication of the Faillace Sequential Tapping Task. On each sequence she performed less than one-half the number of repetitions of each of my five controls.

When I tested her musical abilities, she was able to play and sing with only a few hesitations an overlearned song she had composed five years earlier. This song demonstrated a high level of proficiency in singing, chording, finger-picking, and composing. She was able to name and imitate chords, play chords named, match pitches, and identify musical symbols and their significance. However, she was very deficient in learning new chord sequences, melodies, and rhythms, and had difficulty with simple rhythmic tasks. Her sight reading was very hesitant and unmusical, although this was never a well-practiced skill for her.

This case presents a striking double dissociation with the previous three cases. While the other cases were amnesic for most material and showed some sparing of "action plan" learning including music, my patient had only mild impairments on most memory tasks but had marked difficulty on complex motor sequence learning and particularly music. Her impairment appears to be primarily in learning what Nauta called "action plans."

This conclusion must be very tentative, however. The tasks given to my patient were not strictly comparable to those given to the other subjects. Furthermore, the results are culture-bound. My patient's impairments reflect her aural style of making music — yet there is another case (Teuber, Corkin and Twitchill's, 1977) in the literature of a patient who resumed her work as a church organist after two bilateral cingulotomies. Presumably, her habitual use of sight reading skills of a familiar repertoire allowed her to overcome any complex motor sequence learning problems she may have had, just as my patient was able to perform when new music learning was not required.

As if these complications of musical abilities are not enough to worry about, it has been my experience and, I'm sure, yours too, that there are considerable individual differences in music learning styles, (Table 3). In my marimba band, for example, some people will learn new parts primarily by melodic memory, then pick them out "by ear" on the instrument. Others rely heavily on the visual position of the notes, rather like one would learn the Faillace Sequential Tapping Task. Some use counting, music theory concepts, or other verbal mnemonics. After learning a part the first time, some people will rely on motor memory and sticking patterns (which hand strikes which note) to remember the part at the next rehearsal. Some are very dependent on hearing the other parts in the piece to remember their own, while others prefer to learn their parts alone and then may have difficulty fitting it in with the others. Everyone uses all of these strategies at one time or another, but individual preferences are clearly — sometimes maddeningly — identifiable.

```
┌─────────────────────────────────────────────────────────┐
│                                                         │
│                        TABLE 3                          │
│                                                         │
│           MUSIC LEARNING STRATEGIES AND STYLES          │
│                                                         │
│                    (African marimba)                    │
│                                                         │
│                                                         │
│         Aural (melodic, etc.) memory                    │
│                                                         │
│         Visual memory (positions of notes)              │
│                                                         │
│         Verbal memory                                   │
│                                                         │
│                 Music theoretic ideas                   │
│                 Numeric memory (counting the beats or notes │
│                 and remembering the numbers)            │
│                 Song Text                               │
│                                                         │
│         Kinesthetic memory (sticking patterns, etc.)    │
│                                                         │
│         Memory of one part in relation to other parts   │
│                                                         │
└─────────────────────────────────────────────────────────┘
```

We have looked at music reading and musical memory as illustrations of the importance of developing a psychological analysis of musical behaviors for neurologic studies. These also serve as illustrations of the importance of taking individual and cultural differences into account in that analysis.

Neuromusicology: A Case Study

I will end with a case study of a composer with a right hemisphere stroke in order to illustrate the importance of considering metaphors other than language in trying to understand the nature and cerebral organization of musical behaviors. This work was a collaboration with Artin Arslanian and Lyle Davidson, composers, and Simeon Locke and Hugh Mickel, neurologists. (Judd, Arslanian, Davidson, Locke, and Mickel, 1979).

The patient is a 51 year-old, right-handed, male university professor of music and composer. Ten years previous to our investigation he suffered an innominate artery occlusion as a complication of subclavian artery aneurism surgery. He showed a left hemiplegia which soon resolved except for the arm, a left hemisensory deficit and a left visual neglect, although visual fields were full. A computerized tomography scan obtained 8 years after his stroke revealed a large right fronto-parietal lesion and a separate posterior temporal lesion. Despite some lethargy, he resumed teaching music three months after the stroke, and in a year he took up conducting an orchestra again. In the next several years he spent three summers in Europe and learned two foreign languages while he was there. In the last few years before our study he wrote a music text book which contained many original musical examples.

Despite these accomplishments, he complained to his neurologist of a variety of problems. He had trouble following the logic of conversations. Using a dictionary had become a slow, letter-by-letter process. He got lost in oral foreign language drills because he could not tell which small grammatical part of the teacher's repeated questions had been changed. He failed at attempts to draw in perspective. He frequently got lost, sometimes even in his home town. He had difficulty figuring out what mathematical operations were needed to deal with everyday situations such as making change or leaving a tip in a restaurant.

In the musical realm his piano playing was severely handicapped because of his hemiplegia, although his right hand could play as well as ever. His conducting was less inspired. He found that he had particular difficulties conducting music with shifting meters which had previously presented no problems, such as the *Finale* of *Stravinsky's Firebird Suite* where there are seven beats to a measure with irregular subdivision.

He complained of drastic changes in perceiving and recognizing played notes, giving him total insecurity in taking musical dictation. He also complained of difficulty writing music which is best described in his own words: "The bane of my classroom existence for the past ten years has been an inability to write freely in a given time signature without making any errors in reckoning the prescribed number of beats per measure. The heretofore automatic process of measuring has been supplanted by a tendency to measure in terms of phrase length. Currently I have been reduced to digital computation to check the accuracy of my music on the board." In addition, he said that he frequently failed to space notes on the page appropriately in accordance with their relative durations.

He did not listen to music for enjoyment as frequently as he used to, and he said that he no longer had significant emotional experiences from listening to music, although he had no difficulty in remembering the emotional meanings which he had attached to particular pieces in the past.

Finally, his musical composition since the stroke was very limited, despite efforts. One reason he cited was that he was no longer able to create the appropriate emotional milieu or atmosphere which he felt to be a prerequisite to composing. This latter symptom appeared to be a very important factor for him, even though it is difficult to define or describe. It involved, for him, the ability to recall vividly a series of scenes, situations, or moods, and then use those recollections to generate a coherent piece of music.

He experienced another difficulty with composition as well, which is best expressed in his own words: "I seem to be very aware of an inability to synthesize information and to then draw conclusions based upon the interaction of the factors involved. This particular manifestation of insecurity I consider to be a lack of ability to create a Gestalt. It is in this sense I shall use the term. The compositional process for me at this time seems to lack a Gestalt. Notes are correct, orchestration skills are very much intact and show no diminution. Content, however, is dull, lifeless (soulless). Since the compositional process has for me been one of working at several levels of the ongoingness of the melodic, harmonic, rhythmic flow simultaneously and keeping track of the various factors, I find that I am not able to maintain a thread of continuity and must work in small segments which, while appropriate and significant in themselves, do not interrelate with each other."

"Interestingly, I have little difficulty in writing in a serial technique. I find it relatively simple, but I have never been overawed by the musical content of this style of compositon. The manipulation and the various row manifestations present no problem."

I should mention at this point that his introspections were generated essentially independently of any knowledge of current theorizing concerning brain function.

We tested him extensively, both psychologically and musically, and had chosen ten deficits to describe the changes in abilities he had experienced as a result of his stroke. We described all ten deficits subjectively and objectively, musically and non-musically, (Table 4). I will detail this analysis for the last two deficits, as a model for other case studies.

He experienced difficulty in shifting from one mode of thought or pattern of response to another, especially when dealing with the same or similar stimulus materials. This is reflected in his complaints of difficulties following the logic of conversations, in using a dictionary and in language drills as already described. He also showed impaired performance on tests which required the successive formation of different concepts using the same stimulus material, for instance, on the Wisconsin Card Sort Test. In the musical realm, he reported the difficulty conducting mixed meters and composing which I have mentioned. When I asked him to repeat rhythms I had tapped, he showed a tendency to use the same meter for many successive items, even when it was inappropriate, and when he did switch meter, he showed extra difficulty with that particular item. He also showed impaired Gestalt formation. We use this term in the sense that he used it, that is, he had difficulty drawing conclusions from a set of facts and difficulty appreciating the relationships between several different factors or stimuli. This was seen in his non-musical complaints about drawing and getting lost, and his difficulties with mathematics. He peformed relatively poorly, as well, on verbal abstractions and analogies tasks.

Musically, he complained of a problem of writing the wrong number of beats per bar, and of difficulty composing, as we have mentioned. In the musical tests we gave him, the Gestalt formation difficulty was reflected in his poor performance on counterpoint exercises where he must write several simultaneous melodies which relate to one another according to certain rules. Despite hours of work, he failed in an effort to write a simple canon. Also, he was slow at performing an analysis of unfamiliar pieces given the score, and he at first misused some concepts of advanced analysis.

To summarize, what may be the most surprising finding in this case of a professor of music with a large right hemisphere stroke is that his musical abilities are so well preserved. Nevertheless, he shows a number of subtle cognitive and emotional deficits which are typical of patients with right hemisphere lesions. These are present in musical as well as non-musical functioning, and they interact to produce a serious impairment in his ability to compose.

This case, then, lends support to the position that many different parts of the brain make characteristic contributions to the complex of behaviors which we call musical. It illustrates the point that musical deficits frequently are not specifically or exclusively musical, nor are they simply like language deficits. Rather, we must turn to considerations of other modes of thought to understand the structure of musical behaviors. And, finally, I would like to remind you that we must take individual and cultural differences into account in our attempts to understand the biology of music making.

TABLE 4 SUMMARY OF DIFFICULTIES OBSERVED IN A COMPOSER WITH A RIGHT HEMISPHERE STROKE

Difficulty	Non-Musical Complaints	Non-Musical Tests	Musical Complaints	Musical Tests
A. Left Hemiplegia	weakness	neurologic exam	playing piano, bass conducting	piano playing
B. Left Hemisensory Deficit	decreased sensation	neurologic exam	loss of keyboard sense	piano playing
C. Left Visual Neglect	fails to notice things	neurologic exam Digit Symbol		
D. Impaired Singing			decreased range, quality, and power	singing
E. Auditory Temporal Resolution	hearing change	counting short trains of rapid clicks	difficulty with dictation, and hearing rhythms	duration discrimination, rhythm reproduction, and dictation
F. Memory	difficulty with word-finding and arithmetic	naming, calculations, Wechsler Memory Scale	dictation, and theory	dictation, theory, and melody recall

Difficulty	Non-Musical Complaints	Non-Musical Tests	Musical Complaints	Musical Tests
G. Motor Preseveration		Writing "MN" repeatedly in cursive	rhythm errors in playing and conducting	rhythm reproduction
H. Set-Shifting Difficulty	difficulties with conversation, following directions, language drills, dictionary use, and calculations	test directions, Wisconsin Card Sort Test, Digits Backwards, Shipley Abstractions, Raven's Matrices, Visual-Verbal Test, Arithmetic	mixed meter conducting and composing	rhythm reproduction, melody reproduction, meter determination, and rhythm reading
I. Impaired "Gestalt Formation"	difficulties with drawing, finding his way, conversation, arithmetic, and learning the Russian alphabet	Block Design, Picture Arrangement, Object Assembly, Shipley Abstractions, Hooper Visual Organization Test drawings, stick patterns, 3D blocks, Raven's Matrices, Visual-Verbal Test, Porteus mazes, Wisconsin Card Sort Test	difficulty with writing the correct number of beats per bar, spacing notes on the page, and composing, especially counterpoint	writing, meter determination, excerpt identification, analysis, composing counterpoint, Pitch Stream SegregationecrsedAffective Involvement with Musiclethargy
J. Decreased Affective Involvement with Music	lethargy	less involved, listens less		

Tedd Judd

NOTE

A more detailed version of this paper will appear under the title, "The Varieties of Musical Talent," in *The Exceptional Brain: Neuropsychology of Talent and Special Skills*, L. Obler & D. Fein, (Eds), New York: Guilford.

BIBLIOGRAPHY

Bancaud, J., Talairach, J., Geier, S., Bonis, A., Trottier, S., & Manrique, M. *Manifestations Comportementales induites par la stimulationelectrique due gyrus cingulaire anterieur chez l'homme.* Revue Neurologique, 132, 705-724, 1976.

Bever, T.G., Chiarello, R.J., "Cerebral dominance in musicians and non-musicians", *Science,* 185, 137-139, 1974.

Brust, J.C.M. "Music and Language: Musical Alexia and Agraphia," *Brain,* 103, 367-392, 1980.

Cleall, C., "Notes on a young deaf musician," *The Psychology of Music,* 11, 101-102, 1983.

Edgren, I., "Amusie (musikalische Aphasie)," *Deutsche Zeitschriftfur Nervenheilkung,* 6, 1-64, 1895.

Edwards, E. M., *Music Education for the Deaf.* South Waterford, ME: Merriam-Eddy, 1974.

Faillace, L. A., Allen, R. P., McQueen, J. D., Northrup, B., "Cognitive deficits from bilateral cingulotomy for intractable pain in man," *Diseases of the Nervous System*, 32, 171-175 1971.

Gardner, H., *The Shattered Mind*, Pp. 199-200, New York: Knopf, 1975.

Henschen, S. E., *Klinische und anatomische Beitrage zur Pathologie des Gehirns*, Vol. 5, Stockholm, Nordische Bokhandeln, 1920.

Hill, A. L., "Savants: Mentally retarded individuals with special skills," *International Review of Research in Mental Retardation,* 9, 277-298, 1978.

Hood, J. D., "Deafness and music appreciation," In M. Critchely and R. A. Henson (Eds.) *Music and the Brain,* Pp. 378-397, Springfield, MA: Charles C. Thomas, 1977.

Judd, T., Arslanian, A., Davidson, L., Locke, S., and Mickel, H. A., "Right hemisphere stroke in a composer," Paper presented at the International Neuro-psychological Society, New York, February, 1979.

Judd, T., Gardner, H., and Geschwind, N., "Alexia Without Agraphia in a Composer," *Brain*, 106, 435-457, 1983.

Kimura, D., "Left-right differences in the perception of melodies," *Quarterly Journal of Experimental Psychology*, 16, 355-358, 1964.

Luria, A. R., Tsvetkova, L. S., and Futer, D. S., "Aphasia in a composer," *Journal of the Neurological Sciences*, 1, 288-292, 1965.

Mann, L. "Casuistische Beitrage zur Hirnchirurgie und Hirnlokalisation," *Monatschrift fur Psychiatrie und Neurologie*, 4, 369-378, 1898.

Milner, B., "Laterality effects in audition," In V.B. Mountcastle *(Ed.)*, *Inter-hemispheric Relations and Cerebral Dominance*, Baltimore, 1962.

THE STUDY OF SKILLED PERFORMANCE IN MUSICIANS

George P. Moore
Professor of Biomedical Engineering
University of Southern California

The occasion of this conference is testimony to the renewed interest in the manifold of biological, medical, therapeutic and futuristic concerns surrounding music and music performance. For various reasons music performance has defied, resisted or just not invited the invasions of science and technology visited on almost every other aspect of our civilization. The tentative and sporadic investigations earlier in this century have left little legacy of scientific inquiry into the biology of music or music making.

I have spent most of my professional life studying the nervous system, specializing in the analysis of signals sent between nerve cells, and transmitted from sense organs to the brain. A few years ago when I once again became a music student, I thought it might be interesting to apply some of the techniques of the neural sciences to the study of highly skilled and complex behavior in musicians.

Given the many legends about musicians' speed, precision and dexterity, attributes which would make them ideal subjects for sensory and neuromuscular investigation, I found, to my surprise, that while there is work on musicians related to music pedagogy, and some interesting work in the perceptual aspects of music, there was not any systematic effort to study musicians as a class of extraordinarily skilled practitioners of sensori-motor coordination.

Not for several decades have scientists seriously investigated the biological bases of music making. It is not recognized as a legitimate area of scientific research, nor can any agency be identified as having any interest in its becoming so. Yet now may be an ideal time for study to resume.

We enjoy certain advantages today that our predecessors did not. First, we know a great deal more now about the detailed anatomy of the body, especially the nerves, muscles and bones that are employed in instrumental performance, and about the lips and vocal tract which are the instruments of singers.

Second, we know far more today about the psycho-physiology of sensation and perception, about the physiology of neuromuscular control, and about the hierarchical control of movement and the learning processes associated with it.

Third, much progress has been made in understanding the physics of musical instruments, the relation between the structure of instruments and the sounds they make, and the relation between certain purely physical aspects of playing and their acoustic consequences.

And, finally, we enjoy a technological advantage, possessing a wealth of instruments and computers for measuring, recording and analyzing the component processes of musical performance. These devices allow us to identify, and make accurate, systematic observations of the variables that form the basis of exceptional technique.

It is at this point that our fuller understanding of anatomy, physiology, and physics of musical instruments assumes importance, serving to explain and interpret the meaning of our technology-enabled observations. But the scientific study of music and its performance proceeds from empirical observations that are paradoxical, that cannot be explained or interpreted. These are the observations that lead to significant questions. Skilled performance seems so simple, so unitary, that we are enchanted by it rather than challenged to grasp its paradoxes and contradictions. But when we begin to make careful observations and measurements of skilled performers, or study the behavior of students in whom the components of technique have not been successfully assembled, then we find plenty of questions. Having formulated some general questions of interest, we can then proceed to determine the means, technological and procedural, by which answers might be achieved.

The most general statement of our interest is how, and in what way, the instrument becomes an extension of the body of the performer. In contrast to physicists, who study the relation between the instrument and the sound it produces, we want to understand the relation between the body, the brain, and the instrument. We are interested in what the brain knows about the instrument: its size, shape, position, its physical laws. How is this information represented in the brain, and how does it differ from the representation of natural body parts such as the arm? How does the brain reconfigure the biophysics of the body to match the physics of the instrument, and how are these subtle interactions between body and instrument modified to produce various shades of sound and feeling? What are the emergent properties of the resulting organic combination? How are the component pieces of technique integrated in the hierarchy so that they may be subordinated to the more abstract goals of the performance?

Ultimately, our studies are intended to deepen, rather than trivialize, the sense of awe and respect we have for nature's gifts; to sharpen our awareness of the prodigy of orchestration of mind and body that underlies virtuosity, not reduce it to a simplistic list of components. We do not presume to play a role in helping musicians to play better, or in diagnosing their faulty practices or their medical pathologies. These matters are the proper domain of teachers and clinicians. We see as our responsibility the study of how different people actually produce the sounds we hear from their instruments, not to engage in partisan disputes about whether their particular practices are good or bad, correct or incorrect. Our instrumentation already creates enough anxiety in experimental subjects; any additional judgmental burden would only weaken the trust in our relationship.

Choice of Instruments and Measurements

Since the first task is to make measurements of what actually happens in the performance of a particular instrument, we chose two instruments that afforded certain advantages. The first instrument we chose was the cello because it is representative of an important class of instruments; it is relatively large and, therefore, easier to make measurements on than the violin; and because, not by coincidence, I was studying the cello for my own enjoyment. The second instrument we chose was the piano, again partly for its intrinsic interest, and partly because certain technical opportunities presented themselves. My discussion here will be confined to some results obtained from studying cellists.

The most obvious thing to measure is sound, but we also make video tapes of performance to clarify points that may arise later in interpretation of other data. Then it is important to identify and then measure the variables that both characterize and distinguish various aspects and attributes of performance. It is at this level that the wealth of fascinating detail awaits.

In most instances, we want the variables of interest to be available in electrical or electronic form. For this reason, we employ a class of devices known as "transducers," i.e., devices that convert some variable of interest into an electrical signal that can then be accurately measured. For example, we use force transducers, miniature devices that convert the forces or deformations applied to them into electrical signals which can then be amplified and recorded. A phonograph cartridge is an example.

We use these devices to measure acceleration forces associated with bowing or vibrato in cellists, and have also implanted them in the bow or the bridge of a cello to measure directly the forces within those structures generated by neuromuscular activity in the hand and arm. Other electronic circuits have been developed to track the exact position of the fingers on the string, or the point of contact, and hence position, of the bow in relation to the string.

Other devices for amplifying the tiny electrical signals (the electromyogram) which convey the contractile commands from spinal cord to muscle are also useful in monitoring the complex temporal and spatial arrays of muscle activity that underlie the patterns of movement seen in skilled performance. These allow us not only to determine the muscles that are active, but also the ways that command signals for activity must be modulated in relation to the past, present and future positions of the body.

In the future we expect that the technical devices now becoming available for measuring the three-dimensional movement of the body and its parts will decline in price, making the tracking of complex motions routine and economical. For now, they remain beyond the means of most laboratories.

In what follows, I will describe some of the methods and observations which are typical of the beginning phase of any research program of this type.

Some Observations on Bowing

The movement of the bow in playing a stringed instrument is graceful, variable, and, in its variability, essential to the production of various sounds and shades of meaning. But how would one objectively describe its motion, and how would one distinguish the variations between styles of bowing? Of course, various bowing styles are usually distinguished on the basis of the sound patterns they impart to a sequence of notes, and there are a number of ways of accurately characterizing each style.

One method, which we have found most useful, is to record the bow acceleration pattern accompanying each style. Acceleration measures the changes in velocity and is proportional to the force producing the changes in the speed of the bow across the string. The patterns are quite distinct, making recognition of these styles during performance relatively easy when the acceleration record is available. Given the differences in opinion about the manner in which various styles can or should be executed, and even about the sound

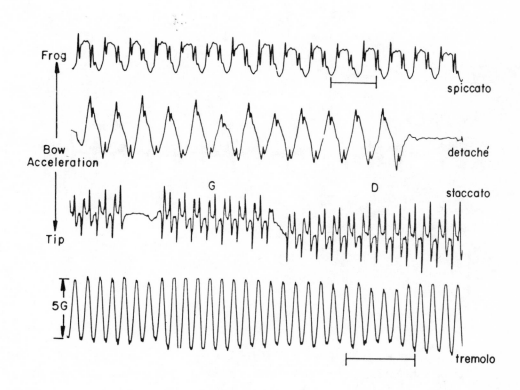

Figure 1

Examples of bow acceleration patterns associated with different styles of bowing in cellists. Acceleration in the direction along the bow is measured by placing an accelerometer at the frog of the bow. Frog-ward acceleration is indicated by an upward deflection, tip-ward acceleration by downward deflections. The zero acceleration level is approximately at the vertical midpoint of each trace.

Bowing styles, from top to bottom, are: spiccato, detaché, staccato, and tremolo. The staccato segments move from the C-string to the G-string. The time scale (timing bars represent 1 second) for the tremolo has been expanded. Peak accelerations are not to the same scale, but the tremolo accelerations are by far the largest (approximately 5G's, peak to peak).

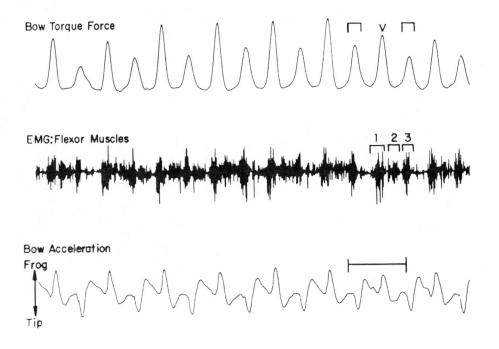

Figure 2

Example of bow acceleration, torque force and muscle electrical activity during the playing of an excerpt of 16 eighth notes from *Perpetual Motion* by S. Suzuki. The bowing style chosen was martelé. An up-down bow cycle has been identified by vertical lines, and the three bursts of muscle activation marked. Time calibration bar is 1 second.

Top trace: Pronating torque force exerted on the bow, measured by a transducer located within the bow just in front of the right index finger. Forces here range from zero at the base to about 300 grams at the peak. Variability in the peak amplitudes of upbow and downbow force can be seen.

Middle trace: Surface electromyogram of the wrist flexor group.

Bottom trace: Acceleration of the bow in its principal direction of motion, measured by an accelerometer placed at the frog. Acceleration in the direction of the frog is upward, tipward acceleration is down. Peak accelerations are about 1/2 G. The point of zero acceleration is approximately halfway between the highest and lowest peaks.

George P. Moore

which is desired, we find this method quite useful. In Figure 1 are shown the patterns of acceleration associated with four different nominal styles of bowing: spiccato, detaché, staccato, and tremolo.

To understand better how these acceleration patterns are produced, we can concurrently monitor the pattern of neuromuscular activity in various muscles of the right arm, and the torque force delivered to the bow by the hand. In Figure 2 are results taken from a cellist performing a simple étude using yet another style of bowing, termed "martelé."

At the bottom is shown the acceleration pattern of the bow, distinctly different from the patterns shown in Fig. 1. At the top is shown the resultant torque force in the bow generated by the pronating (i.e. counterclockwise rotational) force of the hand resisted by the supinating (clockwise) force of the string. In the middle are shown electromyographic (EMG) control signals to the wrist flexor muscles located in the forearm, muscles that contribute to the torque force on the bow. These are monitored in a somewhat non-specific way by an electrode array placed on the surface of the skin, on its medial aspect just below the elbow. More selective recordings of specific muscles are obtained by inserting a very fine wire directly into the muscles of consenting subjects.

Clearly, the bow motion is cyclical, as seen by the repeating pattern of bow acceleration at the bottom of the figure. To produce the desired sound, the rapid movement of the bow is accompanied by an impulse of force delivered to the bow and string at the onset of each bow movement. This force impulse, imparted by the hand and arm to the bow, is clearly seen in the upper trace, one for each note. Each upbow-downbow cycle therefore consists of two impulses of force (top trace), the larger of the two being associated with the upbow.

Corresponding to each bowing cycle, in this style, there are several acceleration peaks. As can be seen in Fig. 2, the largest accelerations in each half of the cycle occur at the moment of maximum bow torque force, i.e. at the beginning of the bow stroke. Within a hundred milliseconds of that event the acceleration changes sign, resulting in an immediate slowing of the bow, then a moment of zero acceleration as the bow, now stopped, is readied for its impulsive change in the opposite direction.

There are three principal muscle command signal (EMG) clusters observed here in each cycle. Each signals the activation of one or more wrist flexors. One EMG burst (marked "3" in Fig. 2) corresponds to the wrist flexion during the onset of the downbow. It can be seen to correspond directly with the increase of torque force in the bow, terminating at the moment of maximum force and maximum acceleration of the bow in the direction of the tip. (One suspects that in the ideal execution of this bowing style the force and acceleration peaks are simultaneous.) The bow is not yet moving at maximum speed, but this will be the moment of maximum loudness of the note. The contraction is associated with movement. A second burst of activity (marked "1" in the Figure) occurs in conjunction with the upbow. It, too, terminates abruptly at the moment of peak bow torque force and bow acceleration.

The third flexor burst (marked "2") arises from a different set of wrist flexors which serve to decelerate the frogward bow motion. Their activity terminates when the bow stops and the acceleration is zero. Their counterparts, wrist extensors, are not monitored in this recording; hence the fourth phase of the bowing cycle, the phase of braking of the tipward acceleration, is not accompanied here by any observable command signals.

If the EMG signal is amplified and fed to a loudspeaker, its burst pattern can be heard simultaneously with the sound of the notes being played. It accompanies the eighth-notes of the score with a pattern of three syncopated "sixteenth-notes" and a sixteenth rest where no EMG signal is recorded.

We observe that the impulse of force associated with the upbow (top trace) is consistently larger than that seen during the downbow. This provides an example of the performer's intuitive, rather than conscious, realization of the basic physics of the bow: to produce the same loudness and timbre, equal amounts of force must be imparted to the bridge by the string, and therefore, by the laws of levers, the torque force exerted by the hand on the bow must be larger when the bow is at the tip. The trick in learning to produce a series of notes that sound identical is to learn the subtle asymmetric patterns of force required to produce them.

The spatio-temporal acceleration pattern of the bow relative to the string is invariant for a certain type of bowing. Still, the manner in which that pattern is produced, the muscles and joints involved, depends on which string is being played and on the dynamic level desired. The point is that while the bow motion has certain invariant features, the means of producing it are quite varied. Thus, production of a variety of tonal textures by various bowing styles requires a mastery of the intricate patterns of movement that correspond to them. Each is learned, presumably, by acquiring unconsciously the acceleration pattern which produces the required sound at the right tempo. How, where and in what form these patterns are stored in the brain, and how these patterns are translated into the constellation of muscle activation patterns

George P. Moore

appropriate for each position of the arm, remains a difficult problem for future research.

Computer Simulation of Bowing

What are the determinants of the complex patterns of arm motions utilized in bowing? In some respects they are determined dynamically by the requirements of the desired sound and the corresponding demands of bow acceleration, as described above. But these motions are themselves constrained by the inherent geometry of the cello, bow, body and bowing arm. To understand these latter constraints more precisely, we used computer simulation techniques to explore some simple ideas about the mechanics of bowing. To do this, we developed programs to calculate, and then animate, the sequence of positions assumed by the arm of a cellist during a bowing cycle.

The programs use general data about the dimensions of the cello and the bow, and particular measurements for each performer concerning the dimensions of the right hand and arm, and the position of the body relative to the cello. The bow is assumed to move perpendicular to the string and remain a fixed distance from the bridge throughout the cycle. Given these assumptions, the arm, bow and string lie in approximately a single plane. Of course, in actual performance the bow may not meet these assumptions.

To understand what happens in the program, imagine that the bow is placed at some position on the string and held there by some unknown force. Now the performer is asked to grasp the bow as he normally would when it is in that position and moving in a certain direction. He will then unconsciously calculate the points of contact of the bow with the hand, and the exact angles of the wrist, elbow and shoulder which enable him to execute the grasp. This is not a trivial matter: there are actually many solutions to this problem. Yet the cellist automatically selects one, the one we normally associate with "good" bowing.

What constraints determine this constellation of joint angles? First, the specific dimensions of the cellist's arm and his postural relation to the cello. Thus the solution will be different for each cellist. The remaining constraints are more difficult to specify, but various guesses (hypotheses) can be explored in each version of the computer program. The computer, operating on a set of assumptions we make about the determinants of bowing position, but not on any actual (measured) positions, calculates a potential sequence of arm positions used in bowing. An example is shown in Figure 3.

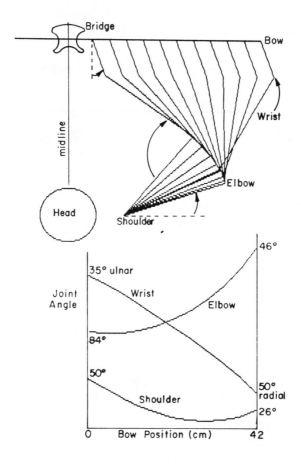

Figure 3

Computer simulation of bowing.

Top: A stick-figure approximation to eleven successive positions of the arm, hand and bow during a single computer-simulated down-bow motion which covers a distance of 42 cm, the plane of the bow arm being viewed from above. The position of the head is shown as a circle. The trajectory of the bow is shown as a straight line at the top. Body measurements of an actual performer are provided to the computer which then calculates the sequence of wrist, forearm and shoulder angles which keep the bow moving in a straight line at right angles to the string.

Bottom: Shoulder, elbow and wrist angles are plotted during the down-bow movement. The angles are measured as indicated in the upper part of the Figure. As the downbow proceeds, the wrist undergoes progressive rotation in the radial direction (from a starting angle of 35 degrees in the ulnar direction to a final angle of 50 degrees in the radial direction). The elbow starts at an angle of 84 degrees, decreases slightly over the next two frames, and achieves a value of 146 degrees as the bow reaches the tip. The shoulder angle starts at 50 degrees; abduction decreases that angle to a minimum of 18 degrees, and subsequent adduction increases it again to the final value of 26 degrees.

86   George P. Moore

The sequence of arm positions can then be animated and observed on a monitor. Some assumptions about bowing, particularly those concerned with the use of the wrist, lead to stiff, clumsy or erratic movements, while others produce a simulated bowing motion that seems to be typical of real cellists. As a result, we can categorically reject certain principles of organization of movement patterns, and focus our attention on others for further study.

This figure brought to our attention some subtleties of bowing which we subsequently confirmed in real performers. For example, in a typical downbow we would expect the elbow to become progressively extended, and the shoulder progressively abducted (moved away from the body midline). This is not the case for many cellists: the computer simulations (Fig. 3) indicate that at the onset of a downbow (near the frog) the elbow may actually flex slightly, and at the end of the motion the shoulder may adduct (move toward the midline), as a simple consequence of the geometry of the arm and the sequence of motion. The situation is reversed, in a complex way, during an upbow. The figure also demonstrates that in the early stages of the downbow, it is primarily the shoulder motion (i.e. the upper arm) that draws the bow across the string, while during the later stages it is elbow extension and movement of the forearm. The motion is thereby transferred from the upper arm to the lower.

Vibrato

Vibrato, like bowing in a certain style, is another example of a "generic motion," i.e., a class of movements designed to impart a small oscillatory change in the contact point of a finger on the fingerboard. This small change in contact creates a slight variation in the pitch of the note and a pleasing sound familiar to listeners. Vibrato is not produced by any fixed group of muscles in an invariant way, but rather depends in its execution on the position of the shoulder, arm, wrist and hand.

We monitored the performance of a cellist playing a scale on the A string in a position at which the elbow angle is roughly midway between between full extension and full flexion. (Fig. 4) At the top of the figure is shown the cyclical pattern of wrist acceleration measured by placing an accelerometer on the outside lateral aspect of the left wrist. In this position, the recorded oscillation will be a simple sinusoidal trace when the wrist and arm are moving in a plane parallel to the fingerboard. In the central part of the figure are vibrations observed during the playing of three consecutive notes. The consistency and rhythmicity of the motions, at about five cycles per second, are quite evi-

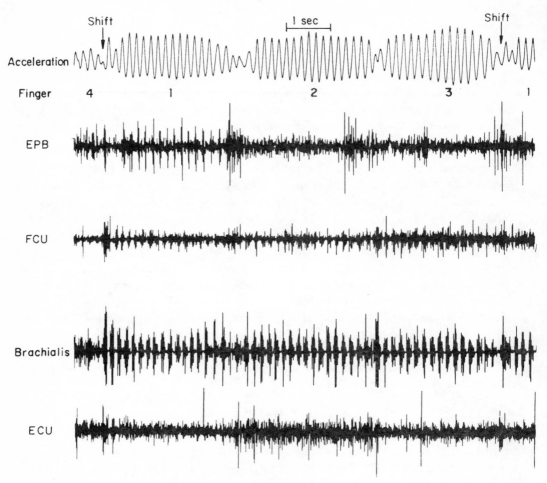

Figure 4

Vibrato motion and associated muscle activity. A cellist plays a simple scale on the "A" string. In the segment shown, two shifts in position occur (at arrows). In the first, the subject shifts from first to fourth position, in the second, from fourth to sixth. Note the very different patterns of arm acceleration and muscle activity before and after the first shift, and the brief pause in vibrato that typically accompanies finger transitiions and shifts. All the muscles shown generate a burst of activity during the shift.

Top line: Acceleration of the forearm, measured by an accelerometer placed on the lateral aspect of the left wrist. Increasing accelerations produced by elbow extension produce upward deflections, downward deflections indicate accelerations produced by elbow flexion. The finger being used to produce the note is indicated just below the acceleration record.

Other lines show electromyographic activity in: extensor pollicis brevis (EPB, a thumb extensor); flexor carpi ulnaris (FCU, a wrist flexor); brachialis (an elbow flexor); and extensor carpi ulnaris (ECU, a wrist extensor). EMG records were obtained using surface electrodes.

George P. Moore

dent, as are the brief interruptions of the pattern that occur between note transitions as first one and then another finger is placed on the fingerboard.

Near the beginning, and again at the end of the passage shown, the performer shifts from a lower to a higher position on the fingerboard, and the pattern of vibration relative to the cello can be seen to change, as does the pattern of muscular activity required to produce it. We have observed in many cellists a switch from a rotational vibrato in lower positions to a translational vibrato at higher positions.

The EMG signals of four muscles of the left arm, three of which have some activity directly time-locked to the vibrato pattern, are monitored in this example. They are (from top to bottom) extensor pollicis brevis (EPB, a thumb extensor), flexor carpi ulnaris (FCU, a muscle rotating the wrist outward and flexing it downward), brachialis (an elbow flexor and a main contributor to the power stroke of the bow at this position), and extensor carpi ulnaris (ECU, a muscle extending the wrist outward and upward and in some respects an antagonist of FCU).

Many muscles of the arm participate in the production of vibrato or in the anti-vibrato stabilization efforts which must accompany it. Indeed many of the muscles of the body — arm, back, trunk and even legs — on both sides of the body are in some way involved in the process of vibrato. But in the particular position highlighted in the central part of this Figure, the main producers of the power required to move the arm in the vibrating pattern are the elbow extensor, triceps (located at the back of the upper arm just below the shoulder), and an elbow flexor, brachialis, located in the general area of the better-known biceps muscle.

Brachialis, in this example, is consistently active at the same phase of the vibrato cycle as it acts both to brake the extension of the elbow produced by triceps (not shown) and begin the return of the arm to a more flexed position. It also shows some additional activity during the shifts to "higher" positions along the fingerboard (actually they are lower in terms of body position and require elbow extension), and this activity is used to stop the elbow extension at the end of the shift. Brachialis also shows an additional burst of activity in the transition between the second and third fingers.

In this particular arm position, both brachialis and triceps must alternate in active contraction to produce the rhythmic movement, but this is not generally the case. At greater or lesser degrees of arm flexion, one or the other of these muscles will be the main supplier of power, while the other acts more passively as an elastic (restoring) antagonist. As the left elbow becomes more extended in higher positions, for example, and the elbow flexor is stretched, it naturally generates more passive force, resists further extension, and serves to return the arm to a more flexed position without a great deal of neuromuscular activation. The electromyographic pattern reflects this by showing an increase in the activation signal to triceps, and a decrease to brachialis. The reverse occurs as the arm becomes more flexed when the player is at "lower" positions. In other words, a muscle may be important for vibrato, yet not always require central activation.

The thumb extensor EPB (top EMG record) acts synchronously with brachialis during vibrato, but only when the first finger is down. As the first finger is raised and the second finger is placed on the fingerboard, EPB no longer exhibits vibrato-related activity, but does show a burst of activity prior to each finger transition. The hand is normally stablilized with respect to the fingerboard by a downward force of the fingers and an equal upward force by the thumb. When the finger is raised during a note transition, this equality of forces is interrupted, and the thumb extensor must become active to counteract the maintained activity of the thumb flexors, which would otherwise lift the cello.

Rhythmically active also is the wrist flexor FCU (second EMG trace). Since the wrist does not appreciably rotate during vibrato, this activity must be viewed as a stabilizing activity, serving to prevent extension of the wrist by the movement of the arm. The extensor for the wrist, however, does not show activity time-locked with vibrato, but does show a noticeable increase of activity when the second finger is on the fingerboard.

The point of this technical description is not to catalogue all the muscles of the arm and body in relation to vibrato at various positions of the arm. This would indeed be a formidable task. Rather it is to point out how the same generic motion is played out in vastly different ways at different times. With each change in position, and even with a single change in finger, the entire constellation of active muscles may change, and the role played by any muscle may change. Yet we perceive the motion as fluid and unitary. Small wonder that vibrato technique is one of the most difficult to learn and impossible to teach by precept; no wonder that it is produced in so many different ways by performers with different arm sizes and proportions. No wonder that any change in its pattern requires new learning by the nervous system. No wonder that many preparatory exercises are only preparatory in a psychological sense.

Conclusions

The results discussed here are but tiny examples of the types of observations that can begin to form a basis for the scientific study of skilled performance in musicians. They remind us of the countless components of performance technique for each instrument that must be described by objective measurements. For each of these components, there is an underlying technical problem in kinesiology, and at even higher levels profound problems of sensory and motor coordination in the brain that are now being formulated by theoreticians and studied by experimentalists in much simpler situations.

In its unique way, music brings together in one medium the highest levels of human intellectual inventiveness, emotional feeling and physical skill. At its best it achieves a unity of expression that conceals the enormous amount of talent and technique necessary for its creation and performance. It is an achievement so deep and mysterious that, while we will always be richer for it, we may never fully understand it.

Yet there has always been a curiosity about music and its performance, about the mysterious workings of the mind and body which make it possible. Perhaps it is now time to begin again, seriously and patiently, the scientific process of investigation.

Acknowlegments

The author would like to express his appreciation to David Hary and Dan Antonelli for numerous discussions and for their contributions to electronic instrumentation; to cellists Paul Diebold, James Kjelland, Sharon Koga, Karen Patch, and Nancy Yamagata for their participation as subjects and consultants; to Susan Kusaka for technical assistance; to the School of Performing Arts, USC, for its materiel support; and to the Ford Motor Company for financial support through a grant to the USC School of Engineering. Finally, I thank The Biology of Music Making and their staff for their energy, support and enthusiasm.

BRAIN MECHANISMS
IN HIGHLY SKILLED MOVEMENTS

Frank Wilson
Assistant Clinical Professor of Neurology
University of California, San Francisco

Musicians are understandably curious about the neurology of the auditory system. This morning we are looking at some other features of human brain functioning which are of interest to musicians. For me, the most captivating questions have to do with the influence of training and experience on the shaping of motor skills. That is, one may ask what are the anatomic and physiologic features of the human brain and muscular system that account for the refinement of muscular control as observed in an artistic musical performance.

We revere the musical virtuoso, just as we revere the trapeze artist who brings us to our feet in a frenzy. But what do we really know about the physical basis of virtuosity, or, for that matter, about the skills of ordinary mortals? Let me pose the question to you in the most direct way I can, with an illustration. What you are about to hear are three brief recordings of a young pianist at ages 8, 12, and 16 years (taped example). A traditional pedagogic question generated by this sequence might be something like: how many hours of Pischna or Philipp exercises went into this transformation? My question is a bit different. I'd like to know what was going on in the brain and muscular system during that eight-year period. Even superficial reflection about this process impels one to the conclusion that the brain mechanisms involved must be of a very high order and among the most complex found in biologic control systems. Our responsibility, as educators and scientists, is to learn what we can about the processes underlying this kind of change, be it in the average or the gifted musician. This means we need to begin to understand the musician as one engaged in an activity which is fundamentally physical in character. The well trained musician is, after all, an individual whose muscular prowess generally surpasses anything encountered on the athletic field.

At first glance, nothing seems more contrary than the notion that musical skills might be muscular in the same sense that traditional sports skills are muscular. Deep within our collective memory is the imprint of the bespectacled, frail, and passive child instantly recognized as being "musical." Having been impressed at an early age with the heroic mythology of the locker room, the word, muscle, evokes for us images of mass, strength, and combat. We all know about biceps, triceps, deltoids, and pectorals, but who ever heard of someone having a knockout set of abductor digiti quinti minimi, or a breathtaking flexor pollicis brevis? Musicians themselves have sometimes fallen prey to the notion that bulk is what counts in the muscle department. It is a colorful notion, and false. Muscles are more than a set of coiled springs. Similar to eyes and ears, muscles are an extension of the brain. They are the action end of an integrated neurophysiologic system designed for interaction of the body with its surroundings. When one examines the anatomy and physiology of this system, one sees in the logic of its organization a message about priorities. This is a system in which flexible control and variable responsiveness represent the pinnacle of development.

Although my focus this morning is not really on muscle, this would probably be the best place to say a few things about this part of the nervous system. Muscle is a specialized tissue whose essential function is to change its length. When it is at rest it just sits there; when it is activated it gets shorter. Obviously, to get anything done a muscle must be attached to something at both ends. In the body, one end of the muscle is usually attached to a bone, and at the other end to a second bone, with a joint or moving surface in between. You can imagine what happens when a muscle is put to work. As it gets shorter, the angle between the two bones changes. There is also another muscle on the opposite side of the two bones. That is so you can put things back they way they were when you started. The principle here is that bodily movement always occurs because of a combination of muscular contractions and relaxations working in cooperation. If all the muscles were contracting at one time, the only thing that would happen is that you would shrink. This actually does seem to happen, as can be seen in a musical performance given under tension. In order for our movements to be effective, the brain, and particularly the motor system, must regulate the degree of contraction and relaxation of every muscle participating in a particular movement, at every instant. Otherwise exact control could not occur.

I would probably be correct if I guessed that most of us in this room have, at some time in our lives, had our hands on a piano or some other keyboard instrument. I would further venture the guess that a large majority of this audience continues to spend a significant amount of time relaxing with or working at an instrument or singing. Anyone left out of that group has surely sat at a typewriter or computer terminal. So I can assume some degree of personal familiarity on the part of every one here with the process of regulating fractionation movements of the digits; the separate, discrete, and highly practiced movements of individual fingers on which keyboard playing is built. Other instruments require the precise regulation of these and other groups of muscles. The organ demands skilled movement of the feet as well as the hands and arms. Wind instruments demand control of facial and intraoral muscles to produce a pleasing tone. Wind instrumentalists, of course, share with vocalists the need to acquire exceptional control of the airstream used to set up vibrations in the oscillator on which their sound depends. String players have the interesting problem of controlling pitch with one hand and arm, normally the left (which is fascinating in itself), and dynamics and timbre with the other. Timing and sequencing of tones are accomplished by collaboration of the pair.

As I just mentioned, muscle has to be attached to something in order to do any real work. Since most musicians use their hands to make music, the hand seems a logical structure to look at. A plaster cast of the hand of Franz Liszt, probably the best known of the piano virtuosi, looks simple on the outside. Underneath the skin, however, the hand is an intricate and compact machine made up of muscles, joints, tendons, bones, nerves, and blood vessels, engineered to permit an endless variety of movements. When the musician is operating this machine, the external movements visible to the audience may be quite simple or complex. In any case, there is a fabulous machine at work responsible for the final result.

How is this done? No one has any real basis for final pronouncements on this subject. Even so, because of the remarkable work of a number of neurophysiologists, particularly since the early 1970's, it *is* possible to formulate some intriguing hypotheses.

As a prelude to the survey of biologic details, it is useful to look at the device the musician must learn to operate, the musical instrument. Reduced to its basics, it is simply a resonant object which the performer must manipulate, strike, or alter aerodynamically so that some sort of sound is produced. The sounds become music when they are formed into patterns of tones whose frequency, rhythm, dynamics, and harmonic quality are controlled by the musician. The human voice is itself a remarkable musical instrument when it is controlled in this way.

The design of the instrument sets the conditions not only on the sound that will be produced, but also on the physical demands imposed on the musician. Perhaps no better illustration of this exists than in the seemingly trivial difference between the harpsichord and piano. The harpsichord, the most important keyboard in use at the time of Bach, is operated by depressing a key which causes a string, or paired strings, to be plucked. Its major limitation is that there is no way for the player to vary the loudness of its sound — that is, to control dynamics by finger pressure. In the early 18th Century, probably in 1709, a Paduan harpsichord builder named Bartolommeo Cristofori invented a mechanism which permitted the strings to be *struck* rather than plucked, so that the instrument might be played soft or loud according to touch. This invention set the stage for the development of the modern pianoforte (the word, as you know, means "soft-loud"). The rapid evolution of the piano as a concert instrument certainly has a great deal to do with its acoustic power and its capacity to satisfy the need for volume in performances in large halls or with large ensembles. It is possible that the piano was destined to eclipse the harpsichord in any event, as it presented the skilled musician with a new and somewhat more interesting set of control problems, namely those associated with its greatly expanded dynamic range.

We may therefore regard the musician, along with the tennis player and archer, as one confronted with what in scientific or engineering parlance is referred to as a "control" problem. He or she must adapt the use of some part of the body to an external object in order to make the object behave in a particular and predictable way. I first heard about this sort of biomechanical stuff when I was in the Navy some years ago, during a summer program meant to introduce midshipmen to the special problems of Navy fliers. Airline and Air Force pilots, you see, have a nice, stable runway a few hundred feet wide and a few miles long to land their planes on. Not to minimize their difficulties, but with all the other things they need to keep track of, at least they don't need to worry about the runway itself tilting and tossing. An aircraft carrier, on the other hand, provides a landing area 90 feet wide and not much longer, which itself is rolling, pitching, bobbing, and forging ahead at approximately thirty knots.

In our course we were told that the suggestion had been made by a number of sensible people that a carrier landing could be turned over to a computer. Our instructor looked at us quietly to see how the thought struck us. Then he said, "But gentlemen, it's really a matter of economics. The human brain is the only non-linear computer that can be mass produced by unskilled labor." Which brings us to the computer.

When looking at a drawing of the surface of the brain one sees two large masses called hemispheres. They are nearly mirror images of one another. The back part is called the occipital lobe. It is the principal receiving station for information from the eyes. The side part (that looks like the thumb of a boxer's glove) is the temporal lobe. It is the auditory analog of the occipital lobe.

When you look inside the brain, at the very top, forming the surface (or mantle), of the hemispheres, is the region called the motor strip. It is the hub of what is called the motor system. It is one of the areas of the brain where we can see a sort of map of the body. Some years ago Dr. Wilder Penfield and his colleagues at the Montreal Neurological Institute discovered that a very weak electric stimulus applied to individual points on the motor strip caused muscles in varying locations of the body to twitch. After doing this repeatedly in a number of patients, they were able to say with a great deal of confidence which parts of the motor strip were responsible for activating which muscles of the body. They were thus able to develop a map of the motor strip and its associated muscle responses. The map is particularly interesting when you consider what musicians do. It shows that this section of the motor control system is predominantly dedicated to the small muscles of the body, among which are the muscles of the hands, arms, and those involved in vocalization.

Making music, however, involves a good deal more than just twitching small muscles. Muscles have to work smoothly in collaboration with one another in complex and constantly changing patterns of contraction and relaxation. Timing, sequence, and precise control of force and speed are also essential. Although much of what is accomplished in finished musical performance is automatized, no two performances are ever the same. Clearly, there must be the possibility of instantaneous changes in control, no matter how well rehearsed and learned a piece of music might be. This incredible flexibility of control is an attribute of the system as a whole, and so we have to look at the rest of it.

The next component of the motor system we will consider is not visible at the surface. It is a group of compact cells referred to as the basal ganglia. They form rounded structures near the center of the brain. These nuclei are known to have a great deal to do with regulating the cooperative efforts of groups of muscles, especially in relation to the adjustment and maintenance of body posture. Think for a moment about the movements of the fingers of a violinist, or a saxophonist, or flutist, controlling the pitch of the strings of the instrument or the movement of the keys. Not only are the fingers moving, but the upper muscles of the arm are also holding the hand in a position so that the fingers can do their job. No matter what else is going on in the body, standing still or moving, it is still necessary for the brain to control the relationship between the hands, and often the mouth, and the musical instrument.

Frank Wilson

Time limitations this morning make it impossible to review in detail the most recent work on basal ganglia activity in skilled movements. Briefly, however, it now appears probable that these important structures are involved in the initiation of limb movements, including skilled movements, in at least two important ways: first, by linking a motor sequence to an environmental stimulus or cue, and second by orienting the distal portion of the limb so that it can effectively interact with an external target. The situation is a bit like the control of a steam shovel, with considerable attention being paid to getting the bucket where it belongs before starting the scoop and dump routine. It is entirely possible that control signals to the distal musculature are held in check until all this prearranging is complete. The degree to which basal ganglia also participate in planning and organization of distal skilled movements remains uncertain. There is, however, some preliminary evidence that suggests they may contribute a great deal.

We are now in a position to consider, in a rather rough way, how the system works as a whole. As an engineer might see the situation, any movement that is intended has to begin with an idea. The translation of that idea into physical movement calls the entire system into play. A series of coded signals begins in the region of the motor strip, causing activation of a group of muscles which move the limb toward the intended target. Simultaneously, the nerves in the muscles, joints, and skin, and the eyes watching the activity, begin reporting back the progress of the intended move. This permits adjustments or corrections to be made, so that the limb can be brought smoothly to its intended target.

To this point our analysis is accurate, but incomplete. It doesn't explain how the body can make movements of the kind necessary to control a musical instrument during fast passages. Here, there simply isn't time to get information back and forth in the nervous system fast enough to make corrections if the movement isn't on target. There has to be another way of to explain how the brain manages to accomplish this task.

The first important clue to understanding the control of these moves was discovered almost ninety years ago. In 1895 Paul Richer took a series of rapid sequence photographs of the quadriceps muscle during a kicking motion. After studying the photographs he said the following about the contraction of the muscle during the kick: "It is very energetic and short lasting. It launches the limb in a set direction and ceases long before the limb will have completed its course of action." Because of the similarity of this kind of move to the firing of a gun shell, it was called, ballistic.

It is now recognized that highly skilled movements, particularly those that are rapidly executed and brief in duration, are under the guidance of a far more complex control system than is required for movements which can be corrected by ongoing adjustment, or so-called "feedback control." The essential characteristic of the control system is that the details of the movement must have been completely worked out in advance, in a lengthy trial and error process, so that the movement can be executed when it is called for with absolute accuracy and consistency, in a nearly automatic way. This means that the brain, or the motor control system, must issue in advance of the move, an ordered series of command signals that specify what the muscles involved must do, from start to finish, before the movement itself actually begins. Since there is no time to correct mistakes once the move has begun, everything must be correct from the very beginning.

Advance programming of skilled movements is one important feature of ballistic control. Another equally significant feature is the striking change in muscle responsiveness that occurs in this condition. The physical fluidity which a performer enjoys when he or she is "on," or is playing unconsciously, almost certainly stems from a marked shift in the physiologic behavior of muscles coming under a ballistic mode of control. In fact, the experienced musician may actively seek an inner state during performance in which the muscles feel warm, relaxed, and light, using that feeling together with auditory information to confirm that things are going well. By contrast, there is probably a specific physiologic explanation for the rather horrifying reversal of that fluidity which sets in when a performer loses confidence and begins to worry about the mechanical details of execution.

At the present time it is not clear how the development of the ballistic mode of control comes about. Most experimental studies point strongly to the repetition of accurately performed short movement sequences as the basis for the physiologic shift that occurs when muscles are under the ballistic mode of control. The cerebellum, and particularly the newest part of the cerebellum called the lateral hemispheres, has been proposed as one possible site of a set of subprograms of movement that can be drawn on to assure accurate performance of highly rehearsed movement. This kind of arrangement would at least partially explain the advantages of certain kinds of rehearsal techniques.

While at the Paris Conservatory Isidor Philipp, the great piano teacher, wrote about rehearsal strategy and said this about speed: "Too much stress cannot be laid upon the usefulness, the necessity of slow work." Stephen Heller's motto was, "Practice very slowly, progress very fast." And Saint-Saens said, "One must practice slowly, then more slowly, and finally slowly."

If one looks to the organization of the nervous system to account for validation of these pedagogic principles, I think there is very little difficulty generating a fascinating hypothesis. The cerebellum and basal ganglia are situated in such a way that they can monitor and store details of ongoing and previous bodily movement. Any movement that is frequently repeated becomes a candidate for automatization, which is to say, for ballistic programming. Obviously, if the goal of rehearsal is to expedite this process, it follows that the best strategy is one that emphasizes accuracy and repetitions. If practicing takes place at a pace too fast for accurate execution, the musician will probably end up with more than one version of the performance, any one of which may present itself in public according to whim. An interesting corollary is that when the rule of slow practice is adhered to, it really *does* produce reliable performance. Practice one version of a work consistently and that's the one you will have for the concert. If, in this context, artistic decisions about a work are postponed much past the beginning of serious practice, the musician will likely join the swarms of unhappy golfers and tennis players struggling to change their swing after it was learned incorrectly.

I must emphasize that we are still a very long way from anything like a comprehensive understanding of the operation of the motor control system as a whole. But if one is curious about how things seem to work during the few hundred milliseconds encompassing a rather simple, highly practiced, self-generated move, the picture certainly seems to be coming into focus. We are fast approaching the day when we will be able to to gather far more detailed and precise information about brain activity in humans engaged in carrying out skilled movements.

In my personal view, as you might guess, musicians are the people we ought to be looking at as we attempt to understand the truly unique operations of the human brain. Let me, however, give you fair warning. You may want to take a moment to consider your reply when a nice person in a white coat asks you with a smile if you would like to assist with a little experiment. I think you should cooperate. Just don't let anyone drill any holes!

VISUALIZATION OF BRAIN METABOLISM IN SKILLED MOVEMENTS[1]

John Mazziotta
Assistant Professor of Neurology
UCLA School of Medicine

I will show you some Positive Emission Tomography (PET) studies. These studies are not of input of musical information but of output motor activity, directed by the brain to do skilled tasks. We look at the source of the training that the brain has, in order to develop hierarchies to perform these complicated tasks. Think for a moment about how complicated just one muscle's behavior is — the timing, the onset, the offset, the force involved for just one muscle to do just one of these tasks; how incredibly complicated it is to control the movements of an entire extremity, all those muscles and joints, in real time, occurring in a dynamic way. How does the brain do this? I won't answer that question for you. What I will show you are some very preliminary and interesting studies suggesting how different tasks could be learned by the brain. We will also look at some ways of examining the brain using what might be the most exotic of the technologies you'll see this evening, the PET scan.

(Showing a slide). I have to describe to you something of the organization of the cortex of the brain. Near the top, in the center, is the motor strip, one of the parts of the brain that is well named for what it does. It is an area that is organized topographically, that is, according to the topography of the body. On it you have the representation of the whole body, each hemisphere controlling the the opposite side of the body. In front of the motor strip, also well named, is the pre-motor area. These are areas that are thought to set up some of the programs that are exclusively run by the motor strip and certain other brain structures.

---

1.   Dr. Mazziotta has kindly consented to the inclusion of his two edited but unrevised presentations in the Proceedings of the conference — *Eds.*

We looked at these areas using the PET scan. We made slices of the brain, electronically, of people doing different tasks. These were not musical tasks. One task was a novel one, newly learned. The other was a very over-learned task. These were compared to a control state where the subject sat without moving his arm. So, there were three studies of each subject. We did a total of twenty-eight sets of these studies.

The novel task was to tap the fingers in a certain sequence; a certain number of taps was repeated over and over. The subject learned this task just before we injected him with a compound to make the PET images. The over-learned task was writing one's name, simply to sign one's name over and over again, for the full period of the measurement. Signing one's name is one of the most over-learned of tasks, and quite analogous to some of the more automatic technical aspects of playing an instrument. These tasks, to a large degree, are performed at the subconscious level.

This is what it looks like when you write your name for thirty minutes, over and over again. Another fellow had to write, "Mickey Mouse," one hundred and eighty times. In both tasks the motor strip was activated. You can see it here in red, indicating high metabolic activity. The right hand is moving. The left side of each image is the left hemisphere of the brain. You can see that the hand area of the motor strip is activated when the subject does either the tapping task, the novel task, or the over-learned task. In addition, areas in front of the motor strip, supplementary motor areas and other areas, also are activated by both tasks. These are thought to be staging areas for organizing such movements.

A difference was seen deep inside the brain in structures called the basal ganglia. In the control study the subject is not moving, not doing anything. This, on the other hand, is the study where the subject is writing his name over and over. You can see the difference. Same subject. There is about a twenty percent increase in metabolism. This occurred only with the writing task, the over-learned task. It did not occur with the novel task.

Why would this happen? These structures are thought to be very crucial in integrating sensory and motor information. They have rich connections with the cortex from all zones, both sensory areas and motor areas. We hypothesized that these areas could be programmed, as one learns a motor task through repetition, to take over some of this task from the cortex, doing it at a fairly automatic level in the deep structure of the brain.

This experiment doesn't prove that, so we're doing another experiment for which I don't yet have the results. It involves scanning the subjects as they write their name with their left, non-dominant, hand. We then train them to that over and over again, every day, for weeks and months, until it becomes relatively automatic. It never becomes as automatic as when the dominant hand is doing it, but, nevertheless, a well learned task. We will see if we can move the activation from the cortex to the deep structures.

One last example involves Huntington's disease, an inherited disease. The manifestations are psychiatric problems, dementia, loss of cognitive abilities, and involuntary movements, especially wild movements of the extremities.

This is a set of Computed Axial Tomography (CAT) scans of the brain. They show the anatomy of the brain, These are a set of PET scans of the brain. They show the metabolism of the brain, much as the scans we've been looking at. This is a normal individual's PET scan. You can see the structure that we talked about, a part of the basal ganglia called the caudate nucleus. That's its normal shape and position. Its metabolism appears black, which is normal. This is a patient with advanced Huntington's disease. The structure is missing. It has atrophied and been lost from the brain. Therefore, of course, we don't see any functional activity in that site. Here we see a patient with very early Huntington's disease. The structure is physically there, but functionally it is not working.

But why bring this up? Here is a population of patients, particularly ones with early disease symptoms, who can write their name. They do the task more slowly, more deliberately, than people free of Huntington's. They can, however, do the writing task. And yet, they are missing, functionally, the very structure that seems to be most activated in doing that task in normals. How does this fit into the complicated issue of learning a task and then trying to maintain that ability when the system becomes rewired or damaged?

We took the subjects with Huntington's disease, those who had early symptoms, and asked them to write. We compared their scans sitting with their hand immobile versus writing. We found that the strip of cortex we initially looked at is activated when writing. That is, it increases its metabolism to a point which is similar to a normal subject doing this task or the novel task.

What about the basal ganglia? When we compare the control study to the stimulated state we find no difference. These subjects perform the writing task without the structure that is maximally activated in normals. One pos-

John C. Mazziotta

sibility is that they have reverted back to a more primitive way, a more novel way of doing this. Each time they run that program, they do it in the cortex, not in these deep structures. When you ask them about it, they say it is a very deliberate thing. They think about it each time.

This is very inferential information about ways that we can look at these complicated and intriguing problems. How does the brain learn how to do something, be it a motor task or mental activity? This is one of the fundamental questions of neurology. When the brain is damaged, how does the subject recover the ability to do something? The patient has an acute injury, say a stroke, and yet can slowly recover the ability to do something; or, as in this case, develop compensatory mechanisms of the brain which allow one to continue to perform a task despite damage.

The relevance to music is, I think, obvious. How does a performer learn to do selected tasks in a technically proficient way? How are those programs built into the system? How does the system control these complicated time tables of all the muscles moving across time and space? How are the artistic capabilities that transform a mechanical proficiency into a type of art imposed on these automatic systems? I think these are intriguing questions for us all. The preliminary studies provide some means of starting to look at these questions. I hope they have been provocative in that regard.

BRAIN MECHANISMS IN AUDITORY PERCEPTION

INTRODUCTION

John C.M. Brust
Director of the Department of Neurology
Harlem Hospital Center, New York

Since Gall and the physiologists a century and a half ago, certain areas of the brain have been held to be particularly involved in different cognitive processes. For example, the left cerebral hemisphere appears to be the major processor of language function, whereas the right hemisphere seems to be crucial for spatial manipulation. Where in the nervous system music is processed is the subject of this morning's and tomorrow morning's sessions. For introduction, I would like to pose two questions. First, over the years, how has the question of music's localization in the brain been experimentally addressed? The answer is, by studying both normal and abnormal subjects. Abnormalities may cause either negative or positive phenomena. By negative, I mean a loss of musical capacity following brain damage from, say, stroke, trauma, brain surgery, or temporary brain anesthesia following injection of barbiturate into the vascular supply to one or another cerebral hemisphere. Positive phenomena consists of seizures. Some seizures are precipitated by hearing music, including particular passages of music. Of a different sort are seizures that take the form of musical hallucinations of one type or another. Seizures can be experimentally produced during surgery by electrical stimulation of certain areas of the cerebral cortex. Localization of the brain damage causing negative or positive phenomena can then be determined by autopsy, at surgery, or, more recently, using such techniques as computerized axial tomography (CAT scanning).

Normal brains can be studied by a variety of procedures, including dichotic listening, a technique which some, but not all, believe is a means of delivering auditory information into one or the other cerebral hemisphere. Positron emission tomography enables one to visualize in normal, awake subjects what parts of the brain are most active during a particular cognitive task.

The second question is, after a century and a half of such studies, what have we learned about where and how the brain processes music? The answer is, not much. Far less, in fact, is known about how information is carried along the auditory pathways than how it is processed through the visual system. A simple to complex physiologic hierarchy such as Hubel and Wiesel described for vision may well exist for hearing, but it remains to be defined. And the question of cerebral hemispheric dominance for music remains unanswered. On that depressing note, then, we will move to the first speaker.

Positron emission tomography, as he will probably stress, is very expensive, and there aren't very many of these machines available. There is no group that has made more impact on this area than Dr. Mazziotta's at UCLA. He will tell us what this machine is and what it has taught us about how the brain handles music.

BRAIN METABOLISM IN AUDITORY PERCEPTION: THE PET STUDY[1]

John C. Mazziotta
Assistant Professor of Neurology
UCLA School of Medicine

It's a pleasure for me to participate in this unique conference, and to show you some of the studies we have done at UCLA to visualize the normal human brain as it is performing, if you will, listening to various types of auditory information, both verbal and nonverbal. Most imaging techniques for the brain or other organs show the anatomy and structure of the organ. Today I will show you images that depict the function of the brain super-imposing on the anatomy. This is an unusual, even exotic technique. It is expensive and not available at many places. In order that you will understand the images that depict this cerebral activity I have to explain to you a little bit about the kinds of experiments we do and how they are performed.

This technique is a way of imaging the brain. It is performed with a device called a Positron Computed Tomograph or PET scanner which makes cross-sectional images of the brain. A radioactive compound injected into the subject circulates in the body. These are radioactive forms of natural substances in the body — water, oxygen, or glucose — or analogues that mimic the behavior of the natural substance, altered to play certain tricks on the system. One of those compounds I will talk about today, deoxyglucose, mimics the behavior of glucose or sugar. Since glucose provides from 95-99% of the energy fuel for the brain, if we can see how much glucose a given piece of the brain is using, we can estimate how active that part of the brain is in doing a task. We inject this compound, wait thirty minutes, and then start to make the pictures. Everything the person does in the thirty minute period should be reflected in these brain images. Anything they did, thought, or performed just

---

1. Dr. Mazziotta has kindly consented to the inclusion of his two edited but unrevised presentations in the Proceedings of the conference — *Eds*.

after the injection counts more than something done at the time we are about to make the images. With the help of some mathematics and some information from the blood, we can construct functional maps based on regional variations in metabolism within the brain. We can use this technique to study a variety of physiologic processes, the behavior of drugs, and other things. There are about twenty PET scanners in the United States, two at UCLA, and about twenty more in other countries around the world, mainly in Europe and Japan. For those of you who have seen an x-ray CT scanner, they look quite similar. The whole device is controlled by a computer and the images are displayed in black and white or color on TV monitors.

We can see the top of the brain and work our way down to the bottom of the brain, seeing the frontal lobes of the brain, the occipital lobes, the visual cortex, and the auditory cortex. The auditory system is crossed, but arranged so that sounds entering either ear are distributed through the brain stem (a structure low in the brain) up to both cerebral hemispheres. Since this is a crossed system, auditory stimulation causes activation of the primary auditory regions on both sides of the brain.

We can see a good deal of detail in these images, and make certain conclusions about how particular areas of the brain are responding, and inferences about what they are doing. To give you a feeling of how these images appear, Mike Phelps and I did a study a long time ago of the visual cortex. As Dr. Brust said, this is a system that is much better understood, from animal studies and also from human experiments, than the auditory system. (Showing PET scan slides) We looked at the visual cortex with the eyes closed, and found it inactive relative to the remaining areas of the brain, the frontal cortex and other areas. When that same subject looked at just a plain bright white light, there was a substantial increase in metabolic activity of the visual cortex. Remember that an ordinary CT scan, an x-ray CT scan, would look the same because it only shows anatomy. The PET scan also looks at function. We did a variety of these types of studies and the most complex stimulus involved subjects who sat outside the campus on Westwood Blvd. and observed whatever happened to go by. On a sunny day in southern California, these can be fairly provocative stimuli. In fact, the metabolic rates measured in the visual cortex of these subjects has only been exceeded by individuals who had epileptic seizures during some of our other experiments. Subjects in this case were male only. We found that the magnitude of response is graded. It increases in proportion to the complexity of the function of the brain. As we turn to the auditory studies, keep that in mind.

We used a large number of normal volunteers, right handed, in a variety of auditory tasks, to study the behavior of the primary auditory areas. We tested when subjects' eyes were open, but with the ears plugged with rubber stoppers and covered with soundproof headphones, and found the auditory cortex to be relatively inactive. Then we had the subjects listen to a verbal stimulus, a narrative story. In this test the left side of the brain was predominately active. These activations were actually quite complicated in that they involved both sides of the brain. But with purely verbal material, activation was seen predominately on the left side in right-handed people. With nonverbal material (in this case one of the Brandenberg concerti) we found the greater increase in the right hemisphere. The frontal cortex was active in both cases. When we allowed the subjects to hear music and language at the same time, both hemispheres were equally active in patterns that conformed to the sum of verbal and nonverbal stimuli. One can begin to look at hemispheric specialization involved in these processes, but must keep in mind that many regions of the brain are involved in these tasks. In fact, I would be hard pressed to name areas of the brain that did not respond. We did, however, identify areas of maximal activity.

We can even look at the effect of hearing the stimulus in one ear at a time. Our subjects who listened to a story played into the left ear develop predominately left hemispheric activations, and when the story is played into the right ear, again develop left hemisphere activations. The levels here are slightly different, but the patterns are very similar. So the ear that one listens with seems to be not very important. The *content* of the information, however, as we shall see, is very important.

This is a set of studies for which there is an example of three different individuals, who fell into different groups. In another experiment we used two different types of nonverbal stimuli taken from the Seashore tests of musical aptitude. These were originally developed to test separately skills on perception of music rhythm, pitch, tone, tone memory, etc. In one, the subject hears a chord, a pause, then another chord, and has to decide whether the two chords are the same or different. We found in all our subjects, ten of them now, right hemisphere activation and asymmetries much in excess of anything we had recorded in the left hemisphere using verbal stimuli. This was true of all the subjects.

In the tonal memory test the subject hears a simple melody, 3-5 notes, all of different frequency. After a pause there is another sequence of notes, and subjects must decide if the second sequence is the same or different from the first, when the frequency of only one note may be changed. Our rather simplistic hypothesis was that this would be primarily a right hemisphere task, and in fact in most of the subjects — two-thirds, to be exact — we saw an asymmetry compared to the subject's own control results. We asked our subjects, "How did you do the task? What was the way you performed the task?" A few said they had no strategy at all, they just listened, waited, and then made a decision when they heard the second group of notes. A few said that they would mentally re-sing the notes silently until the second playing, and then make their decision.

There was a subgroup, about a third of the patients, in whom the left hemisphere became more active, particularly in the parietal and temporal region. These subjects, when asked how they solved the task, reported they had used some sort of visual imagery. One was a computer sciences graduate student who said, "I made frequency histograms of the notes." In other words, he made a little bar graph in his mind, proportional to the frequencies, and compared the sequences in a visual mode. Another subject said, "I see dots in space, their height proportional to the frequency, and I compared it again visually." These left hemisphere responders, like all the right hemisphere responders, were musically naive in that they could not read sheet music and that they did not play a musical instrument. One subject in the left hemisphere group, however, was a professional musician. He told us that not only did he see the notes on a musical scale, but also that he could identify them.

What might we conclude from these results? It may be that we need to look not at the content of the stimulus, or the ear that one plays it into, but consider the specific strategy that one uses to solve the task. The development of a strategy through particular training, be it musical or otherwise, represents learning, which may alter physical or anatomically based processes in the brain. In all our test subjects, the maximal response, the maximal change in metabolism from the control state where they heard nothing, to the stimulated state was always in the primary auditory areas which received the first input from deeper structures. These responses varied from left hemisphere to right, depending on whether the task was verbal or nonverbal, or on the strategies the subjects used. The patterns were complicated but consistent.

In another test, a subject listened to a mystery story, and was told he would be paid in proportion to how much he could remember about the story on a post-test interview. What did we find? As in all the other studies, the primary auditory cortex was activated in both hemispheres. But in addition, there was a new structure for us to see, namely the middle portion of the temporal lobe. This area of the brain contains structures known as the hippocampus, the parahippocampal gyrus, and fusiform gyri. These are structures that are believed to be very important in memory — storage and retrieval — the processing of information or information destined to become memorized. We never saw this in a control study, do not know if this was just an unusual effect of auditory stimulation, or was an effect of paying careful attention to a stimulus. Did we find the greed center of the brain, or is this an effect specific to memory? We have not answered that question yet, but we are closing in. It may be possible to use these techniques, and with progressive change of the experiment design to understand how the brain responds to complicated and multifactorial situations.

What have we learned from these auditory studies to this point? I would say that we have learned that the cortex of the brain, the outer portion of the brain I have been showing you, responds in ways determined more by the content of the stimulus than by its location. It does not matter so much which ear one plays into; but *what* you play is very important. And it may also be that the strategy used, formed by past experiences of the auditory or other systems, may be important in shaping the cerebral strategies involved in perception and integration of that information. The responses, these changes from the control state to the state where the brain was active, were small in magnitude. They only changed about 10-20%, but the patterns were very consistent, and the sites were always the same for a given set of stimuli.

We feel this technique, positron CT or PET scanning, offers a way to look not only at the primary receptor areas of the brain, but also at more complicated abstract processes of the brain, such as strategy, activation occurring in association with perception, and appreciation. This is important to be able to do in humans because the auditory system is species specific. If you did similar experiments in rats, it would be difficult to extrapolate the findings to humans. When we make an observation in the human brain, it has special meaning. I would reiterate that these responses are very complicated. We cannot say that music is appreciated in the right hemisphere or the left hemisphere. Many factors are involved; it is going to be a very interesting story, but not a simple story. With the techniques we saw this morning, we can begin to examine all sorts of processes in the human brain. We have seen visual and auditory responses, and later tonight I will show work we have started on motor responses of the brain, when a subject does a novel task vs. an over-learned task such as playing a musical instrument. We can look at issues about memory. We can look at cognition, thinking processes, perhaps even emotions like performance anxiety.

John C. Mazziotta

These experiments were limited in their interpretability because of the complicated tasks given our subjects, but there is some prospect that we can look at these issues objectively and quantitatively, and we can begin to look at more than the most primitive responses of the brain to a given stimulus.

THE PERCEPTION OF MUSICAL CONFIGURATIONS

Diana Deutsch
Department of Psychology
University of California, San Diego[1]

Suppose you are in a concert hall listening to an orchestra. The mixture of sounds that reaches your ears is produced by many instruments playing in parallel. These sounds may be organized in an infinite number of ways, yet in general people show remarkable consensus in describing what they hear. People generally agree, for example, as to which sounds combine to form melodies, which combine to form chords, and so on. This paper is concerned with the principles underlying such perceptual organization, and in particular with the effects of different spatial arrangements on how music is perceived.

Organization by pitch and by timbre

The tendency of the perceptual system to separate out patterns of tones on the basis of pitch range has long been acknowledged in musical practice. This is reflected, for example, in the law of stepwise progression, rules governing the crossing of voices in counterpoint, the technique of pseudopolyphony, and so on. But what, specifically, are the consequences of such perceptual organization?

In one situation to investigate this issue, listeners are presented with strings of single tones in rapid succession. When these tones are drawn from two different pitch ranges, judgments concerning their orders are often very poor. In taped Example No. 1,[2] you will hear a repeating string of six tones that are

---

1. This work was supported by UPPHS Grant M1-21001. Requests for reprints should be sent to Diana Deutsch, Department of Psychology, C-009, University of California, San Diego, La Jolla, California, 92093.

2. A cassette of the sound examples described in this article is available from the author.

drawn from two different pitch ranges. Many listeners are unable to order these tones correctly (Bregman and Campbell, 1971).

Even when the presentation rate is slowed down, so that order perception is easily accomplished, there is a gradual breakdown in temporal resolution as the pitch disparity between two alternating tones increases. This is illustrated in taped Example No. 2. A rhythmic irregularity is quite apparent in a sequence of alternating tones that are close in pitch, but as the pitches of these tones diverge this irregularity becomes gradually less perceptible. The example begins with tones that are far apart in pitch, then they converge and the rhythm becomes apparent, then they diverge again and the rhythmic irregularity is lost (Van Noorden, 1975).

Dowling (1973) demonstrated another sequence of grouping by pitch proximity. He presented listeners with two well-known melodies interleaved in time, and required them to identify these melodies. When they were in overlapping pitch ranges the performance levels were poor, since the melodies were combined into a single perceptual stream. However, when one of the alternating melodies was transposed to a different pitch range, performance levels rose considerably.

Another advantage to pitch proximity involves short term memory for single tones. In one study, I presented subjects with a test tone, which was followed by a sequence of further tones that they were asked to ignore, and then by another test tone. The second test tone was either identical to the first or it was a semi-tone removed, and the subjects judged whether the test tones were the same or different. The experiment examined the effect on recognition accuracy by varying the average size of the melodic intervals formed by the tones in the interpolated sequence. These are plotted on Figure 1. It can be seen that as the average size of the intervals decreased the error rate also decreased. This finding leads us to conclude that the interpolated sequence forms a framework of pitch relationships to which the test tones are anchored, and the more proximal the relationships the stronger the framework, and so the more accurate the pitch recognition judgments (Deutsch, 1978).

Grouping by pitch proximity is responsible in part for a powerful illusion which occurs when two streams of tones emanate simultaneously from different regions of space. A perceptual reorganization occurs so that the higher tones all appear to be coming from one spatial location and the lower tones from from another (Deutsch, 1975a,b). This illusion is described in detail below.

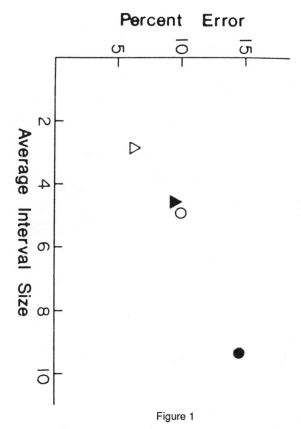

Figure 1

Percent errors in pitch comparisons as a function of average size of melodic interval formed by tones in interpolated sequences (from Deutsch, 1978).

When sounds are presented in rapid succession, the listener may group these on the basis of sound quality, or timbre. Warren, Obusek, Farmer and Warren (1969) constructed repeating patterns of four unrelated sounds: a high tone, a hiss, a low tone, and a buzz. When the sounds were 200 m/sec in duration and followed each other without pause, listeners were quite unable to to name the order in which they occurred. It was necessary to increase the duration of each sound to over 500 m/sec before this task could be carried out.

Wessel (1978) demonstrated grouping by timbre in another way. He generated repeating patterns of tones which consisted of three pitches and two alternating timbres (i.e.,...A1, B2, C1, A2, B1, C2..., with A,B,C, representing pitches and 1,2 representing timbres). When the timbres were

Diana Deutsch

similar, listeners described the patterns in terms of the pitch sequences. But when the timbres were dissimilar, listeners described two parallel streams instead, distinguished on the basis of sound quality (see also Risset and Wessel, 1982).

Organization in space

We now turn to the situation in which different regions of space are involved. Here some surprising findings have emerged. Consider, for example, the pattern shown in Figure 2a, taken from Deutsch (1975a,b). This consists of a major scale, with successive tones alternating from ear to ear. The scale is presented simultaneously in both ascending and descending form, such that when a tone from the ascending scale is in the right ear, a tone from the descending scale is in the left ear.

One can easily imagine how this pattern should sound if perceived correctly.

Figure 2 (a above, b below)

a. Pattern giving rise to the scale illusion. A major scale is presented simultaneously in ascending and descending form, such that when a tone from the ascending scale is presented to one ear a tone from the descending scale is presented to the other ear.

b. Percept most commonly obtained. The higer tones are all heard as in the right ear, and the lower tones as in the left ear (Deutsch, 1975a).

However, I have played it now to hundreds of listeners and, with rare exceptions, an illusion is always produced. The type of illusion varies from listener to listener, but the most common one is shown in Figure 2b. The correct sequence of pitches is heard, but as two separate melodies; a higher one and a lower one, that move in contrary motion. Further, the higher tones all appear to be coming from the right earphone and the lower tones from the left. When the earphone positions are reversed, this perception is still maintained. So it seems to the listener that the earphone that had been producing the higher tones is now producing the lower tones, and that the earphone that had been producing the lower tones is now producing the higher tones. Other listeners perceive the sequence differently. Some hear all the higher tones in the left ear and all the lower tones in the right ear, with earphones placed both ways. For yet other listeners, when the earphone positions are reversed, the apparent locations of the higher and lower tones also reverse.

The illusion has another surprising aspect: right-handers and left-handers show different patterns of localization for the higher and lower tones. The findings from Deutsch (1975) are shown in Table I. Right-handers tended significantly to hear the higher tones on the right and the lower tones on the left, and also to maintain this percept when the earphones were placed in reversed position. But the left-handers as a group did not preferentially localize the higher and lower tones either way.

We know that in the overwhelming majority of right-handers the left hemisphere is dominant; this is, however, true of only about two-thirds of left-handers, the remaining one-third being right hemisphere dominant (Herron, 1980). So this pattern of results indicates that we tend to perceive the higher tones as coming from the side of auditory space that is contralateral to the dominant hemisphere, and the lower tones from the opposite side.

Finally, a proportion of listeners hear only the higher tones, and little or nothing of the lower tones. Table II displays the findings from Deutsch (1975), showing the numbers of listeners who heard all the tones and of those who heard only the higher tones, tabulated separately for right-handers and left-handers. It can be seen that the two handed populations differed significantly on this measure also. Most of the right-handers heard all the tones, but only about half of the left-handers did so.

What was uniformly found in this experiment was that listeners formed perceptual groupings on the basis of pitch range. They either heard all the notes as two non-overlapping pitch streams that moved in contrary motion, or they heard the higher tones and little or nothing of the lower tones. It is particularly interesting that no listener heard a full ascending or descending scale, since both these scales were present in the sequence, and the major scale is a very familiar pattern in our musical culture. As a further test of this effect, I presented the same pattern to a group of listeners and then only the ascending scale component, and asked them whether this had been embedded in the

TABLE I

Numbers of right-handed and left-handed listeners perceiving both streams and numbers perceiving a single stream.

Handedness	Streams	
	Both	Single
Right	34	7
Left	15	14

From Deutsch (1975b).

TABLE II

Localization patterns for the two streams in listeners who perceived all the higher tones in one ear and all the lower tones in the other. Figures show numbers of right-handed or left-handed listeners obtaining a given localization pattern.

RR: Higher tones localized in right ear and lower tones in left on both presentations.

LL: Higher tones localized in right ear and lower tones in left on one presentation; higher tones localized in left ear and lower tones in right on the other.

Both: Higher tones localized in right ear and lower tones in left ear and lower tones in right on the other.

Handedness	Localization		
	RR	LL	Both
Right	21	1	8
Left	2	5	4

From Deutsch (1975b)

full pattern. All replied that it had not. So we must conclude that the mechanism responsible for grouping tones by pitch range is so powerful as to prevent the listener from perceiving a familiar musical scale which is present in this pattern.

What is the relationship of these findings to perception of more complex music? This question was addressed by Butler (1979a), who was concerned, among other things, with testing the generality of these findings to music which is presented in a natural environment. A further question that he raised was whether the illusion only holds for sine wave tones, or whether streams of complex tones might also be segregated into channels according to the ranges of their fundamental frequencies. Further, he wondered how such factors as improperly timed attacks, unequal attack strengths, and unequal durations, all of which exist in natural musical sounds, might affect the illusion.

To investigate these issues Butler presented the scale configuration through spatially separated loudspeakers rather than earphones. The listeners noted separately the sequence that they heard as coming from the speaker on the right and the sequence that they heard as coming from the speaker on the left. In some conditions the tones were generated on a piano. Further, differences in timbre and loudness were sometimes introduced between the tones presented through the different speakers. Despite these variations, virtually all responses reflected channeling by pitch proximity, so that the higher and lower melodic lines were perceived as each apparently coming from a different speaker. A further interesting finding was that when differences in timbre were introduced between the tones presented through the two speakers, a new tone quality was perceived, but as though coming from both speakers. So not only were the spatial locations of the tones perceptually rearranged, but their timbres were rearranged also.

Such effects can be found in performed music. For instance, at the beginning of the last movement of the *Pathétique Symphony* there is a passage in which notes from the theme and accompaniment alternate between the first and second violins, as shown on Figure 3. But the listener instead perceives the theme as coming from one set of instruments and the accompaniment as coming from the other. This is true even when the orchestra is arranged in nineteenth century fashion, with the first violins to the left of the audience and the second violins to the right.

Diana Deutsch

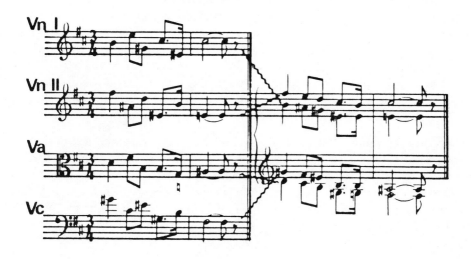

Figure 3

Passage from the final movement of Tschaikowsky's Sixth (Pathétique) Symphony. The combination of the Violin I and Violin II melodies results in the percept shown on the upper right. The combinations of the viola and violincello melodies results in the percept shown on the lower right (from Butler, 1979b).

So far we have been considering situations in which signals emanating from the two locations are simultaneous. What happens when temporal differences are introduced?

To examine this issue, I presented subjects with two simple melodic patterns, and they identified on each trial which one of these they had heard (Deutsch, 1979). The patterns were generated in four different ways. In the first condition the melody was presented to both ears simultaneously, and here a high level of identification performance was obtained. In the second condition the component tones of the melody were distributed randomly between the ears, and here identification performance was, in contrast, very poor. Subjectively, one feels compelled here to atte nd to the pattern coming either from one earphone or from the other, and it is very difficult to integrate the two patterns into a single perceptual stream. The third condition was exactly like the second, except that the melody was accompanied by a drone. Whenever a tone from the melody was in the right ear the drone was in the left ear, and whenever a tone from the melody was in the left ear the drone was in the right ear.

So both ears always received input simultaneously, even though the components of the melody were still switching from ear to ear. Identification of the melody was greatly improved in this condition, and subjectively the difficulty in integrating the two streams essentially disappears. In the fourth condition a drone again accompanied the melody, but now it was presented always to the same ear as the melody component. Input was, therefore, again to only one ear at a time. Identification performance in this condition was again very poor (see also Judd, 1979).

These findings show that with signals delivered to two spatial locations, temporal relationships are important determinants of grouping. When the two ears receive input simultaneously, grouping by pitch range occurs readily so that identification of the melodies is facilitated. However, when the signals to the two ears are separated in time, grouping by spatial location is so powerful as to virtually abolish the listener's ability to integrate the signals from the two ears into a unified stream. Identification of the melodies therefore becomes very poor.

What happens in the immediate case, where the signals arriving at the two ears are not strictly simultaneous, but rather overlapping in time? To find out I investigated the effects of temporal asynchrony between the components of the melody and the contralateral drone. This intermediate case was found to produce intermediate results. Identification of the melody in the presence of the contralateral drone where the two were asynchronous, was at a higher level than when input was to one ear at a time, but at a lower level than where the melody and drone were synchronous (Deutsch, 1979).

How do these results relate to normal listening? Berlioz wrote in his Treatise on Instrumentation:

"I want to mention the importance of the different points of origin of the tonal masses. Certain groups of an orchestra are selected by the composer to question and answer each other; but this design becomes clear and effective only if the groups which are to carry on the dialogue are placed at sufficient distance from each other. The composer must therefore indicate in his score their exact disposition. For instance, the drums, the bass drums, cymbals and kettledrums may remain together if they are employed, as usual, to strike certain rhythms simultaneously. But if they execute an interlocutory rhythm, one fragment of which is given to the bass drums and cymbals, the other to kettledrums and drums, the effect would be greatly improved and intensified by placing the two groups of percussion instruments at the opposite ends of the orchestra, that is, at a considerable distance from each other." (Berlioz, 1948).

We can see from the above experiments that the spatial disposition of instruments should indeed have profound effects on how music is perceived. When two sets of instruments are separated in space, and a clear temporal separation also exists between the sounds generated by these instruments, the resulting perceptual dissociation may be so strong as to prevent the listener from integrating the different sounds into a unified stream. However, a certain amount of temporal overlap between the instruments will facilitate such integration. Yet there is a tradeoff; the greater the degree of temporal overlap, the greater will be the loss of spatial distinctiveness; and as simultaneity is approached, spatial illusions may occur (see also Deutsch, 1982).

We now return to the issue of how perception of two simultaneous tones may be affected by whether the higher is to the right and the lower to the left, or whether this configuration is reversed. In the scale illusion, right-handers tend to perceive higher tones as on the right and lower tones as on the left, regardless of where in fact they are coming from. Examining the pattern producing this illusion and the precept most commonly obtained shown in Figure 2, we find that the illusion may be described as a correct localization of "high-right/low-left" combinations, combined with an incorrect localization of "high-left/low-right" combinations. For the second type of combination, the higher tone is perceptually displaced from left to right, and the lower tone is perceptually displaced from right to left. It can be seen that reversing the earphone positions would not alter this precept, since any "high-left/low-right" combination would still be organized in space to sound like a "high-right/low-left" combination instead.

This leads to some further issues. For example, is the perceptual displacement of higher tones to the right and lower tones to the left simply a peculiarity of the scale illusion, or does it occur more generally? Second, is this effect found only in divided attention tasks, or does it also occur when the listener is focusing attention on one side of space and ignoring the other? Third, given the impairment of localization accuracy for "high-left/low-right" combinations, is there also perhaps an impairment in perceptual accuracy for tones in these combinations regardless of how they appear localized?

To investigate these issues I presented musically trained subjects with two sequences of tones, one to each ear, and asked them to write down in musical notation what they heard. An example of such a pattern is given in Figure 4.

Figure 4

Pattern such as emplyed in two experiments to examine perceptual accuracy for tones in 'high-right/low-left' combinations, compared with 'high-left/low-right' combinations.

As can be seen, this may be described as six dyads, each of which is either of the "high-right/low-left" type, or of the "high-left/low-right" type.

In one experiment subjects were asked to attend to the sequence of tones delivered to one ear, and to notate this sequence ignoring the other. It was found that significantly more tones from "high-right/low-left" dyads were correctly notated than from "high-left/low-right" dyads. In contrast, however, significantly more tones from "high-left/low-right" dyads were notated as intrusions than from "high-right/low-left" dyads.[3] In other words, there was a tendency to hear higher tones that were presented to the left ear as though to the right, and to hear lower tones that were presented to the right ear as though to the left. This experiment shows, therefore, that the mislocalization of higher tones to the right and lower tones to the left is not simply a peculiarity of the scale illusion, but occurs with other types of patterns also. Further, this mislocalization effect occurs despite attention focusing on one side of space, ignoring the other.

As a concrete example, Figure 5 gives the reports of a subject when presented with one of the stimulus patterns. This pattern consisted of B♭-A-F-D-C-G presented to the right ear together with D-F-G-C-B♭-A presented to the left ear. However, when asked to report the pattern heard in his right ear the subject notated D-A-G-D-C-A; thus substituting the higher left ear D for the B♭, the higher left ear G for the F, and the higher left ear A for the G. When asked to report the pattern heard in his left ear the subject notated B♭-G-F-

---

3.   For both types of dyad, and for both ccorrect notations and intrusions, significantly more higher tones were notated than were lower tones.

Figure 5

A subject's report on one stimulus pattern. Higher tones that were presented to the left ear were perceived as though in the right, and lower tones that were presented to the right ear were perceived as though in the left. As a result, the melodies that were perceived by the subject were quite different from those in the stimulus pattern.

B♭-A-G, substituting the lower right ear B♭ for the D, the lower right ear F for the G, and the lower right ear G for the A.

Findings from this experiment lead us to question the popular interpretation of patterns of ear advantage that are obtained in dichotic listening to melodies (Kimura, 1964). To test for such ear advantages, the following procedure is generally employed. On each trial the subject is presented with two simultaneous melodies, one to each ear. This dichotic presentation is followed by four binaural melodies in succession. Two of these are identical to the melodies that had been presented dichotically and two are different. The subject identifies on forced choice which two melodies he had originally heard. If more melodies are identified from the left ear, this is held to reflect greater involvement of the right (or nondominant) hemisphere in processing the melodies. Analogously, if more are identified from the right ear, this is held to reflect greater involvement of the left (or dominant) hemisphere instead.

This inference, however, relies on the assumption that dichotically presented melodies are heard either veridically, or as degraded in some nonspecific fashion. The asymmetrical distortion in perception of these melodies found here clearly provides a source of artifact. In the Kimura paradigm, the binaural melodies that are presented for identification cannot be compared by the subject with the melodies that had been presented dichotically because he did not perceive these melodies in the first place. The "identification judgments" made by the subject must rather be judgments of *similarity* between the binaural melodies and the illusory melodies that had been originally perceived.

Referring again to Figure 5, we can see that the illusory melody perceived as the right ear contains more extraneous high tones than the illusory melody perceived as in the left ear. Further, the illusory melody perceived as in the left ear contains more extraneous low tones than the illusory melody perceived as in the right ear. If, in general, melodies were rendered more dissimilar by the addition of extraneous high tones than extraneous low tones, then right ear melodies should be more disrupted by this perceptual reorganization, so that artifactual left ear advantages should be obtained. Analogously, if melodies were rendered more dissimilar by the addition of extraneous low tones, then left ear melodies should be more disrupted instead, producing artifactual right ear advantages. Since the present anisotropy has not so far been controlled for, we cannot assume that patterns of ear advantage that have been obtained with the Kimura paradigm reflect greater involvement of the hemisphere contralateral to the ear associated with the larger number of identifications.

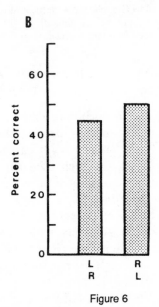

Figure 6

We now turn to whether there may be a difference in perceptual accuracy depending on whether tones are presented in "high-right/low-left" combinations, or in "high-left/low-right" combinations, where localization is not at issue. To examine this

Percentages of tones correctly notated in correct serial positions, classified by whether they came from 'high-left/low-right' dyads $\left(\begin{smallmatrix} L \\ R \end{smallmatrix}\right)$, or from 'high-right/low-left' dyads $\left(\begin{smallmatrix} R \\ L \end{smallmatrix}\right)$.

I asked subjects to listen to patterns such as in the experiment just described.

Diana Deutsch

However, instead of focusing attention on the input to one ear and ignoring the other, they were asked to notate the entire pattern without regard for ear of input.

Figure 6 shows the percentages of tones that were correctly notated in the correct serial positions, classified by whether they came from "high-right/low-left" dyads or from "high- left/low-right" dyads. Performance was significantly better from the former type of dyad than from the latter.[4] Further, there were significantly more "high-right/low-left" dyads from which both tones were notated correctly, and significantly fewer "high-right/low-left" dyads from which neither tone was notated correctly. We can thus conclude that there is

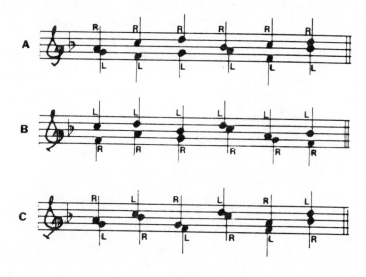

Figure 7

Patterns such as employed on varying spatial arrangements. A. All dyads of the 'high-right/low-left' type. B. All dyads of the 'high-left/low-right' type. C. Dyads of the 'high-right/low-left' type alternate with dyads of the 'high-left/low-right' type.

an advantage to presenting tone combinations in such a way that the higher is to the right and the lower to the left, both in terms of how well these tones are localized, and also in terms of how well their pitches are perceived.

---

4.   For both types of dyad, higher tones were more accurately notated than were lower tones.

Is there a perceptual advantage when higher tones are coming consistently from one spatial location and lower tones from another, compared with the situation in which higher and lower tones frequently exchange locations? To find out, I devised a set of patterns such as shown on Figure 7. In the first type of pattern the higher tones were always presented to the right ear and the lower tones to the left. In the second, the higher tones were always presented to the left ear and the lower tones to the right. In the third, "high-right/low-left" dyads alternated with "high-left/low-right" dyads.

Visual analogues of these patterns are shown in Figure 8, in which the closed circles represent tones to the right and the open circles represent tones to the left. In displays A and B, analogous to the first two types of pattern, two groupings are readily perceived; one corresponding to the filled circles and the other to the unfilled circles. But in display C, analogous to the third type of

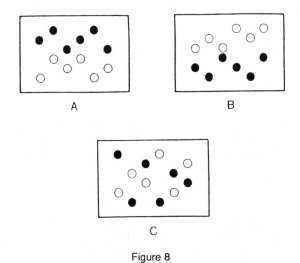

Figure 8

Visual analogues of the three types of pattern represented on Figure 7. Closed circles represent tones to the right, and open circles represent tones to the left.

pattern, perceptual grouping are not readily perceived. One might then hypothesize that, because of this impaired ability to form perceptual groupings, performance on the "alternating" type of pattern should suffer relative to the others. Accuracy in notating this type of pattern was indeed found to be

Diana Deutsch

lower than in notating the patterns in which the higher and lower tones were each consistently associated with a particular spatial location.

The enhanced processing of tone combinations in which the higher is to the right and the lower to the left appear at first to be paradoxical. It can, however, be accounted for on a simple model, which is here presented.

When a tone is presented monaurally, this gives rise to activity in frequency-specific units in both hemispheres, though predominantly in the hemisphere contralateral to the ear of presentation (Syka and Aitken, 1981). Let us assume that neural units responding optimally to a given frequency are linked in reciprocal inhibition, such inhibition being mediated by callosal pathways. Let us also assume that the unit in the left (or dominant) hemisphere would tend to exert a stronger inhibitory influence than the unit in the right (or non-dominant) hemisphere. Let us further assume that frequency-specific units within each hemisphere are linked in reciprocal inhibition, with units activated by higher tones exerting a stronger influence than units activated by lower tones. (Recall that in the present experiments higher tones were better perceived than were lower tones). This would lead to the baseline patterns of

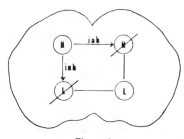

Figure 9

Patterns of inhibition hypothesized to give rise to the perceptual advantage to 'high--right/low-left' combinations over 'high-left/low-right' combinations. See text for details.

inhibition shown of Figure 9. The unit representing the higher tone in the left (or dominant) hemisphere should tend to win out over the unit representing the higher tone in the right (or non-dominant) hemisphere, and also over the unit representing the lower tone in the left hemisphere. As a result, the unit representing the lower tone in the right hemisphere should tend to win out over the unit representing the higher tone in that hemisphere, and also over the unit representing the lower tone in the left hemisphere.

When the higher tone is presented to the right ear and the lower tone to the left, the stronger activation of the contralateral auditory pathways should reinforce these baseline patterns of inhibition, and so result in enhanced patterns of activation in response to the presented tones. But when instead the higher tone is presented to the left ear and the lower tone to the right, these baseline patterns of inhibition should run counter to the stronger activation of the contralateral pathways, so that weaker patterns of activation in response to the presented tones would result.

One consequence of this model is that, since tones in "high-right/low-left" combinations give stronger patterns of activation, their pitches should be more accurately perceived than those of tones in "high-left/low-right" combinations. A second consequence concerns localization accuracy for tones in these two types of combination. It has been shown that when activity in one hemisphere gives rise to a perceived sound, the sound is heard as though on the side of space that is contralateral to that hemisphere (Penfield and Perot, 1963). We can therefore assume that the perceived location of each tone will be determined by which of its representatives in the two hemispheres is more strongly activated. Thus the stronger activation of the unit representing the higher tone in the left hemisphere should result in perception of this tone as on the right, and the stronger activation of the unit representing the lower tone in the right hemisphere should result in perception of this tone as on the left.

Finally, a note concerning musical practice. In his article, "Space as an essential aspect of musical composition," the composer Henry Brant remarked:

"Even today (1965) the resource of space is still, by most composers, considered an optional or peripheral aspect of music, in some cases applicable, but requiring no essential fixed scheme or extensive fund of detailed knowledge based on practical experiment. This view, as it now seems to me, places serious constrictions on musical expressiveness — it could almost be compared to a method of composing which made no specific provision for the control of time values or pitches." (Brant, 1967).

At the time that this was written there had been very little formal experimentation on the effects of different spatial arrangements on perceived music. The finding described in the present article document and elaborate on Brant's point by showing not only that spatial disposition can affect perceptual clarity, but even that given certain spatial configurations, the listener's precepts may well run counter to the intentions of the composer. A deep understanding of this issue is therefore essential if optimal communication between composer, interpreter, and listener is to be achieved.

References

Berlioz, H., in *Treatise on Instrumentation,* I.R. Strauss, Ed., and T. Front transl. (E.F. Kalmus, 1948).

Brant, H., "Space as an essential aspect of musical composition," in E. Schwartz and B. Childs (Eds.) *Contemporary Composers on Contemporary Music,* New York: Holt, 1967.

Bregman, A.S. and Campbell, J., "Primary auditory stream segregation and perception of order in rapid sequences of tones." *Journal of Experimental Psychology,* 1971, Vol. 89, 244-249.

Butler, D., "A further study of melodic channeling." *Perception and Psychophysics,* 1979, Vol 25, 264-268. (a)

Butler, D., "Melodic channeling in a musical environment" *Research Symposium on the Psychology and Acoustics of Music,* Kansas, 1979. (b)

Deutsch, D., "Musical illusions," *Scientific American,* 1975, Vol. 233, 92-104. (a)

Deutsch, D., "Two-channel listening to musical scales," *Journal of the Acoustic Society of America,* 1975, Vol. 57, 1156-1160. (b)

Deutsch, D., "Delayed pitch comparisons and the principle of proximity," *Perception & Psychophysics,* 1978, Vol. 23, 227- 230.

Deutsch, D., "Binaural integration of melodic patterns," *Perception & Psychophysics,* 1979, Vol.25, .399-405.

Deutsch, D., "Grouping mechanisms in music." In D. Deutsch (Ed.), The *Psychology of Music,* New York: Academic Press, 1982.

Dowling, W.J., "The perception of interleaved melodies," *Cognitive Psychology,* 1973, Vol.5, 322-337.

Herron, J. (Ed.), *Neuropsychology of Lefthandedness,* New York: Academic Press, 1980.

Judd, T., "Comments on Deutsch's musical scale illusion," *Perception & Psychophysics,* 1979, Vol. 26, 85-92.

Kimura, D., "Left-right differences in the perception of melodies," *Quarterly Journal of Experimental Psychology*, 1964, Vol 16, 335-358.

Penfield, W., and Perot, P., "The brain's record of auditory and visual experience," *Brain,*1963, Vol 86, 595-596.

Risset, J.C. and Wessel, D.L., "Exploration of timbre by analysis and synthesis," In Deutsch (Ed.) *The Psychology of Music N*ew York: Academic Press, 1982.

Syka, J. and Aitken, L. (Eds.), *Neuronal mechanisms of Hearing.* New York: Plenum, 1981.

Van Noorden, I.P.A.S., "Temporal Coherence in the Perception of Tone Sequences," Unpublished doctoral dissertation, Technische Hogeschoel Eindhoven, The Netherlands, 1975.

Warren, R.M., Obusek, C.J., Farmer, R.M., and Warren, R.P., "Auditory sequence: Confusion of patterns other than speech or music," *Science,* 1969, Vol 164, 586-587.

Wessel, D.L., "Low dimensional control of music timbre," *IRCAM Report,* Paris, No.12, 1978.

Section III

The Voice of Experience

INTRODUCTION: THE VOICE OF EXPERIENCE

Frank Wilson
Conference Director

In the years before Velcro, kids had to learn how to tie their shoelaces. I think this generally happens before the age of five. I remember that I had been struggling for months over the instructions I had been given to lead me through the steps of this complex ballet demanded of my little fingers. I recall vividly the first time I got it right — it was during my after-lunch nap, and suddenly the whole thing just fell together. After recovering from the shock, I remember untying the shoelaces and running through the routine again to make sure that it hadn't been an accident. Then I hopped out of the crib and ran excitedly to my mother to show her what I had done. I knew two things immediately as a consequence of this experience: first, that I had accomplished something very difficult and very important; and second, that I was too old to be confined to my crib after lunch.

As we get older we encounter all sorts of opportunities to exercise this special human ability, to build our repertoire of skilled movements. We learn to write, draw, shoot marbles (and rubber bands), to throw strike-out pitches, to do needle point and to fix watches or cars. If we are the sort of people who take pleasure in the building of these physical skills, we also tend to join soccer teams, baseball teams, basketball teams or ski teams, or we take music lessons. In the process of doing this we generally seek out a teacher or coach. We do this because we want to make the process more efficient by taking advantage of the experience of someone older and wiser — someone who will help us to take full advantage of our own potential.

This morning we are going to be looking at the problem of acquiring physical mastery through the eyes of the teacher — several teachers, actually — in order to gain a foothold on what we all recognize as very challenging terrain.

The teachers who are with us this morning are here because of a strong commitment in their own work to this principle, namely, that one cannot expect to bring one's own innate abilities to their full potential without an understanding of the physical basis of musical skill.

THE OBOE IS A WIND INSTRUMENT

Joseph Robinson
Principal Oboe
New York Philharmonic Orchestra

I've been waiting for months for this gathering, marveling at the assemblage and wondering about the common ground we all share. I come to you as a professional player and teacher, without any kind of medical expertise except that deriving from my own manifest ailments. When Dr. Wilson told me that Bob Freeman (Director of the Eastman School) had recommended me for this conference, I believed it was because Bob knew better than most the psychologic and physiologic damage twenty years of oboe playing have accomplished. He and I were at Princeton together when I was a more or less happy, normal, bright-eyed and bushy-tailed student.

I joined the New York Philharmonic in 1978. In our big-league, high-octane performance pressure cooker, we do 220 concerts per year. Most of them are taped for broadcast, some are recorded, others televised. Along about April or May, most of the insulation is burned off the wires. To recuperate, I go to Wyoming in the summer to perform in the Grand Teton Music Festival. That is where I've been for the past few weeks.

I think I'll leave any discussion of my own peculiar kinds of music pathology to Dr. Leonard Essman, the New York Philharmonic's tour physician, and to Dr. Ivan Shulman, his counterpart with the Los Angeles Philharmonic. In this address I will talk from a layman's point of view about what I understand, namely, the physiology of oboe playing.

First, let me mention that the New York Philharmonic recently began a chamber music series. It has given all of us in the orchestra, particularly those string players who labor anonymously, a chance to collaborate in a more individual and personally satisfying way. It was my privilege to begin the series with the *Trio for Oboe, Bassoon, and Piano* by Poulenc. I remember as I walked out with Judy LeClair and our pianist that afternoon, hearing some lady in one of the front rows whisper loudly, "Which one is the oboe?" Fearing there might be one or two among you who are uncertain about the oboe, I thought I'd start today by playing a two-minute piece by Benjamin Britten for solo oboe, written about 1959, to demonstrate the tonal range and character of the instrument. The piece is entitled, *Pan, Who Played Upon the Reed Pipe Which was Syrinx, His Beloved.* (The Britten is performed).

It is probably obvious, even at so short a hearing, that breath control, especially in this mile-high city, is the quintessential capability of oboe players. Of course we have to wiggle our fingers and flap our tongue in order to pronounce notes and articulations correctly. This is no easy matter, as the persistence on audition lists of such finger-breaking examples as Ravel's *La Tombeau de Couperin* and tongue-splitting excerpts from *La Scala de Seta* by Rossini attest. Still, it is wind control which is primary for singers and woodwind and brass instrumentalists. It is, after all, the wind which creates and shapes the musical tones we produce, which sculpts the musical line (the interpretive artist's highest challenge), and which gives life to our music.

Before pursuing the methodologic aspects of oboe playing and the physiologic aspects of technique, let me digress to an earlier time in my musical career. In 1963 I was studying the nature and extent of government support to the arts in Germany. This gave me an opportunity to be in Europe and to explore the wellsprings of our musical culture. It also gave me the opportunity to travel to France and to meet Marcel Tabuteau, the founder of the American school of oboe playing. He was principal oboist with the Philadelphia Orchestra for forty years, and is, from an American point of view, the most important player and teacher of the instrument in modern times, Heinz Holliger not withstanding.

Tabuteau retired from the Philadelphia Orchestra in 1954. By that time literally every major oboist in this country was a student of his or a student of a student. It is an amazing pedagogical achievement that he not only created a distinctive approach to playing, but that he disseminated it so effectively. When I first met him he had not taught for ten years. The invitation for me to study with him was not based on any dramatic or obvious talent. (I had, in fact, left my oboe in Paris to be repaired). Rather, I came to him as an eager admirer. My writing skills appealed to him, and he hoped I'd help him write his method book. In exchange he said he would help me join the club of his star pupils. What success I have had as an oboist I credit to him.

Until I met Tabuteau in 1963, my playing was concerned with playing more notes faster. I might tell you of the first lesson I had with him in June of that year. He played and then I played. We spent the afternoon sort of testing one another. I left feeling quite let down, thinking that if this was Mecca for oboe players, it didn't amount to much! Before leaving I asked him, "Can we work on the Mozart Oboe Quartet while we're together? I have to play it in October." I remember his eyes narrowed into slits. "Yes, of course we can play the Mozart. Bring it tomorrow, 8:30 in the morning." When I arrived the next day he was gouging cane, ignoring me. I said, "Good morning, how are you today?" He gouged another piece of cane, turned, looked over his shoulder and said, "Robinson, you are a very *sick* oboe player." Then he gouged another piece of cane. While I was thinking over his response he said, "I think I know the cure, but you're not going to like it." At that moment I thought, "if he destroys me as an oboe player I'll just do something else. I can stand it."

The cure was much worse than I supposed. He took the oboe away from me and made me peep on a tube of cane for about ten days; just the reed stuck on a tube. I had to play 1-2-3-4-5-4-3-2-1, creating little tonal building blocks that had to have exactly the right proportions in their getting larger and smaller. "2" had to have the same exact shape on both sides of the progression, not something different. While this may sound like kindergarten stuff, in practice it is very, very difficult to achieve. When Tabuteau was satisfied that I could play little rectangular notes that had the same shape and were proportional to one another, he then said the notes had to be triangular, not rectangular. That meant that when I played "1" I had to begin softly and diminuendo down to nothing, then "2" was played with a crescendo, "3" was louder but again with a diminuendo, "4" louder yet with a crescendo, and "5" again a diminuendo, the process continuing until again arriving at "1" with a diminuendo down to nothing. This sculpting in sound was something I never had practiced, certainly not with such meticulous care. But this activity was absolutely primary to Tabuteau's aesthetic outlook, where the performer has a creative role in the realization of a composer's work. Basically, what Tabuteau said was that the notes indicated on the page, while significant, are just a blueprint. The interpreter's real art is to give life to the edifice of music, sculpting it through time so that every presentation is unique, having about it, when properly done, a spontaneous, creative life of its own.

After the aforementioned exercises Tabuteau said, "Look, the numbers don't mean shape alone, they also mean color." (A single pitch could be played on a scale of 1-10, depending upon one's degree of sophistication, from dark to bright). The discovery of that interpretive realm was quite a shock. It meant that sense could be made of music in terms of the evolution of the color of the notes. Then there was the matter of vibrato, a difficult and elusive technique for wind players, which emanates in a pulsing fashion from the throat or diaphragm, or from both. There was also the need to connect notes so that slurred intervals and phrased notes were unified, not by just the absence of articulation, but by the use of a much more sophisticated bonding. The idea was to create one impulse of musical energy upon which were carried the various pitches. This technique of playing very legato intervals and phrases was something very challenging and difficult.

Articulations in music are basically the same as in speech. It is a matter of defining — giving separate and distinct character to — the pitches. In this there is a whole realm of possibilities, whether rendered very loud and percussively or in a very soft, sibilant sort of way. Tabuteau had an entire interpretive outlook regarding articulations which was new to me. There was also the potential for rhythmic nuance, which is really a matter of creating a rhythmic pulse and then deviating from it, to create tension or release of tension. Finally, there was ornamentation.

I've now listed seven or eight techniques which go into the interpretive artist's repertoire. Success was not just a matter of getting a gold star for playing a piece correctly, for putting the notes in more or less the right places with a pleasing sound and more or less correct intonation. That was just the starting point. Tabuteau would demonstrate all these things by making up an eight note phrase to which was applied some prescription for dynamic shape, inflection, color, and articulation. One had to have a computer to figure out all the interpretive combinations and permutations. It was all so mind-boggling — and so dramatically effective. He would say, "Now, you see, I have reversed the numbers; I reversed the inflections and see what happened." What he did was to open up my conceptual field of vision. He made me appreciate the fact that any musical utterance is infinitely complicated, infinitely challenging, limited only by the performer's sensitivity, discretion, discrimination, and discipline.

I think that great art in any form rewards scrutiny. It behooves all of us who care about music to try to sharpen our own sense of discernment, if only to be able to separate sophisticated musical artistry from what is less distinguished. Now six years into my career with the Philharmonic, I think this is something which critics, for the most part, fastidiously avoid. Why is Harold Gomberg, as an oboist, different from Heinz Holliger? What makes one school of French horn playing different from another? We need to have an understanding of what the creative achievement of an artist like Pablo Casals was all about, what his raw materials were, and what his interpretive task was. The performing musical artist takes separate, disparate pitches and communicates them to an audience as coherent musical statements, in a way which is comprehensible, persuasive, and affecting. The highest form of our calling is to communicate something about our human predicament, something which is otherwise, it seems to me, largely ineffable.

We, as performing musicians have the wonderful opportunity, as well as the serious obligation, of interpreting some of the most profound and important feelings experienced by humankind. This means that the composer's intention can never be completely categorical, exclusive, or absolute. It is much too limiting to think of it that way. Music possesses the potential of infinite complexity, limited only by the performer's power of imagination.

So much for musical purpose; let's get back to physiology. I taught for four years at the North Carolina School of the Arts in Winston-Salem, a place that's close to home. I watched the development of that unusual institution from its beginnings in 1965. One of my jobs there was to play woodwind quintet concerts, which I did eighteen times a year for sixth graders. It was a particular challenge to keep sixth graders interested in oboe playing for even five minutes, so I would demonstrate the instrument and, of course, play *Peter and the Wolf*. But what captivated everyone was to challenge those eleven-year-olds to hold their breath while I played the opening of the second movement of Tchaikovsky's *Fourth Symphony"*. The more troublesome were the little boys, the more they responded to the challenge.

A surprising accident occurred at the last of these concerts. While holding his breath, one eleven-year-old boy in the front row collapsed. I thought he was kidding, but he wasn't. The nurse rushed out to check on him, and sure enough, he had passed out. I thought I would be sued. Clearly, I'm not about to demonstrate that challenge to you now.

Breath control, getting back to the point, is the most important of the basic oboe techniques. Tabuteau used to say that conservatories were full of string players who could finger their way through all the concerti, but the soloists knew what to do with the bow. And so it is for wind players; the potential for sculpting, for changing vibrato and color, all these things derive from control of the wind.

Another thing Tabuteau said was that oboists were always suffocating from a surplus of air. This predicament is somewhat unique to oboe players. We have a very small opening between the reeds through which our breath must pass. During the time we are moving the air through this small outlet, our oxygen supply is being depleted — and probably a little gray matter dies every time I play the Tchaikovsky *Fourth*! Since only a small amount of air can pass between the reeds, oboe players are left with a fair amount of air in their lungs at the completion of a musical passage. The problem is how to get rid of this oxygen-exhausted air.

Joseph Robinson

Oboists must also endure a very high degree of internal air compression. I think that's the most unnatural thing about playing the oboe. It is not like the clarinet, or the saxophone, or flute, or most of the brass instruments, in which the air passes more freely through an aperture. Performing on these instruments is much more like singing or speaking. The oboe involves a constipated feeling of air entrapment, and players must learn to accept the discomfort of high internal pressure in order to produce a good tone.

A couple of years ago a teacher at the University of Texas sent me an article from *Musical America* (printed in 1944). In it was a discussion by Tabuteau about the fundamentals of oboe playing, noting that students at the Curtis Institute would spend one year just learning how to produce a tone. The most important basic technique for oboists, he said, is the ability to vary the air pressure behind the reed. I'm going to belabor this a bit, and hope that you will bear with me because esoteric as it is, it is the most difficult physiologic problem oboe players have.

From the beginning, students resist the compression of air in their mouths as being unnatural. There is really nothing in our normal lives which is akin to that. The problem is that from birth, or possibly before it, internal pressure from the throat down *is* natural, as in grunting. Moreover, we have very few sensory receptors in the glottal area, which makes it very difficult to monitor differences in pressure. If, as Tabuteau said, it is most important for oboists to be able to vary the pressure behind the reeds, it is then crucial for them to be able to experience the difference between high and low pressure in the mouth. There was a teacher at the Eastman School, Bob Sprinkle, who developed a very ingenious teaching tool. He had someone make a pressure gauge which measured ounces of pressure per square inch. When a short length of surgical tubing was inserted into the side of an oboist's mouth, the player could observe a pressure gauge needle moving as he or she played. This was a wonderful frame of reference because it accurately showed what was going on in the mouth cavity behind the reed.

Let me briefly mention two other basic techniques related to oboe playing. First, oboists must spend a great deal of time and energy being carpenters in a kind of Medieval craft which hasn't advanced for hundreds of years. We import raw cane and frantically, day after day, try to make it responsive and capable of producing tones which are expressive. I think it must be akin to what would beset surgeons if they had to make their own knives, never knowing if or how long they might function. Typically, in the New York Philharmonic I will play one concert and completely deplete the potential of a reed.

This, as many of you may know, contributes immensely to the psychologic problems of oboe players. It is a fact that we never know what kind of instrument we are going to be playing. The reed is affected by temperature, altitude, by humidity, and all sorts of obscure things about which we don't know very much. So, for twenty hours a week I whittle on cane!

The instrument, too, is fickle and undependable. Oboe keys and springs, unlike the flute, are uneven and unequal. Every separate fingering has its own special feel. The pads are affected by humidity, and spontaneous condensation in an octave well can wipe out all the oboe's high notes in an instant.

It is a very primitive instrument, and I have had to learn to replace hundreds of pads on my own oboes over the years. To play on the double reed we have to cover our teeth with our lips. This constancy of the lips against the teeth can be very painful. Moreover, the pitch of the reed can be changed by the pressure of biting, depending on how open or closed the aperture of the reed is. So, besides the several techniques I've mentioned, there is the need to open and close the reeds with the jaw.

The lips also cover or uncover the cane, determining whether the tone will be darker or brighter. There are, therefore, basically three variables involved in oboe playing, besides fingering and tonguing techniques: (1) the speed of the wind, faster or slower, which I'll call variable "X"; (2) the biting pressure to open and close the reeds, variable "Y"; and (3) the moving of the reeds in and out of the mouth, to cover and uncover them, variable "Z." These, as far as I'm concerned, are the *only* variables which impact tone, its color and shape. It is very important that any good oboe player be able to vary these along as wide a continuum as possible, and to move in as free and supple a way as possible within the range of potential afforded by each.

Getting back to interpretive techniques for a minute, the sculpting of sound involves making bigger or smaller sounds which, in turn, depends upon the interrelationship of the first two variables, blowing and biting. Playing loudly requires that I blow hard. In that circumstance I have to play with my mouth as far open as possible, or, as Tabuteau said, like a fish coming up for a bug. Playing at the other end of the dynamic continuum, whispering, involves very little wind and considerable biting. So it can be seen that pianissimo is really a creature of embouchure while fortissimo is a creature of wind. The third variable complicates things a great deal. Allow me to show you the difference between dark and bright. (Robinson performs). So, you can see and hear that by moving the reed further in or out of my mouth I can change the color of the note.

The greatest physical need for all performers is, I think, flexibility. This is where medicine, in terms of physiologic (and possibly neurologic) interest, and music intersect. What medicine has done in the sports field applies just as well to musicians, because we are athletes who emphasize a very particular physical discipline. I have jaws of steel, and can probably generate more ounces of air pressure per square inch in my mouth than one might imagine. This highly refined physical capability, developed over twenty-five years, is susceptible to the same kinds of functional disability as any other physical techniques.

The worst affliction is what I call isometric tension. Speaking as a performer, I would like to see this problem addressed by medical professionals interested in physical functioning. Most oboists — 90% or more — are, without being aware of it, afflicted by this tension. When they play softly, instead of blowing slowly, as if they were speaking, they tend to work very hard in the abdominal region, choking off the air flow to the reeds with their throats. The reason for this is, partly, that from earliest instruction beginning students are told to support, support, and support; *more* for piano than for forte. To students this always means some sort of physical effort, so they work harder. This is one of the sources of the isometric tension trap. The other is breathing. Preparation to play involves taking a breath. Once the breath is taken, the air is withheld from the reeds by a glottal reflex (that's what I've been calling it all these years). What this means is that the source of throat constriction problems begins the first day a student takes a breath in preparation to play.

This isometric tension, this throat constriction, inhibits the free expulsion of air, with the result that most oboists are topping-off the air in their lungs the way people topped off their gas tanks in 1973. (Remember when there were gas lines to buy one dollar's worth of gas?). So, too, oboists are always taking in a little more air on top of a lung full of air, until they are quite literally about to explode. This is a very difficult and unnatural predicament. Imagine that you want to play Brahms' "Lullabye" in such a physical state!

At this point I'm going to lay it on the line. I have a very dogmatic approach to breathing which derives, as does everything I do musically, from something Tabuteau told me. There was produced, just before he died, a series of tapes in the form of lessons, which would have been the core of the method book we were going to write. The first thing he says on these tapes, a kind of legacy from his long career, is about breathing: "Today, for a first lesson, most important for the attack, get rid of the air in your lungs. Say, *aahhhhhhhh,* and play with the pressure left at your command against the resistance of the reed." For most people this is just so much mumbo-jumbo. How can you play after exhaling?

For many years I, too, thought this was a severely overstated pedagogic insight, namely, that we have the most control over wind when there is the least air, and conversely the least control when there is the most air. Today it makes eminently good sense to me, so much so that I exhale before very important, poignant, expressive, and difficult solos in the orchestra. Those passages which are of short duration I play nearly without air. I tell my students that it is a little like taking a sponge out of a tub of water and allowing it to drip until it stops dripping. Once the dripping has stopped, one can take the sponge and squeeze out another cup of water. That squeezable part, in the wind analogy, is the air we should employ when we play. What this does is invert the typical breath support process. It forces me to move that air which otherwise lies dormant in the bottom of my lungs. In other words, I must act upon my body to produce air flow instead of acting upon the air to withhold its flow. Instead of holding back, I do something to make the air move. Thus, the tonal output exactly reflects my physical output.

Bear with me one more time. There are three basic approaches to wind supply and delivery. The first and most widespread is for players to breathe up and in and down and out. The second way is to breathe down and in and down and out. The third way is the only way that allows for real flexibility, which is to breathe down and in and up and out. This allows me to impel my wind with a kind of controlled Heimlich maneuver. I make my stomach wall the handles of a bellows, and throw my viscera under my diaphragm in exact proportion to the wind flow. In this way, when I blow slowly I barely move my stomach, and when I blow fast I convulse, as it were. You can almost diagram my musical phrases by how much my stomach moves in or out, or by how much my chest leaps upward in response to my stomach movement.

I know that this is all somewhat esoteric, and I apologize for that. This discussion does, however, address the most important physiologic problem for oboe players, and to some extent other wind players as well. We need to function as efficiently as we possibly can through the elimination of this kind of isometric tension.

The shaping and sculpting potentials I discussed earlier are ways of varying the sounds that are produced. At the Marlborough Festival, Casals would bellow whenever someone played a straight note. He said it was dead and ugly. So, the amount of variance in a sound is in effect the amount of life in the music. What we as musicians need to be able to do is to deal discretely with smaller and smaller units of sound, as if we were playing connect-the-dots, through time. I believe that one measure of the sophistication of an interpretive artist is seen in how small the units are which are controlled and manipulated.

I believe strongly that one cannot play a musical line as supple and fluent as a ballerina's movement while acting and looking like a cigar store Indian. There must be a physical analog to the musical output. This means that the parts of our body which impact musical output, which produce it, must function freely and efficiently. In my six years with the Philharmonic I've seen a great deal of physical disability deriving from tension. A colleague's career was shortened because of convulsions of his left arm, so much so that in moments of high stress he would throw the reed from his mouth. Another had a jaw so painful that she couldn't sleep for nights on end. Still another colleague had his career terminated by nervous colitis as a result of playing with great tension. I have a twenty-five year old colleague playing in a major American orchestra who suffers from shoulder and back pains and now has developed ulcers. Finger rigidity is everywhere. Oboists with crocodile bites abound. But the most common dysfunction has to do with control of the wind.

In conclusion, allow me to apologize if this discussion has been too particularized or arcane, or if it has appeared to be irrelevant to the larger purposes of this conference. There surely are very significant psychologic elements impacting upon musical performance, and you'll be hearing about them in great detail, I'm sure. My concern is whether the challenge of musical excellence is more intimidating than invigorating, more threatening than promising. It seems important that the musical performer and the music pedagogue be able to identify clearly and correctly the kinds of voluntary motor functions which have a positive effect on one's music making; to nurture their more supple and subtle response throughout the widest possible range of function, so that physical efficiency is as much an attainable goal for the musician as artistry itself.

A TEACHER'S PERSPECTIVE ON MUSICIANS' INJURIES

Dorothy Taubman
Founder, The Dorothy Taubman Institute of Piano

Presented by Edna Golandsky
Associate Director

Thanks to the public revelations by both Gary Graffman and Leon Fleisher, no one today doubts that there is a real problem of injured musicians. Now is the time to face the fact that the enormity of the problem removes it from the realm of accident. Nor can we fall back on the romantic notion of "over-practicing." Musicians like this explanation because it suggests extreme sacrifice for one's art. Too many musicians practice very long hours without sustaining injury to give credence to that explanation.

In my many years of involvement in piano instruction I have never encountered injuries that came from too much practicing, only *wrong* practicing. Through the generations, in attempting to help students, teachers have developed a mass of exercises without any investigation into the anatomic correctness of the movements involved. It is believed that to develop finger strength and dexterity requires a long term, gymnastic approach. This view is held in spite of the fact that prodigies as young as seven or eight years of age often emerge with stunning techniques without those many years of practice, while most of us never develop that kind of virtuosity after years of practice.

At the core of the problem is the fact that our profession lacks a body of knowledge, of researched, tested, and proven material such as exists in many other fields of learning. Ours is a hearsay tradition carried through the generations by word of mouth from teacher to student. Scientific study in our profession has been minimal, and even that little bit has all too frequently been overlooked. Students in our music schools are not required to read books on piano technique, even though they are working many hours a day to develop the necessary skills. The prevailing philosophy can be summed up in the idea that when it comes to technique, you either have it or you don't.

Harold Schoenberg, in his book, *Great Pianists,* describes pedagogic chaos. "Just as C.P.E. Bach had codified clavier technique as it was known in the 1750's, so the bridge pianists from Clementi onward tried to codify piano technique. Glorious confusion and disagreement resulted. But that is the rule in piano technique to this day. Clementi commanded the student to hold his hand and arm in a horizontal position, but Hummel and Henri Bertini wanted the hand turned outward. Clementi said that the palm of the hand should be stationary with only the fingers moving. Dussek said that the hand should lean toward the thumb. Hummel wanted the fingers to lean outside. Kalkbrenner said that the secret of playing octaves was a loose wrist, but Mocheles recommended a tight wrist."

It is this kind of confusion that is greatly responsible for so many musicians no longer playing. The tools needed for music making are physical tools. Our hands function according to physiologic principles of hand and arm movement. The instrument has its own mechanical principles. When these are all put together a science of technique emerges that permits the body to function perfectly without stress or strain.

I have spent forty years developing a comprehensive approach to piano technique that allows for an ordered and rational approach to solving all technical problems. Not only has this approach produced many virtuoso pianists, it has also achieved an extraordinary success rate in curing injured pianists most of whom are performing again.

It is not, however, cures that I want to address, but rather prevention. These injuries need never have happened. Let us examine some traditional approaches to the teaching of piano technique and see how they cause injury. First would be the basic finger positioning. Round fingers are still the most widely taught position. It has been such an important part of the training that when Horowitz performs on television, musicians are horrified at his straight fingers. I do believe there is a reaction of almost a physical revulsion against fingers that are not "beautifully" rounded. We need to pause a moment to reflect that Horowitz has been playing for most of his eighty-plus years without injury while many other pianists playing with rounded fingers are no longer performing. Let us find out why.

Please curl your fingers and move them up and down quickly. Now open your fingers as they fall naturally and move your fingers up and down. You will feel the difference in the freedom of motion. Now curl your fingers and move your hand up and down quickly. Again, open your fingers and move your hand up and down quickly. The difference is unmistakable.

Let me explain. In these movements we have used two different sets of muscles, long ones which extend from the tip of the fingers to the elbow and short ones from the tip of the fingers to the end of the hand. When you pull the nail joint inward, curling the fingers, the long flexor is being used. It pulls tightly under the fingers and the wrist. This creates the restriction of motion you experienced in both the finger and hand motions. When fingers are allowed to fall naturally without any anticipatory molding of a position, the fingers will drop freely from the knuckle. This motion is done by the short flexor, the muscle that does not extend over the wrist. The short flexor moves the fingers only downward, not exerting any pull on the fingers or wrist. The danger of the constant pull is exacerbated when power is needed, for then the pull becomes even greater. Eventually these muscles can weaken and spasm causing numbness, clenching, and pain.

The most common injury is damage done to the fourth finger. Symptoms vary from pain in the finger to pain extending into the forearm, clenching, and weakness. It is the myth of the weak fourth finger that is most responsible for this. It is believed that the fourth finger is inherently too sluggish for speed and too weak for power. This view is held in spite of the fact that most virtuoso pianists evince no such weakness. The weakness is said to result from the finger's inability to lift independently, because of tendons and ligaments that cross over the fourth finger and connect it to the third and fifth fingers. The other fingers are not connected on two sides in this way. To prove this weakness the pianist is told to hold all the fingers down on the piano keys and then to try to lift the fourth finger. In this situation the connecting and crossing tendons and ligaments exert a pull with the slightest amount of lifting, and bring the fourth finger to the extreme range of its motion, where it is in danger of injury. Also, in this situation, when the fourth finger finally plays down into the key, it has no support or weight from the arm. The strain of forced lifting plus the lack of arm support in key depression both contribute to the feeling of weakness and sluggishness.

The existence of crossing tendons and ligaments is totally irrelevant. In a coordinated technique finger movements are never isolated from the hand and arm. The fact is that tendons and ligaments cross over on top of the fingers, not on the bottom. This means that the fourth finger can drop down, away from the other fingers, without any interference from muscular pulling. This makes possible a totally different organization of the alignment of the finger and arm motion. Instead of lifting any finger away from the other fingers and arm, the fingers that do not play can all be raised together and the finger that must play can drop down individually. With no restricting ligaments and tendons under the fourth finger there will be total freedom in the dropping motion. The arm will then accommodate the downward motion by balancing on the playing finger. It has nowhere else to go because it is no longer resting down on the unused fingers. The playing finger now has the full support of the arm. When the arm balances equally on each finger, all fingers will feel strong, free, and controlled; the fourth finger will not feel different from the other fingers. When it plays it will feel "individualized" because the arm gives it power and the absence of pulling tension permits speed.

The fourth finger problem is a classic example of a lack of synchronization of the fingers and arm. If the fourth finger is limited in any way, it is only because a technique has been devised that places that finger at a disadvantage. As a result of these misconceptions, pianists are trained to overcome this so called "obstacle" even before it appears. Many of the naturally well coordinated pianists would not develop this problem at all if left alone.

Exercises are often assigned to overcome this supposed fourth finger weakness. Ironically, it is these exercises for stretching the fourth finger that often are responsible for creating the problem to begin with. A more apt term for finger individualization exercises is "finger isolation." In his book, *The Physiological Mechanics of Piano Technique,* Ortmann points out that no amount of practice can overcome the lifting limitation. This was written in 1928, and still the exercises are being used.

Any exercises that are for the purpose of stretching are dangerous and unnecessary. No matter how large the hands, the distances between notes are often too large for any fingers to reach. Open your fingers as much as possible; feel the tension. Now open your fingers to the point of comfort. Obviously reaching lateral distances across the keyboard cannot be the role of the fingers. Since there are arm movements that provide all necessary lateral motion, the fingers are relieved of any stretching whatsoever.

There is also the matter of speed. Exercises are assigned to develop strong finger muscles so that the fingers can move fast. Speed into the keys produces powerful sounds, but not faster tempos. On the contrary. Ortmann's research using high speed cameras showed that a fast finger action into a key actually retards tempo. The finger striking with force against a key, actually bounces away from the key several times before the key is fully depressed. The pianist wonders why speed is not forthcoming, even though he is working hard to move his fingers as rapidly as possible.

Clearly then, if one is to avoid rebound there must be a limit to finger speed. You might be surprised at how much less finger speed is required to play at great speed. What has been missed is that the tempo of a piece comes from the *horizontal* speed, the movement from key to key, not the vertical speed.

Horizontal motion is produced by arm movements carrying the fingers across the keyboard. This the arm can do easily at great speeds. The distance the finger must move to depress a key is so small that when it moves somewhat slower it does not interfere at all with the horizontal speed. Remember that pianists can play fast and softly at the same time, and must depress the key slower for soft playing.

Fast finger training is an example of the gymnastic approach which invariably overworks the fingers, creating spasmodic motions and a jerkiness that interferes with arm participation. The unfortunate result of this is risk of injury to the fingers and hands from the unnecessarily forced finger action. Another by-product of fast fingers is smudging and missed notes. The pianist did not actually miss the key but was thrown from it, thereby missing it altogether, hitting the next key, or playing both keys together. It all happens so fast that the pianist does not realize that initial contact was made with the correct key.

If we cannot use much finger speed into the key, how do we get power? To begin with, the fingers themselves are small and light; their muscles are not equipped for power. The weight of the arm, however, is such that it easily can transmit its power into the keys without being thrown from the keys as are the fingers.

It is clear that we lack a basic technical philosophy that can prevent serious injury. In order to arrive at such a philosophy we must be aware of what causes the trouble. Fortunately, wrong motions feel tense, awkward, and difficult. Therefore the first and foremost principle should be, if it does not feel good and wonderful it is wrong. Students raised with this philosophy will not be injured. We must rid ourselves of the prevailing belief that pain means developing muscles. If the pain lasts a lifetime, when can it be said that the muscles are finally developed?

My experiences have revealed that stretching to the extreme range of motion, either in exercises or in repertoire, is one of the main causes of injury. If so, a more realistic view of legato playing must be developed. It is in trying to connect the unconnectable that injuries occur. The pedantic notion that legato can only be achieved by connecting fingers is responsible for this. We have all heard pianists play connecting each finger, yet the total effect was not legato. On the other hand, passages that could not possibly be played legato physically have sounded legato. Since it is our task to create aural illusions, not to win gymnastic contests, all we need to do is sound legato. The how of it must not include the destruction of the hand. We will find healthier ways of achieving legato if we realize that legato is a quality of sound rather than a physical fact. When necessary we will think of connecting *tones* rather than fingers.

Intelligent pedal use is one of the important ingredients for producing legato. What always amazes me is that pianists see nothing wrong with holding the pedal down on runs, smearing them, while thinking they are cheating when they use the pedal to achieve legato, thereby sparing the hands. The quality of tone together with the control of timing and duration can produce the melting effect which is the essence of legato. That, together with the pedal, will create all the legato ever needed.

The incoordinate handling of legato is usually produced by incoordinate fingering as well. Since pain and fatigue have been an acceptable adjunct to playing an instrument, little thought has been given to fingering from the viewpoint of coordinate motion. Much of the edited fingering shows little comprehension of the physical requirements for execution of a passage. Fingerings which demand stretches must be changed. If a passage feels awkward, the first thing to check for is the possibility of a better fingering. Proper fingering allows the fingers and hand to move freely and easily while facilitating speed and overall execution.

On the issue of practice, we have accepted some formulas that need to be reexamined. One of them is the concept that slow practicing is always beneficial. Ortmann conducted tests to compare the choreography of motion used in fast and slow playing. By placing lights on the hands of pianists he was able to record hand and arm movements as they played scales and arpeggios. This yielded some very interesting information, especially that the movements in fast playing were totally different from the movements in slow playing. This poses two interesting questions: can one practice with one set of movements in slow practice and a different set of motions in fast practice, and, is slow practice valid? There are pianists who seem to make a good transition from slow to fast playing. However, it is an unconscious process and is often inconsistent. When these pianists fail to make the transition they become as confused as those who complain that despite hours of slow practice, playing does not go well at performance tempo.

For pianists who cannot make the change from slow to fast practicing, slow practice can be a mire. Among these can be pianists who intuitively develop speed movements when playing fast, lose them in slow playing, and then cannot find their way back to full speed. These students invariably report that they play better when they practice less. They also claim to play new pieces more freely.

This would seem to pose a dilemma because slow practice is essential to the development of control, evenness, and texture. The answer is that *one must know the motions required for speed* and use those motions in slow practicing. Only then will slow practice do the job it is supposed to, which is to make fast playing possible and beautiful. In fast playing each group of notes has its own special shape made up of a combination of hand and arm movements. The correct shape of these movements must be analyzed and brought into slow playing. In this way, when practicing slowly you are not really playing slowly; you are playing fast, slowly. It is as if you photographed your fast playing and then ran the film back in slow motion. In slow practice you are teaching yourself to play fast while developing the refinements necessary for expressive performance.

I would now like to turn to the issue of relaxation. In the early 1900's some teachers became aware that their students were suffering crippling tensions. In attempting to help them they developed systems based on relaxation which are still in use today. Unfortunately, the cure has often been worse than the disease.

Relaxation of the fingers, hand, and arm as a general approach to piano pedagogy is no more valid than those based on tension or fixation. The feeling of being relaxed is not the same as, for example, actively relaxing the hand. Being relaxed is the comfort felt from coordinate movement. Conscious attempts to relax the hand not only fail to create correct motion, but also can destroy correct movement. When we give any limb the message to relax, all the muscles relax, including the muscles that must move. The result is inertia and a collapse of technique. The delicate balance of contracting and relaxing muscular behavior has been interfered with.

The relaxation approach has been responsible for much pain, especially in the upper arm and back. Too much relaxation of the hand forces the upper arm and back muscles to hold the hand on the keyboard. These unneeded contractions can cause spasm in those muscles. Worse still is the disorganization of technique that results from double messages; now move, now relax. Retraining those injured from too much relaxation is much more difficult than retraining those suffering from too much tension. Most of all, it should not be necessary to teach relaxation. Instead, one should be taught to move correctly, thus obviating the need to learn to relax from tension.

A particularly common practice, and a dangerous one, is conscious relaxation of the wrist. When a student complains of tension in the wrist, often, instead of finding the reason for the tension, he will be told to drop the wrist to relax it. Tension in the wrist may be caused by pressing the fingers too hard into the bottom of the keys. Dropping the wrist will not remove the tension; it may simply compound the problem. The wrist is a fulcrum whose stability is essential to motion. In dropping the wrist a vital link in coordinate motion is destroyed.

Ortmann's tests showed that the dropped wrist motion was incoordinate. With the use of a metal arm, he showed how the weight of the arm dropped into the wrist when the wrist relaxed. This can produce pain in the wrist itself, as well as back pains, since the back muscles will compensate to keep the hand on the keyboard. The dropped wrist also deprives the fingers of arm support. Pianists so trained complain of spaghetti fingers. The collapsed wrists and lack of arm support have led to that feeling.

This does not mean that we cannot move the wrist up or down. There are necessary wrist movements that balance the arm over each finger. These movements are not relaxations; they are controlled movement. The sudden relaxed wrist drop is spasmodic, and therefore incoordinate.

Over the years there has gradually developed an awareness that the arm played a role in technique. This resulted in a teaching method that trained pianists to use "upper arm leadership." This approach is uncoordinated because the upper arm does not move efficiently at high speeds. The muscles of the upper arm and back are "slow" muscles that work well in slow movements. When forced to move quickly they tend to spasm.

If a coordinate technique means that the fingers, hands, and arms must move together as a unit, then there must be an arm motion that can comfortably move as fast as necessary. It is the forearm, not the upper arm, that can assist the fingers in getting across the keyboard quickly without bringing on tension and pain. The upper arm will move along with the forearm motion. The concept of upper arm leadership is tantamount to the tail wagging the dog, and is responsible for much of the disabling neck, back, shoulder, and upper arm pain experienced by pianists. It is also destructive of technique in that when the upper arm pulls the fingers along the keyboard, the fingers tend to become very sluggish. In a coordinate technique all parts essentially move together. The guiding limbs, however, must be those with fast moving muscles.

Another widespread practice is training for endurance. This implies that fatigue is the inevitable price of a virtuoso technique, and one must therefore be trained to endure it. One strategy is to make the passages more difficult in practice than they really are, in the belief that the passages will seem easier in performance. For example, if there is an extended series of octaves which cause fatigue, then repeat them twenty times as you practice the piece. In that way, when the passage is performed as written it will seem easier. This approach, the repeating of the octaves over and over again, is a path to injury. Fatigue, like pain, is a symptom of incorrect playing.

To me endurance is a horrid word. It suggests that one must accept suffering instead of dealing with the causes of fatigue. Endurance training is nothing more than obliviousness to symptoms. When we understand that there is no reason for fatigue, we then will be motivated to correct the problem.

Good habits are developed through repetition. So are bad habits. With enough repetition, even using incorrect technique, one can learn to play a passage. But there will be a price to pay in fatigue, insecurity, and, too often, injury. In the example of the octaves, the first step would be to analyze the movements involved, identifying those that allow the line to be played as written without fatigue. Only then should one practice the octaves, repeating them until the new movements become habits.

Pianists are able to play unlimited hours without any fatigue or strain, providing they are playing correctly. Coordinate playing is physically euphoric, as are all movements that are achieved with great skill. Inculcate the beginning student with the concept that playing can be euphoric and there is a good chance that the child will not become a "practice problem."

To conclude this discussion I would like to comment briefly on the treatment of injured musicians. Doctors have played a major role in bringing this problem to the attention of the public. In doing so they have performed an important service for all musicians. The treatment of injuries to musicians is becoming better understood, and the incidence of successful treatment is increasing. However, if after medical treatment a symptom persists, one must look to the technique of the player for answers.

Here I should like to caution about some therapies that I consider harmful. Among the more common I include the following:

- *Squeezing a ball.* This can lead to overflexed fingers which, as I explained earlier, can cause considerable problems.

- *Exercises that pull or stretch the fingers.* I again caution that it is the stretching exercises pianists use in their daily practice which account for so much ligament, tendon, and muscle damage.

- *Splinting.* Splinting promotes sensations of isolated finger movements which are destructive.

Finally, I should like to address a major concern — the use of surgery on the hands of musicians. In my many years of dealing with injured musicians, I have taught many pianists for whom surgery had been recommended. In many cases their problems were resolved without surgery by rebuilding their technique. Some of the indications for surgery were clenched fingers into the palm of the hand, clenched fingers pulled upwards, pain and numbness in the fingers, pain in the thumb and wrists, pain in the fourth and fifth fingers extending into the arm, and pain in the elbow extending down the arm.

I have seen many pianists for whom surgery was performed with negative results. The danger of surgery was clearly brought home to me via a report given at a recent medical conference by Dr. C.R. Ashworth, an orthopedic surgeon at the Los Angeles Orthopedic Hospital. He reported operating on a violinist who had a clenched second finger. After the operation the finger could only move sideways, not up or down. Clearly, this violinist will never play again. Dr. Ashworth said he would now hesitate to recommend surgery because not enough is known about its effects on the movements necessary for playing a musical instrument.

To sum up, musicians and doctors will benefit if they keep an open mind and ear to each other. We are all interested in prevention. To that end doctors must help alert the music profession about the necessity to become part of the solution by reexamining the training of music performers.

SUCCESS AND FAILURE IN MUSICAL PERFORMANCE

BIOMECHANICS OF THE HAND

Christoph Wagner
Professor of Physiology of Music
Institut für Experimentele Musikpädagogik
Hochschule für Musik und Theater
Hannover, West Germany

Legend has it that Artur Rubinstein once said that he owes his career to his hands. Obviously he was joking. More seriously, the great pedagogue Heinrich Neuhaus (1967) wrote in his well-known book: "Look upon the hands of our great contemporary virtuosos, Richter, Gilels, Horowitz. You will after the first impression immediately be convinced that these are hands of peculiar, *rare* and unusual qualification for great piano playing." How much of the success is determined by the hand, really? As you know, there are extremely differing opinions.

A widespread view, as expressed by Kochevitsky (1967), is the following: "Any abnormal bone-muscle apparatus is sufficient for the development of a high degree of technique because of the brain behind the hands." However, the assumption of a so-called "normal bone-muscle apparatus" of the hand contains the same fallacy as the notion of the "average man" (Hertzberg, 1972). It is, in my opinion, the origin of many fruitless discussions in the field of instrumental training.

Nearly fifty years ago, Otto Ortmann (1929) devoted a special chapter of his book to "individual differences of the hand." At the same time the physiologist Wilhelm Trendelenburg (1925) also noted the large extent of individual differences of joint mobility in respect to string playing. Their observations and arguments were hardly taken seriously and remained largely unknown, despite the instrumentalists' daily experience that, in the words of Ortmann, "...in the fine adjustments used in piano playing even the slightest restriction is a hindrance." It is this aspect of our question that interests me. How do we explain the thousands of instrumental students, professionals and amateurs, who even after ten or fifteen years of concentrated training do not reach that "high degree of technique"? Is the hand, due to its individual nature, responsible for the failure in these cases? And if so, was it merely a matter of training which had been neglected? The teacher would then be responsible for the student having failed. Or is it a question of manual characteristics genetically determined and therefore resistant to training?

There are many variables related to success or failure in music performance. I am not going to discuss the relevance of manual factors in comparison with other factors. I want to ask only one question — is it possible that the individual biomechanics of the hand can be a limiting factor in instrumental training?

Biomechanical Factors — Measuring; Reliability

The biomechanical characteristics which are, in principle, able to influence the dexterity of the hand can be summarized in the following groups:

1. Shape and size of the hand (and of the arm)

2. Mobility of the joints of the hand (and of the arm)

3. Strength of the muscles which act upon the joints of the hand (and those of the arm).

The manual requirements for the various instruments are quite different.For this reason it is necessary to examine separately the essential biomechanical factors for each instrument. We have largely restricted ourselves to the piano and string instruments in relation to factors of the first two groups, shape and mobility (see Figure 1).

Shape of the Hand: This includes the length of hand, breadth of hand, breadth of wrist, length of the back of the hand, length of the middle finger, and difference of the fingertip 1-3 and 5-3.

Active Mobility: Included here are the ten maximum spans between the fingers of one hand, the range of flexion of the basal joint of the thumb, the range of ulnar and radial abduction in the wrist as well as the range of supination and pronation in the elbow joint.

Passive Mobility: This includes the range of passive lateral movement of the basal joints of the fingers 2, 3, 4, 5; the range of passive abduction of the thumb; the range of passive hyperextension of the basal joints 2, 3, 4, 5; and the range of passive supination and pronation, each under the effect of a given external torque. Measuring passive joint mobility means determining the

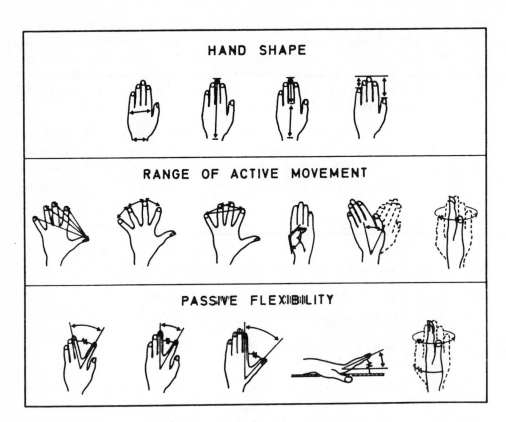

Figure 1

Characteristics of the hand which had been recorded in the investigation. The symbol
— — indicates the application of an external torque when measuring passive flexibility.

amount of mechanical resistance which every individual joint offers to movement.

The combination of measurements is different for each instrument. An examination of the range of supination is of interest for playing the violin and hardly of interest for playing the cello. In the case of the piano, both hands are examined, whereas in string playing we have until now examined only the characteristics of the left hand. Apart from the strength of the muscles, some other factors of joint mobility have not been included, e.g., control of passive wrist mobility. What was decisive for the compilation of data was the time requirement necessary to carry out the tests. In its present form, the examination lasts about twenty minutes with stringed instruments and about forty minutes with pianists.

It would be going too far to describe the technique of measurement here in detail (see Wagner 1974, 1977). The shape of the hand is measured according to the rules of anthropometry. We have developed our own methods for the testing of active and passive mobility. Figure 2 provides a survey of the measurement instruments and procedures.

The reliability of the methods was tested in test-retest measurements by two independent examiners on the right and left hands of 30 test subjects. That they might provide different degrees of variability with various joints is not surprising and has been reported before (Hellenbrandt et al., 1949; Wagner and Drescher, 1984). Apart from this, the size of the external torque plays a

MEASURING HAND SHAPE

MEASURING ACTIVE MOBILITY

MEASURING PASSIVE MOBILITY

Figure 2

Measuring Equipment

Success and Failure in Musical Performance   157

role in the control of the passive mobility (Wagner, 1977). On the whole, the reliability attained seems to us to be satisfactory. Of the 79 test-retest correlations, 44 lie above .9, 66 above .8, 9 between .7 and .8, and 4 between .6 and .7. We hope to improve consistency by technical changes. However, like other investigators, we have noted that determination of joint mobility of the hand presents considerable difficulties (Hamilton and Lachenbruch, 1969; Hasselkus, et al., 1981; Wagner and Drescher, 1984).

Variability of the Musician's Hand

Up to the present time we have examined approximately 600 professional musicians and 130 adult non-musicians according to the methods described. In addition we have examined 160 young people as well as 130 children with and without instrumental training. The majority of pianists were enrolled as students in the piano classes of six German State Colleges of Music. Music teachers at the high school and college levels and free-lance pianists also took part in the study. The majority of string performers were intentionally drawn from professional orchestras ranging from smaller provincial orchestras to large well-known orchestras.

First I would like to show those results which are important from a methodologic point of view, namely the question of variability of the musician's hand. I will show an investigation of 91 male pianists aged 16-33 years. The variability of the left hand of the 31 characteristics investigated is shown in Figure 3. (At the suggestion of B. Scheider, 1981, instead of the coefficient of variation, I use a non-parametric coefficient which provides a ratio of the interdecile range to the median. This is done because we cannot make any assumptions about the form of distribution of the various characteristics or, alternatively, we have indications that in some cases the distribution may not be normal).

Shape

Shape factors as a group show considerably more limited variability than the factors of active and passive mobility. It is interesting that the relative length of the fifth finger is apparently the least consistent characteristic.

Active Mobility

In assessing the pianist's hand one often thinks first about the 1-5 span. As the data show, it is precisely this span which shows the least variability among the ten spans studied; the 3-4 span almost doubles this variation.

VARIABILITY

	CHARACTERISTIC	0 20 40 60 80%
SHAPE	HAND LENGTH	
	HAND BREADTH	
	WRIST BREADTH	
	FINGERTIP DIST. 1-3	
	FINGERTIP DIST. 5-3	
ACTIVE MOBILITY	FINGER SPAN 1-5	
	" 1-4	
	" 1-3	
	" 1-2	
	FINGER SPAN 2-3	
	" 3-4	
	" 4-5	
	" 2-4	
	" 3-5	
	" 2-5	
	THUMB FLEXION	
	WRIST ULN. ABDUCT.	
	WRIST RAD. ABDUCT.	
	ELBOW PRONATION	
PASSIVE MOBILITY	FINGER SPREAD 1-5	
	AT 50 Ncm " 1-4	
	" 1-3	
	" 1-2	
	FINGER SPREAD 2-3	
	AT 50 Ncm " 3-4	
	" 4-5	
	" 2-4	
	" 3-5	
	" 2-5	
	FINGER EXT. ⌐ AT 37 Ncm	206
	2-3-4-5 ⌐ AT 75 Ncm	

Figure 3

Variability of the pianist's hand. Decile coefficients (Interdecile Range x 100/Median) of characteristics of shape and mobility of the left hands of 91 male pianists, 16-33 years.

Much greater differences are also found in the active flexion mobility of the basal joint of the thumb and in the active lateral mobility of the wrist.

Passive Mobility

A graded picture, one similar to active mobility, is also found with passive mobility in that the level of variability as a whole is considerable. The decile coefficient of the active span 2-3 is 31%; the coefficient of the passive spread 2-3 is in contrast, 66%. This means that only with measurements of *passive* mobility does the actual extent of difference in the biomechanical pre-requirements become clear. Finally, gross variability is found in the *passive* extension mobility of the basal joints of fingers 2-5.

Knowledge of this graded variability is also of interest for instrumental training as well. From this it is possible to derive a type of ranking order in respect to the teachers' observing manual characteristics with their students. As you see it is precisely the shape of the hand which tells us least of all.

Quite apart from the *inter*individual variability, the *intra*individual variability is also of interest. If at least some of the characteristics measured here were in close relationship to one another, then the number of factors to be examined could be reduced. For example, to what extent can we draw conclusions from the size of the hand on the hand spans, or from span 1-5 on other hand spans? In the practice of instrumental training such conclusions are constantly drawn unconsciously.

The calculation of correlations provides a number of surprises in this connection (see Table 1). In the test series with 91 pianists there was, at most, a correlation of .49 between the length of the left hand and its spans. The breadth of the hand has a correlation of .32 with the span 2-5. Several spans have a closer relationship if a common finger is involved. Between spans 1-2 and 3-4 there is a correlation of only .23. In the matrix which considers thirty characteristics of the left hand of this pianist group, there are 435 rank correlation coefficients. Of these, 319 are below .5, 407 below .8, with only 27 values over .8. Even a correlation of .8 is an unsatisfactory basis when we are considering the assessment of individual preconditions for piano performance. The correlation between spans 1-2 and 1-4 amounts to .84. As Figure 4 shows, we must nevertheless reckon with the fact that, for example, with a span 1-2 of 220mm, spans 1-4 can differ by 35mm. That corresponds to a distance of a third on the piano! It hardly needs to be pointed out that, under such circumstances, general statements about manual preconditions for piano performance should not be made.

At this point it is worth recalling the investigations concerning the problem of generalization of dexterity which were carried out by Henry (1958) and Fleishman (1958) which essentially speak in favor of the *specificity* of motor skills. The question seems to be whether the non-generalized biomechanical characteristics of the hand could not also, perhaps, be part of the cause of these findings. I am reminded of J.P. Guilford who wrote in 1958, "The properties of bones and muscles, and the manner in which they are put together, should have much explanatory significance in accounting for many psychomotor abilities."

Christoph Wagner

Table 1

Matrix of rank correlation coefficients for shape and active spans of the right hand of 91 male pianists, 16-33 years.

	Hand Length	Hand Breadth	Fingertip dist. 1-3	5-3	Active span of fingers 1-5	1-4	1-3	1-2	2-3	3-4	4-5	2-4	3-5
Hand breadth	.56+	—											
Fingertip distance 1-3	.52+	.33+	—										
Fingertip distance 5-3	.36+	.27+	.05	—									
Finger span 1-5	.49+	.42+	.41+	.13	—								
Finger span 1-4	.40+	.25+	.48+	.16	.86+	—							
Finger span 1-3	.38+	.08	.50+	.22	.76+	.89+	—						
Finger span 1-2	.26+	.04	.32+	.26+	.74+	.84+	.92+	—					
Finger span 2-3	.34+	.16	.49+	.01	.47+	.60+	.58+	.40+	—				
Finger span 3-4	.19	.34+	.24+	.07	.40+	.47+	.28+	.23+	.56+	—			
Finger span 4-5	.14	.35+	.14	-.14	.49+	.33+	.16	.14	.35	.50+	—		
Finger span 2-4	.21	.18	.37+	-.11	.66+	.73+	.54+	.43+	.81+	.93+	.54+	—	
Finger span 3-5	.30	.27	.35+	-.20	.72+	.61+	.43+	.40+	.63+	.85+	.78+	.87+	—
Finger span 2-5	.36+	.32	.32	-.15	.80+	.65+	.50+	.48+	.65+	.80+	.66+	.86+	.91+

+p <.05

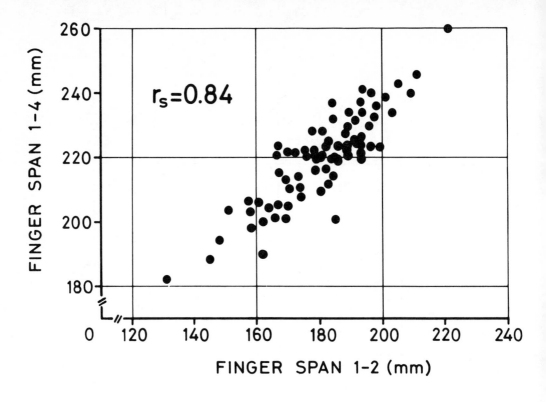

Figure 4

Correlation between active span of fingers 1-2 and 1-4 of the left hand; male pianists, 16-33 years.

Success and Failure Criteria: Comparing Two Groups

In the search for essential biomechanical factors for instrumental performance one could first of all compare musicians with non-musicians. We did this in an earlier investigation with violinists (Wagner, 1975), where we were able to show with a range of characteristics the biomechanical advantages of the violinists' hands. It seems even more instructive to contrast very successful instrumentalists with a group of players who have had serious difficulties with the instrument during or after training. The implementation of such investigations is, however, problematic. For example, the grouping of successful and problem cases for statistical purposes must be done carefully. One depends on successful people who, in spite of their success, have enough time and interest to undergo a biomechanical examination. Also needed is the cooperation of musicians who can recognize their technical difficulties and speak openly about them. For these reasons only a relatively small amount of data are available for contrasting both groups.

Christoph Wagner

It would be desirable to select well-known soloists and winners of international competitions for the "Successful Performers" group (Group S). This restriction would, however, have failed because of the considerable time and effort required. Moreover, I don't consider rigorous limitations to be required. Our investigations are, after all, looking only for biomechanical causes of *technical* success or failure — not causes for a performer's *musical* success as a whole!

For acceptance of an instrumentalist into Group S it was sufficient that they meet one of the following criteria:

- mastery of major works from the virtuoso literature

- participation in international competitions

- membership in a top orchestra

- regular concertizing activity

It would be inappropriate to designate the other group as a failure group for also here it is a matter of professional musicians who have reached a corresponding level of technical achievement.

The group of Problem Cases (Group P) included:

- instrumentalists who had to struggle with selected technical problems over a long period of time, e.g., lack of speed, lack of manual security, lack of endurance, and difficulties with grip and spacing

- instrumentalists with acute functional or organic disorders related to the locomotor system in connection with instrumental performance, e.g., tendinitis, epicondylitis, neuritis, and coordination disorders of the fingers.

We were able to contrast a total of 110 "successful" instrumentalists and 46 "problem" cases. We further divided the subjects according to instrument, sex, and age.

I would like to report on two of these comparisons — other comparisons have yielded similar results. The null hypothesis that both samples (successful and problem cases) originate from one and the same population was tested within each characteristic using the U Test of Mann and Whitney (Sachs, 1969). This means the comparison does not take into account the intraindividual combination and weighting of the factors being examined. We should, therefore, neither over-value the presence of statistically significant differences with particular characteristics nor the lack of significant differences with other characteristics. The analysis serves to describe the present status of results and to call attention to specific tendencies. Later we will want to apply other statistical methods which do justice to the intraindividual combination of the factors. At this time we are not recording a number of biomechanical factors which will be of undoubted importance.

Comparison I: Successful Pianists to Problematic Pianists

(Males, 18-30 years old, right hand. See Table 2)

Table 2 shows both the median and decile coefficient for each of the characteristics examined. Also shown is the indication as to whether a significant difference is or is not present at the .05 level. A two-tailed test was applied to the characteristics of shape of the hand so that arguments for a difference in either direction might be put to rest. We can see that in the selected characteristics of hand shape there were no significant differences.

Characteristics of mobility, however, are quite another matter. All ten active spans are larger among the successful group when compared to the problem group. The same is also true with the active range of flexion in the basal joint of the thumb. There were no differences in the active lateral mobility of the wrist and in the active angle of pronation. With passive mobility we find no differences in the angles of spread in which the thumb is involved. In contrast, higher mobility is seen among successful performers in the six angles of spread without the thumb. The passive extension mobility of the basal joints of fingers 2-5 is also higher among the successful performers.

Comparison II: Successful Violinists to Problem Violinists

(Females, 18-30 years old, left hand. See Table 3)

Included in the Successful Violinists group were 11 female violinists appearing at an international music competition. Quite by chance, the Problem Violinists group also included 11 female subjects. The two-tailed test was applied to the characteristics of the shape of the hand, and the one-tailed test was applied to the characteristics of mobility. This procedure is similar to that used in Comparison I.

In contrast to the comparison of pianists, here we found differences in the shape of the hand — although not those we might have expected. The hands of the Success group were on an average shorter and the wrist narrower when compared to the Problem group. There was, however, no difference in the relative length of the fifth finger, even though it is precisely here that an

Comparison of the samples of "Successful Pianists" (Group S) and "Problem Pianists" (Group P) with respect to shape and active mobility of the right hands. (Males, 17-33 years)

Characteristic		Group	N	Median	Decile Coeff.%	U-Test α=0.05
HAND SHAPE						
Hand length	(mm)	S	37	192	11.5	—
		P	10	89	18.7	
Hand breadth	(mm)	S	37	86	9.3	—
		P	10	83	8.4	
Wrist breadth	(mm)	S	37	57	10.9	—
		P	10	58	21.2	
Fingertip distance 1-3	(mm)	S	37	74	19.7	—
		P	10	72.5	20.3	
Fingertip distance 5-3	(mm)	S	37	36	29.4	—
		P	10	39.5	33.9	
PASSIVE MOBILITY						
Finger span 1-5	(mm)	S	26	233.5	11.6	sig.
		P	10	220	27.3	
Finger span 1-4	(mm)	S	26	228	13.5	sig.
		P	10	213	32.1	
Finger span 1-3	(mm)	S	26	217	13.8	sig.
		P	10	202	36.0	
Finger span						
1-2	(mm)	S	26	184.5	18.8	sig
		P	10	167.5	47.4	
Finger span 2-3	(mm)	S	26	97	20.2	sig.
		P	10	90	43.6	
Finger span 3-4	(mm)	S	26	82	32.0	sig.
		P	10	72	37.1	
Finger span 4-5	(mm)	S	26	93	33.4	sig.
		P	10	83	50.6	
Finger span 2-4	(mm)	S	8	131.5	28.8	sig.
		P	6	119	34.6	
Finger span 3-5	(mm)	S	8	134	19.7	sig.
		P	6	124	26.2	
Finger span 2-5	(mm)	S	8	174.5	14.2	sig.
		P	6	155	34.6	
Thumb flexion	(°)	S	36	55	59.8	—
		P	10	44	103.0	
Wrist ulnar abduction	(°)	S	26	34.5	49.0	—
		P	9	35	77.1	
Wrist radial abduction	(°)	S	26	25	48.8	—
		P	9	23	56.5	
Elbow pronation	(°)	S	21	82	29.0	—
		P	5	81	31.9	

Table 2b

Comparison of the samples of "Successful Pianists" (Group S) and "Problem Pianists" (Group P) with respect to passive mobility of the right hands. (Males, 17-33 years)

Characteristic	Group	N	Median	Decile Coeff.%	U-Test α=0.05
PASSIVE MOBILITY					
Finger spread 1-2 at 50 Ncm (^{o})	S	10	97	41.3	—
	P	6	87.5	42.6	
Finger spread 1-4 " (^{o})	S	10	83	42.8	—
	P	6	75.5	45.2	
Finger spread 1-3 " (^{o})	S	10	90	41.4	—
	P	6	81	50.9	
Finger spread 1-2 " (^{o})	S	11	57	43.2	—
	P	6	56	45.7	
Finger spread 2-3 " (^{o})	S	37	40	62.0	sig.
	P	10	34.5	60.3	
Finger spread 3-4 " (o)	S	37	27	73.3	sig.
	P	10	23	87.4	
Finger spread 4-5 " (^{o})	S	37	42	48.1	sig.
	P	6	37	58.7	
Finger spread 2-4 " (^{o})	S	10	52.5	92.6	sig.
	P	6	38.5	91.2	
Finger spread 3-5 " (^{o})	S	10	55	59.5	sig.
	P	6	45.5	43.1	
Finger spread 2-5 " (^{o})	S	10	65.5	57.4	sig.
	P	6	53	43.4	
Finger extension 2-3-4-5 at 37 Ncm (^{o})	S	8	20.5	134.6	sig.
	P	6	12.5	127.2	
Finger extension 2-3-4-5 at 75 Ncm (^{o})	S	37	35	105.1	sig.
	P	10	25.5	138.4	

Christoph Wagner

Table 3

Comparison of the samples of "Successful Violinists" (Group S) and "Problem Violinists" (Group P) with respect to shape, active and passive mobility of the left hands. (Females, 18-30 years)

Characteristic		Group	N	Median	Decile Coeff.%	U-Test α=0.05
HAND SHAPE						
Hand length	(mm)	S	11	172	11.9	sig.
		P	11	184	17.3	
Hand breadth	(mm)	S	11	74	13.5	—
		P	11	77	15.1	
Wrist breadth	(mm)	S	11	50	10.8	sig.
		P	11	53	15.5	
Fingertip distance 5-3	(mm)	S	11	37	26.5	—
		P	11	38	23.2	
ACTIVE MOBILITY						
Elbow supination	(°)	S	11	109	35.6	sig.
		P	11	100	28.2	
PASSIVE MOBILITY						
Elbow supination at 16 Ncm	(°)	S	11	103	34.8	sig.
		P	11	59	111.5	
Elbow supination at 32 Ncm	(°)	S	11	108	28.0	sig.
		P	11	80	71.0	
Elbow supination at 64 Ncm	(°)	S	11	120	26.7	sig.
		P	8	91.5	40.3	
Finger extension 2-3-4-5-	at 75 Ncm (°)	S	11	58	72.1	sig.
		P	11	43	74.8	
Finger spread 1-2 at 50 Ncm	(°)	S	11	60	49.3	—
		P	11	61	25.6	
Finger spread 2-3 "	(°)	S	11	50	67.2	sig.
		P	11	38	83.2	
Finger spread 3-4 "	(°)	S	11	37	89.2	sig.
		P	11	28	85.7	
Finger spread 4-5 "	(°)	S	11	56	45.0	sig
		P	11	42	69.1	
Finger spread 2-4 "	(°)	S	11	67	81.5	sig.
		P	11	49	82.5	
Finger spread 3-5 "	(o)	S	11	73	47.7	sig.
		P	11	58	63.1	
Finger spread 2-5 "	(°)	S	11	82	44.2	sig.
		P	11	66	69.4	

anatomic difference would be plausible. The data also show that except for the passive range of abduction of the thumb, the Success group is on average at an advantage with regard to active and passive mobility.

We will repeat these comparisons at some future date when a larger amount of data have been collected. Current data show greater variability in the Problem groups than in the Success groups. Even so, present results confirm and explain a number of things that students and teachers experience in an attempt to overcome performance difficulties.

The Individual Behind the Data

I would like to speak about certain basic connections which from a physiological and pedagogical point of view, perhaps also from a medical point of view, seem of interest. In the test series with 91 pianists we noticed that the greatest variability occurred in factors of passive mobility (Figure 3). Passive mobility factors were also seen as having the largest relative difference of medians in the comparison of Success and Problem groups (Tables 2 and 3).

It is important to keep in mind what *individual* differences lie behind these data, and what the data suggest in terms of instrumental performance. Particularly striking are the data related to passive mobility, especially the passive extension mobility of the basal joint of the finger. In the case of hand shape factors, the 9th decile exceeds the 1st decile by at most 30%. (Figure 5) In the case of passive mobility the 9th decile exceeds the 1st decile by 200%, 300%, sometimes 500%, 700%, and even more. This means that in an unfavorable case the joint must be moved against two or three times the resistance, sometimes even against five or ten times the resistance, than might be moved by a person with favorable manual preconditions.

What can an individual affected by five or ten times higher joint resistance do? He can try to reduce the disadvantage by assuming individually favorable postures and movements — something which is seldom done because of a belief that there is only one correct playing posture. Typically, the performer will try to compensate for higher joint resistance by using a correspondingly higher muscular effort, which causes an increase in the basic tension of the affected muscles. Muscle tension is a component of joint resistance which, according to Barnett and Cobbold (1969), comprises an average of 50% of the total resistance when the joint is moved in its middle range. This is the range which is used above all for rapid and precise movements. When muscle tension increases, the affected joint is harder to move — a phenomenon known to many musicians suffering performance anxiety. The increased muscular effort

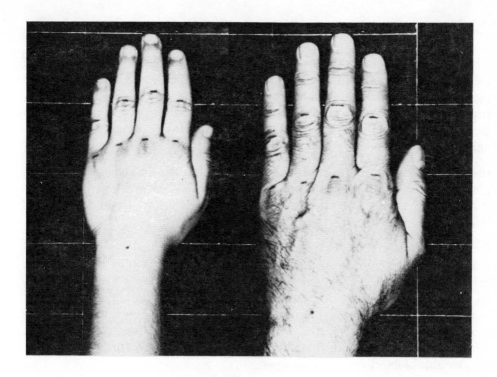

Figure 5

A "large" hand as compared to a "small" hand of two successful pianists. In regard to hand length, the large hand exceeds the small hand by 28%, in regard to hand breadth, by 30%.

needed to move the joint requires a correspondingly higher central nervous control to overcome these unfavorable conditions (Bernstein, 1975). Perhaps the most important effect of biomechanical disadvantages of the hand lies in the increased load on the central nervous system.

Problems of Performance

Once one becomes conscious of these connections, some negative aspects of musical practice are more easily seen. There is, for example, a considerable amount of work needed to acquire such technical skills as trills, ornaments, and repetitions which rely primarily on quickness of execution. For some players, the development of these skills is achieved relatively quickly; for others the process is laborious and time-consuming. For years I have observed that players who have difficulty in attaining speed of execution show high extension resistance in the basal joints of the fingers. This is completely understandable from a physiological point of view. It is known that the speed of contraction is dependent on the loading of the muscle. Differences in the range of 1:5 or 1:10 must make themselves noticeable! No one would expect the same performance from two 100-meter runners where one is dressed in racing attire while the other wears hiking boots, heavy clothing, and carries a backpack. Long hours of practice would be of little use to the weighted-down runner.

It is not surprising that in cases of particularly limited passive mobility, complaints are heard and injuries occur in the hand and arm. Injuries may include tendinitis and epicondylitis resulting from excessive demands of performance.

Despite the best preparation, some musicians are never able to rely completely on their technique. It is understandable that they develop anxiety. I am convinced that this anxiety, more often than we suspect, is biomechanically based. It may originate in the barely conscious realization that one has reached the limits of central compensation for peripheral weaknesses. Therefore, before anxiety is treated with beta-blockers and tendinitis with cortisone, one should be sure that the primary cause of such troubles is not an unfavorable biomechanical condition.

I would like to finish this comment on the topic of failure with an earlier finding because in this, something of the "safety interval" becomes visible. It is a matter of the measurement of the passive supination flexibility of the left elbow joint with non-musicians, non-selected orchestral violinists and participants in an international violin competion (see Figure 6). The noticeable difference between the medians is not found between violinists and non-musicians but between non-musicians *and* orchestral violinists as compared with competition participants. (By the way, the lower variability of the active mobility can once more be read here.) Biomechanical advantages such as we see here are naturally not the reason for success but are a part of the background for the success.

Training or Talent?

If successful and less successful performers can be shown to be different in respect to certain biomechanical characteristics of the hand, one then may ask how these differences came to exist. It is, indeed, difficult to imagine that the left hand of the female violinist becomes shorter by playing the violin (compare Table 3), but that the spans of the pianist increase in the course of training. It is the opinion of most musicians and instrumental teachers that

Christoph Wagner

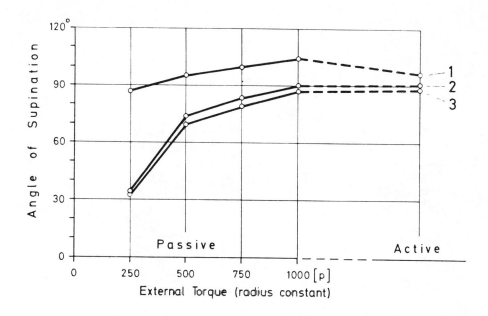

Figure 6

Passive and active supination of the left elbow joint (medians) examined with different groups:

1. 11 violinists, participants in an international music competition (19-29 years)

2: 19 violinists, members of orchester (24-35 years)

3. 13 non-musicians (18-30 years)

mobility can be taught. Our investigation, however, gives no definite answer whether and to what extent selected characteristics are teachable. An initial review of present data indicates no general tendency of increasing mobility in the case of any of the mobility factors. Regarding the average value in relation to time, we can see either no shifting at all (compare Figure 7) or a more or less decreasing tendency in general (compare Figure 8).

In order to complete the survey about development of age we have presented in Figure 9, apart from data on professional musicians as far as was available, also data on children and young people. This example should remind us of the following points:

1. The amount of joint mobility of the hand at early childhood can obviously not be maintained at the same level in any case, even under the condition of daily training.

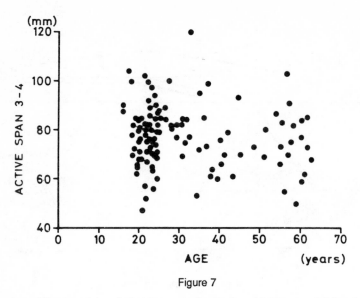

Figure 7

Active span of fingers 3-4 in relation to age; male pianists, 16-33 years, left hand

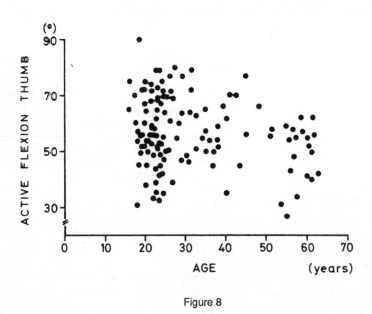

Figure 8

Range of active flexion of the basal joint of the thumb in relation to age; male pianists, 16-33 years, left hand.

Christoph Wagner

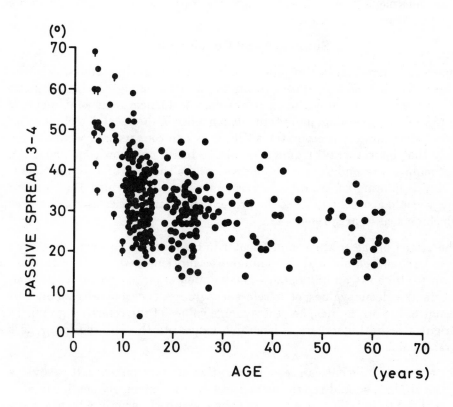

‑Figure 9

Range of passive spread of fingers 3-4 in relation to age (pre-set load 50 Ncm). Male pianists (●) 16-63 years; boys (●) ; girls (●) 4-16 years, left hand.

Success and Failure in Musical Performance

2. The variability with children and young people, seen in absolute terms, is already very high, sometimes just as high as with adults.

3. On the basis of high variability of joint mobility, it can happen even with a decreasing tendency in general that a 60-year-old has a considerably higher mobility than a 20-year-old or even a 10-year-old.

In view of these facts I once again think about Artur Rubinstein, remembering his marvelous performances at age 80. Perhaps his remark about his hands was more than just a joke.

Summary and Conclusion

We have considered (1) the variability of biomechanical characteristics of the hand; (2) the lack of uniformity within one and the same hand; (3) genetic determination as probably the more relevant influence upon joint mobility than the effect of training; and (4) the dependence of the level of technique on certain biomechanical preconditions. There is one conclusion I would draw, namely that instrumental training should be based on knowledge about the actual manual preconditions of the individual. To this end an examination at the very beginning of training is recommended. It is hoped that such a strategy would also contribute to the prevention of some occupational diseases to which musicians are prone.

At the State College of Music and Theater in Hannover we provide those who wish to be informed about their manual preconditions with a "Hand Profile." (Figure 10) It shows an individual's constellation of measured values as compared to the decile values of a reference group. The central column corresponds to the 5th deciles, i.e., the average values of the reference group. To the right are the higher, more favorable values; to the left the lower, less favorable values.

In the given example one can see a frequently found irregularity. It is obvious that the student should try to compensate for the extremely small range of flexion of the thumb (Figure 10, line 16) by moving the arm in advance when the thumb passes under in scales and arpeggios.

Two further examples are given in Figures 11 and 12. The former is of a violinist who won prizes at national and international competitions; the latter is of a student who came to us because of pain in the forearm after doing finger isolation exercises. For years his teacher had admonished him to relax. The student's comment: "I just can't hear that word anymore!" — and with good reason.

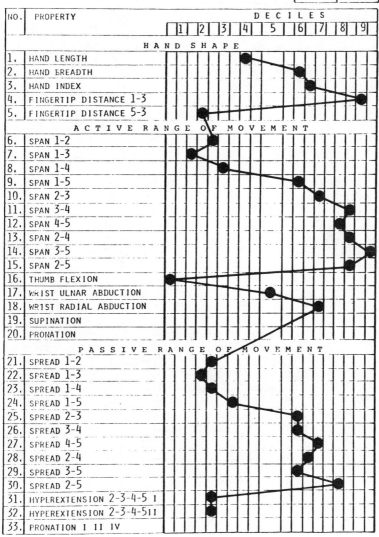

Figure 10

Hand profile of a piano student. Description in text

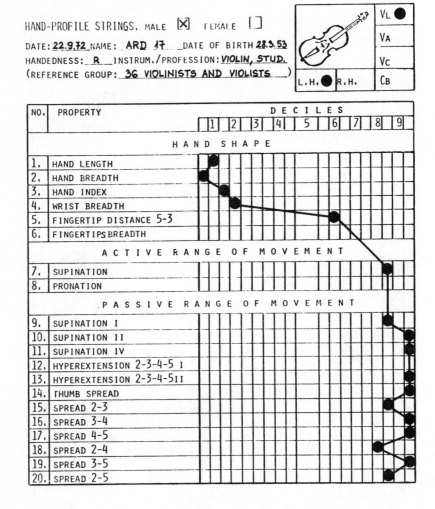

Figure 11

Hand profile of a violin student. Description in text.

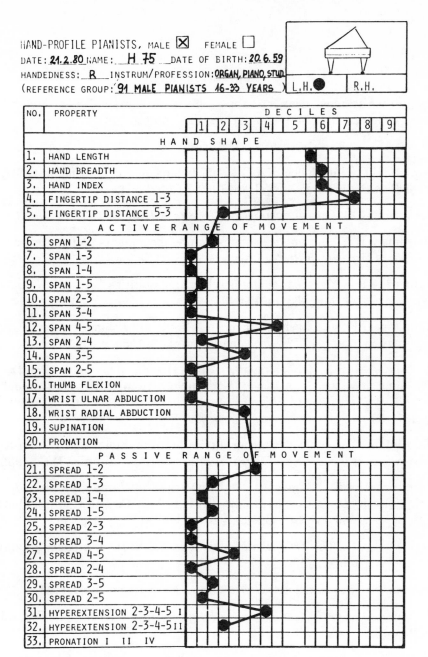

Figure 12

Hand profile of a piano student. Description in text.

Acknowledgment

The author acknowledges the support of the "Stiftung Volkswagenverk," Hannover which enabled him to undertake this study.

References

Barnett, C.H., and Cobbold, A.F., "Muscle tension and joint mobility," *Annals of the Rheumatic Diseases,* Vol. 28, 1969, pp.652- 654.

Bernstein, N.A., *Bewegungsphysiologie, Barth: Leipzig, 1975, pp.59-62.*

Fleishman, E.A., "An analysis of positioning movements and static reactions," *Journal of Experimental Psychology,* Vol. 55, 1958, pp.13-24.

Guilford, J.P., "A system of the psychomotor abilities," *American Journal of Psychology,* Vol. 71, 1958, pp.164-174.

Hamilton, G.F., and Lachenbruch, P.A., "Reliability of goniometers in assessing finger joint angle," *Physical Therapy,* Vol.49, 1969, pp.465-469.

Hasselkus, B.R., Kshepakavan, K.K., Houge, J.C., and Plautz, K.A. "Rheumatoid arthritis: A two-axis goniometer to measure metacarpophalangeal laxity," *Archives of Physical Medicine and Rehabilitation,* Vol.62, 1981, pp.137-139.

Henry, F.M. "Specificity vs. generality in learning motor skills," *61st Annual Proceedings of the College of Physical Education,* Washington, D.C., 1958.

Hertzberg, H.T.E., "Engineering anthropology," In *Human Engineering Guide to Equipment Desig*n (revised edition), H.P. Van Cott, R.G. Kinkade (Eds.), U.S. Government Printing Office, Washington,D.C., 1972 p.471.

Kochevitsky, G., *The Art of Piano Playing: A Scientific Approach,* Summy-Birchard, Evanston, IL, 1967, p.17.

Neuhaus, H., *Die Kunst des Klavierspiels,* Gerig: Koeln, 1967, p.98.

Ortmann, O., *The Physiological Mechanics of Piano Technique,* 2nd Edition, Dutton, New York, 1962, p.311.

Sachs, L., *Statistische Auswertungsmethoden,* 2nd Edition, Springer, Berlin, 1969.

Schneider, B., Personal communication, *Medizinische Hochschule,* Hannover, 1981.

Trendelenburg, W., *Die natuerlichen Grundlagen der Kunst des Streichinstrumentenspiels,* Berlin 1925, Reprint Hamecher: Kassel, 1974, p.84f.

Wagner, Christoph, "Determination of finger flexibility, " *European Journal of Applied Physiology,* Vol.32, 1974, pp. 259-278.

Wagner, Christoph, "Physiologische Voraussetzungen fuer das Geigenspeil," In V. Schwarz (Ed.), *Violspiel und Violinmusik in Geschichte und Gegenwart.* Universal Edition, Vienna, 1975, pp.196-210.

Wagner, Christoph, "Determination of the rotary flexibility of the elbow joint," *European Journal of Applied Physiology,* Vol.37, 1977, pp.47-59.

Wagner, C., and Drescher, D., "Measuring mobility of the metacarpophalangeal joints II, III, IV, and V in the dorso-volar plane," *Engineering in Medicine,* Vol.13, 1984, pp.15-20.

HIGH SPEED PHOTOGRAPHY
OF CELLO PLAYING

Helga Ulsamer Winold
Professor of Music
Indiana University

High speed photography intrigued me first when I saw a small segment of a Heifetz film in slow motion. Suddenly I could see preparatory movements, reaching for groups of notes, and minute adjustments required by particular passages in Heifetz's hand, a hand that had seemed almost motionless at regular speed.

In sports we have scientists studying every part of a movement that could make an infinitesimal difference in competition; in music we usually have the master-apprentice approach, where the master "unveils" his musical ideas and, if he gives any technical solutions, he only describes those musical sensations he feels. How much physics, biomechanics, and physiology should a teacher know? Ideally, the body should be an unconscious playing apparatus that responds perfectly to one's musical intentions. But, if in spite of practice, certain passages don't work, it is necessary to analyze what causes the hindrance.

In my first attempts to do movement analysis I studied basic left hand movements, including vibrato, trills, shifts, and scales. I took films with two cameras simultaneously, one at regular and one at high speed. Five cellists were used as subjects. We studied shifts, trills, scales, and vibrato. I will limit this discussion to selected aspects of cello vibrato.

Prior to the filming I gave the subjects the following questionnaire:

1. Do you vibrate from below the note to the center of the note? *Two thirds of the respondees said yes.*

2. What part (upper arm, wrist, and fingers) do you use mainly to increase vibrato? *Respondees were equally divided etween upper arm, wrist, and fingers.*

3. Do you use the same vibrato movement for neck, three finger, and thumb positions? *Two thirds of the respondees thought they used the same vibrato, one third thought they used a different vibrato.*

4. Does your arm position change if you vibrate a different finger? *All respondees said yes.*

It is clear that opinions on how vibrato is produced vary greatly among highly trained musicians, even without esthetic and emotional considerations.

What is vibrato really? It is a cyclic pitch change created by moving the finger tips up and down on the string. It is an even wave generated by a pendulum movement around an axis that continues once it is set in motion. The ideal vibrato, like most ideal playing functions, requires the entire body to be ready to move. It especially requires flexibility of the shoulder, elbow, wrist, and finger joints to transfer the movement to the finger tips. The angles of all these joints and the curvature and spacing of the fingers determine the angle of the finger tip and the leverage of the arm weight on it.

There are at least four possible ways to generate vibrato:

1. Finger vibrato. The wrist is shaken with the vibrating movement transferred to the finger tips. The finger tips move in the same direction as the hand. This type of vibrato is used mostly by violinists.

2. Wrist vibrato. This is a dorsal-volar rotating movement, where finger and thumb form the axis around which the forearm turns. The finger tip is rolled from one side to the other. Only cellists use this type of vibrato.

3. Forearm vibrato. The upper arm muscles swing the forearm up and down into a slanted or adducted hand. The finger tips move in the same direction as the hand.

4. Upper arm vibrato. The shoulder muscles rotate the upper arm, which in turn shakes the forearm. This vibrato is distinguishable by the flapping underarm muscles and can be used only in the neck positions of the cello.

I have selected excerpts from films of two players to demonstrate differences in vibrato. The first is an advanced undergraduate student; the second is a well known concert artist who has several recordings and has played with most major orchestras in Europe and the United States. The subjects were instructed to vibrate, then to increase the vibrato, and then to decrease it.

Subject #1

She uses a rotating forearm vibrato. The thumb presses against the finger-board. The non-playing fingers are bunched together and pulled away from the string. The third and fourth fingers are also curled up. The fingers roll from one side to the other. The transfer of vibrato from finger to finger takes a long time. The finger is stretched toward the note. The arm axis changes, then the vibrato is set in motion. The motion increases mainly in rolling amplitude, hardly in speed. There is a strong movement in the upper arm where the rotating causes the muscles to flap in the opposite direction of the motion of the forearm. There is no such movement detectable in the three finger or thumb positions. There a different vibrato is used.

Subject #2

He uses a swinging forearm vibrato. The forearm and hand seem to rest on the finger tip. No thumb pressure is detectable. The non-playing fingers circle above the strings. The fingers have enough spacing to allow each finger to swing freely in its own ground joint. There is a fluid line from the shoulder joint to the elbow. Hardly any movement of upper arm muscles is detectable. The elbow, wrist, and finger joints are flexible and rebound from the impact of the finger. The increase in speed can be seen in the faster swinging arm. Some rolling is used to widen the amplitude. The same vibrato is used in all positions. There is an easy transfer to the next playing finger with almost no time lapse in vibrato motions. The fingers are always ready to play double stops, shifts, or finger changes.

After seeing the films, all players agreed that the vibrato moved around the center of the note, regardless of their previously held view. We saw that the rotating wrist vibrato does not lend itself well to the transfer of vibrato from finger to finger, to changing positions, or to uniformity of vibrato in all positions. It is a surprise to most players to see the movement of the vibrating finger in the ground joint, which requires not as much fixation as most advocates of the "strong" fingers suggest. Furthermore, it becomes obvious that all the fingers must have space, that is, they should not be bunched together. The circling of the non-playing fingers above the string is not detectable with the bare eye. Neither does the eye catch the subtle change of axis from finger to finger.

High speed photography allows for the possibility of studying the differences between good players and excellent players. It perhaps allows us to glimpse into that mystic realm where good performance turns to magic.

TECHNIQUES FOR TRAINING
AND REMEDIATING VOICES

Oren L. Brown
Voice Faculty
The Juilliard School of Music

There are probably as many methods as there are pedagogues in teaching voice. This is because the human voice is so difficult to research scientifically, leading teachers to rely on personal experience.

At the numerous conferences where I have been asked to speak on the fundamental principles of vocal technique, I frequently ask the audience to think along with me in the same manner that I would with a private student. I would like to use this same approach with you today.

First, let me ask you to think about the significant differences between speaking and singing. In singing there is a prolongation of the vowel sound, a rhythmic time or duration factor, plus definite pitches or frequencies, each indicated by a musical notation. In singing, in other words, the voice is used as a musical instrument.

All musical instruments have three properties in common: a vibrator, an activator, and a resonator. The vocal folds function as the vibrator. The activator is the energy created by the expiration flow of air from the inflated lungs. The whole body acts as a resonator, as do the the pharynx and the mouth.

Next, let me ask what you consider to be the human sound. A dog barks, a cat meows, etc., but what is *the* human sound? I often get the reply that speech is human sound. But speech is a man-made development which utilizes our ability to make sound and then modify it with a variety of articulatory forms which give it meaning. These forms vary in different parts of the world, thus showing that speech is indeed a man-made development. In fact, one could communicate without sound as deaf people do. To demonstrate, watch my mouth and tell me what I am saying (silently shapes the numbers 1, 2, 3, 4, 5). The majority of you could tell me what those shapes represented even though there was no sound. We find, therefore, that a spoken language requires varying shapes and, under normal circumstances, a simultaneous phonation.

We still have not defined the human sound. Let's consider it as a moan, groan cry, laugh, etc. These sounds express feelings, but do not convey ideas or specific thoughts. But what is the sound we make when we are not quite sure what we want to say? It is, "uh," the schwa sound. We also say "uh huh," meaning "yes." We laugh with a kind of "huh, huh, huh." In none of these cases are we trying to shape any particular vowel or consonant. In the normal, healthy human the muscles of the mouth, tongue, and pharynx are in a relaxed, natural state.

In that the flow of air from the lungs is the activator that has made these sounds audible, we ask, how does one breathe? Would you all stand and, without thinking of breathing, place one hand on the chest and the other just under the ribs. Now observe what happens when you simply stand tall. The majority of you will notice that the chest is now more elevated and that the area just under the ribs has come in a bit. Now, with the hands in the same position, maintaining an easy sense of standing tall, expel all the air from the lungs and do not allow any air to come in until your system needs oxygen. When that time comes, see if you have any sensation inside the body as well as observing what happens under the upper and lower hands. Almost unanimously people feel a primary expansion first under the lower hand, although no willed action brought about the inspiration. Some of you might also have sensed the nerve impulse to the diaphragm inside the body at the moment the body signaled its need for oxygen.

Another way to experiment with the natural manner that inspiration takes place is to expel all the air from the lungs, even bending forward to help. Then, without letting any air in through the nose or mouth, stand tall with your hands in the same position as before, and suddenly open the mouth and experience where the air goes. There was less air pressure in the lungs than in the atmosphere outside, so air rushed in to fill the vacuum. Again, more motion is felt under the lower hand.

An exaggerated and not completely scientific image of easy inspiration and expiration is to compare it to the swing of a pendulum. Empty lungs would be represented by the full swing of the pendulum to one side. As all expiratory muscles are relaxed, air rushes into the lungs resulting in increased air pressure, represented by the swing of the pendulum in the opposite direction. When the lungs are relatively full, if the air is not held, it goes out. This image helps to take the effort out of the process of breathing.

We know that inspiration is an active process and expiration a passive one. So next I would like to see whether the natural expiration of air would do any work. Take a comfortably full breath, and as the air goes out like a sigh, provide a small resistance by shaping the lips and teeth into a hissing position (hisssss). Part of the way through the expiration, release the hissing position and allow the remaining air to escape as a sigh. Did you feel that you were pushing the air out during the hissing? Try it again and see if you can become aware that what you feel is a compression of the air in the lungs rather than any muscular effort. This compression is due to a law of physics known as the Venturi effect. It states that the smaller the opening for a flow of air or liquid, the greater the pressure behind it according to the inverse square of the opening.

Now see what happens if we substitute the approximation of the vocal folds for the hissing. Before we do this, however, we should know how the vocal folds are activated for phonation. Just for the fun of it, everyone take a breath and then sing the tone I am thinking of. (Audience sings). I'm sorry but the jumble of sounds you just made was not the tone I was thinking. I apologize for not having given it to you. Let's try again as I give you A-220 Hz for men and A-440 Hz for women. (Audience sings). That's better. This proves the point that the voice responds to the mental concept. And how does it happen that the pitch, A, resulted rather than some other pitch? It is because the adjustment of the vocal folds is automatic, having been preconditioned over a period of time.

One other point. Observe what happens as I blow between two pieces of paper. Another law of physics, the Bernoulli effect, is demonstrated. Moving air exerts less pressure than stationary air, so we have created a suction which draws the papers together and sets them into vibration. In a similar manner, as we start to release air from the lungs, think of a sound at the same time. The motor nerves in the vocal folds have gone to work to preset the multiple muscle fibers according to a preconditioned reflex, and the moving air completes the closure of the glottis. A cycle of puffs of air is activated which oscillates the folds in response to a pattern of muscle set, air pressure, and elastic recoil which we hear as sound.

Let's again take an easy breath but not hold it. As the air goes out, think of a lazy, sighing inflection such as "huh," prolonging it just a bit. Let's try it again. You will notice how natural it is for this kind of sound to follow a downward slide or inflection. We know that the vocal folds respond to the thought of sound more quickly when the lungs are full. Also, we know that higher frequencies require greater air pressure than lower ones. So, as we progressively release the air, the tone is moving toward lower frequencies which naturally compensate for the presence of less air pressure.

Try this once more, starting randomly just a bit higher and carrying the sound lower. You are now doing everything that is necessary to produce a basic sound for either singing or speaking, except to think of a particular pattern, goal, or task. When there is no fundamental interference, the voice will respond to the mental concept.

For the singer, this is a bare beginning. We next introduce the target of a definite pitch and let the voice slide down either a fifth or an octave. I follow this with a target one-half step lower and proceed in this manner until a comfortable low range has been reached. Then we start again, but this time at a higher note than was given at the beginning, followed by a downward progression of half steps. The sound used can be an easy "huh" or perhaps an "m" hum, which is the same as "huh" with the lips closed. I avoid the "n" or "ng" humming positions because I am seeking an absolute minimum of articulatory involvement.

Next comes the filling in of scale passages or arpeggios, always starting from the top in the beginning stages. These note patterns help establish automatic vocal responses to the thought of particular frequencies. No attempt is made at first to have the tones either loud or soft. After five or ten minutes of these exercises, we rest for a short period and then review what we have done. A student must learn and understand how to practice, since he is his own teacher between lessons. I always recommend that it is much better to do too little than too much.

Let me quickly state that I feel it is very important to explore the upper part of the voice and begin to exercise it as soon as possible since we never use this potential area in normal speech. Therefore, the muscles needed for these ranges must be discovered and used a little at a time, with regularity, so that they can become conditioned to perform their share of making pitch adjustments.

Another very important reason for finding the upper notes and bringing them down through the voice is that in wind instruments, an increase in pressure can raise the pitch. We seek to discover the natural, automatic adjustments of the muscles free from any excess pressure. In time, of course, higher notes are approached from below, but only after the upper adjustments have been sensitized and exercised. By then we have learned to let up on any feelings of tension in the throat as we go to higher pitches.

We are training muscles in much the same sense that an athlete trains, but with one big exception. We must constantly bear in mind that the vocal folds were not developed primarily for making sound. According to the Drs. Jackson, phonation for emotion or speech are only two of nine vocal fold functions. It takes a little at a time over a long period of time to develop a healthy professional singing voice. A concentrated tone is the objective of all training, but a big voice is a gift from God. Each voice has its own potential and must develop at its own rate. No two are alike.

This leads us to the area of remediating problems. I like to quote a statement of the Drs. Jackson that "95% of all who study voice with the thought of becoming a professional singer fail because of overuse of the voice." By far the greatest cause of misuse stems from hyperfunction rather than hypofunction. I found this true during the years I worked at Washington University School of Medicine where I treated over two thousand patients, all of whom were referred by otolaryngologists. I find it equally true today as I work with singers at Juilliard and at my private studio in New York.

It goes without saying that a complete history and diagnosis of each condition is essential for its treatment. Because of the limits of time, I have chosen to present two case histories which came to my attention this spring. The first is that of a high school student who was studying in the pre-college division of Juilliard. She started with me in September, 1983. I found her previous instruction had included primarily vocal exercises starting from the bottom up. She held the position of cantor in her local church and had sung leading roles in several of her high school musicals. Exercising the upper portion of her range and carrying it downward was an entirely new experience for her, and it was some time before she had the confidence to use it in a song. We prepared a recital including some twelve to fourteen songs which she was required to give at Juilliard. The recital lasted approximately fifty minutes. Included in her program was Mozart's *Alleluia* which has a number of coloratura passages, including a "high C" at the end. The program was a great success for a girl her age.

After the recital, which took place in February, she came down with one of those nagging, persistent "flu" colds which bothered so many vocalists that spring. Her school had started rehearsals on a new musical in which she had a leading part. Between the special rehearsals and her cold, our lessons occurred quite irregularly. By mid April she was very worried because she could no longer sing her high notes (she also had to sing the Bach-Gounod *Ave Maria* at a friend's wedding). Although she was not entirely clear of the after effects of her cold, we managed to rediscover how she could perform the wedding piece. She still, however, had her final exam at Juilliard ahead of her, as well as the school musical which required some rather strong singing in her lower voice range. I asked her, "How are you practicing the music for your show, especially those notes at the top of the staff?" To my amazement, she replied, "I thought that if I pushed a bit harder they might come out better." She was reverting to old habits — and we learned a big lesson in a hurry. She got through the musical with success and received an "A" on her final jury, which included the Mozart *Alleluia*. She was also accepted at the Mannes College of Music for the next fall.

The other case is that of a young, up and coming tenor in his early thirties who had a paralyzed vocal cord with abnormal speech. He had virtually no singing voice when he came to me by referral from his voice teacher. It seems that during a performance in the fall he felt something "snap" on the left side of his throat. We can only conjecture that he pulled one of the ligaments in that area as he sang an intense, high note. He had always had an easy, high, lyrical quality in his voice, one which carried well in the house. I happened to have heard him sing the lead tenor at the Kennedy Center in Washington several years previously. During the last year or so before his trauma, he had been trying to get some of the fullness of his lower voice into his upper register by practicing ascending scales.

His case was indeed a challenge. Hyperfunction had produced a condition of hypofunction! We proceeded very gently, working first only on speech. Easy head rolls, yawning, and checking jaw and tongue for stiffness were practiced for a few minutes six times daily, with at least an hour in between. This was done to obtain as absolute a condition of non-interference as possible from all extrinsic activity.

Breathing was evaluated within a body framework of good posture. By experiencing the "hissing" exercise, we established the feeling that a release of air would provide enough energy to produce a sound. This was followed in about a week by the lightest possible, almost whispering, breathy phonation. The "oo" vowel seemed to produce the best result. The "oo" vowel position reflexively induces an easy, low larynx position. We also found we could use a repeated "hoo, hoo, hoooo," thus inducing the reflexive assistance of a light laugh. For the first two weeks we met for three one half hour sessions. I then left town for one week. On my return I found that he had grasped the principles of practicing so well that I only saw him on an average of once per week for three months, at which time I stopped my appointments for the summer.

We had gradually extended the range of sliding inflections, added different vowel positions, letting the sliding inflections move down, back up, and down again. Definite pitches were added as the voice began to strengthen. Talking in a light, loose, almost childish and pressureless manner was begun within the second week.

This young man was most receptive to the exercises and, since he could examine his own larynx, he could see changes taking place. He was not only receptive to the exercises because he knew he had to conquer his condition or give up his career, but also because when he was younger he had pulled a muscle in his shoulder when playing baseball and had to give up the sport. He had canceled all singing engagements, of course, as soon as he had first encountered the injury to his larynx.

When I left for the summer, he was contemplating the possibility of accepting a long term oratorio engagement. We had gone over the most difficult parts of the music and found he could give a professional level performance. I left the decision to him, knowing he would not perform if he felt at all insecure.

The basic principle in voice therapy is one of opposites. Many years ago I read in the book, *Voice Building and Tone Placement* by Dr. H. Holbrook-Curtis that two young students of singing had come to him at about the same time, one with bowed vocal cords and the other with vocal nodules. He recommended to each that they study with the other's teacher, with excellent results.

With the knowledge we have today about anatomy, physiology, physics, psychology, maturation of the voice, neurology, and the fundamentals of muscle growth, it would seem that it might be entirely possible to train a group of teacher-therapists who, at the very least, would not injure a voice and, at best, would be able to develop it to a healthy, professional level.

Several years ago, when I heard of a certified voice therapist prescribing the so called "pushing exercises" for half a year to correct a condition of hyperfunction, I became a bit skeptical as to how much work remains to be done in this field. I am, however, happy to hear more and more that success is being achieved in various locales. This gives me hope that voice therapy may be rounding a corner towards greater therapeutic success.

BIOFEEDBACK IN VIOLIN
AND VIOLA PEDAGOGY

William LeVine
Professor of Psychiatry
University of Kansas Medical School

Biofeedback techniques may help musical performers in several different ways. One way is by promoting general relaxation. A second way is that biofeedback may reduce clinical symptoms such as performance anxiety or "stage fright." A third way is that biofeedback techniques are useful in the treatment of specific functional disorders affecting musicians, such as craft palsies (Levee, Cohen, and Rickles, 1976; LeVine, 1982). And finally, biofeedback techniques may also constitute a new pedagogical tool for the training of musicians. The latter is the subject of this report.

Adequate left-hand technique for the violin or viola requires rapid cycles of contraction and relaxation among agonist and antagonist pairs of muscles. Although there are different opinions among pedagogues of violin and viola regarding the desirable amount of muscle "tension" necessary for good performance, all agree that excessive rigidity of the left hand decreases finger speed and interferes with necessary quick changes of hand position. Excessive muscle tension in the left hand is usually caused by simultaneous contraction of agonist and antagonist pairs of muscles, such as a thumb or finger flexor, against an object of resistance, which results in an isometric contraction.

In the usual playing posture, the neck of the instrument rests upon the palmar surface of the metacarpo-phalangeal joint of the index finger. Because the instrument is primarily rested on the shoulder, only a slight upward force of the left hand is required to support the instrument. Squeezing the neck of the instrument between the thumb and index finger is unnecessary and deleterious to performance. However, some players have acquired the habit of squeezing the violin's neck. We sought to discover whether techniques derived from those used in muscle retraining (Brudny, Korein, et. al. 1976; Baker, 1979) can provide assistance to violinists and violists in removing unwanted left hand tension.

Subjects

Nine volunteer violin and viola players were recruited by word of mouth. All nine displayed tension in the left thumb or hand that interfered with their performance. None had craft palsy, stage fright, or psychiatric disorders. Six were members of a professional symphony orchestra, and three were undergraduate students majoring in violin or viola or in music education with a minor in one of the two instruments. Six were women. All of the subjects were aware of an undesired level of muscle tension in the left hand or thumb. Most also experienced at least one other symptom: cold or sweaty hands or tension in the trapezius muscles. Most of the subjects also reported that the problem of excessive left-hand tension was chronic and worsened by anxiety (including performance anxiety), as well as by the anticipation of playing difficult passages. In most of the subjects, the excessive left-hand tension had been the focus of remedial work in the form of lessons and exercises.

Procedure

Electromyographic electrodes (Autogenic Systems, Inc.) were attached to the left hand in such a way as to detect signals from the adductor pollicis, as well as other intrinsic muscles involved in movements of the thumb and the index finger. Some subjects had small hands or other anatomic considerations that required alternative placement of the electrodes. For subjects with small hands, better results were obtained from gold-cup EEG electrodes (Grass Instrument Co.) used with EEG electrode paste and covered with a small amount of 3M Micropore tape. Use of the EEG electrodes also interfered less with the subjects' access to higher positions on the instrument's neck. For other players, extension of the left index finger caused feedback sounds even though the subject was not gripping the violin too tightly. In such cases, an alternative placement was sought.

The EMG electrodes were connected to an Autogen 1500 B (Autogenic Systems, Inc.) feedback myograph. When EEG electrodes were used, they were connected to the myograph by an adapter cable. The sensitivity of the meter was adjusted so that an easy musical passage (usually a scale) played with the relaxed left hand produced a reading near the middle of the meter. A non-derivative audio feedback mode was used. A click sound proved most audible over the sound of the musical instrument. The feedback threshold was adjusted to produce the click whenever the EMG activity exceeded the level observed during the easy scale passages.

The subjects then played their usual, more difficult material. In most cases, the EMG reading was above the meter's range. The subjects were instructed to stop playing immediately when the click was heard and to repeat the passage until they could play it without producing the click. Thus, the feedback tone signaled the presence of increased EMG activity. Initially, the threshold was set so that the subjects could play the majority of their music without sounding the feedback tone. Unusually difficult maneuvers, such as double-stops, caused transient clicks and were disregarded.

Thirty-minute training sessions were held at the subjects' convenience once or twice a week. During the second or third session, we taught the subjects to apply the electrodes, to operate the apparatus themselves, and to find the threshold setting at which they could still play most of their music without sounding the alarm. We had them lower the threshold setting gradually so that they would have to decrease EMG activity still further to prevent the feedback tone from sounding. A specific number of sessions was not recommended; subjects were told to continue as long as they believed they were benefiting. Attendance records were kept, and the results were assessed by structured telephone interviews three to seven months after the student stopped participating in the study.

In the telephone interviews, the subjects were asked to rate the degree of their disability caused by left-hand tension on a scale of 0-5, with 0 designating no problems and 5 designating complete incapacity. The ratings were made retrospectively for "before training," "immediately after training," and "now" (i.e., at the time of follow-up). Comparison of the "before" and "immediately after" ratings were taken as a measure of efficacy; comparison of the ratings "immediately after" and "now" served as a measure of relapse. An open-ended question about new symptoms assessed the possibility of symptom substitution, that is, the appearance of new symptoms following the disappearance of old ones. Other open-ended questions assessed the subjects' belief about how biofeedback worked in this application.

Results

Results are shown in Table 1. Eight of the nine subjects (89%) believed that the biofeedback technique decreased the tension in their left hands immediately after treatment. One of the nine subjects (Subject No. 9) gave a numerical rating that indicated improvement, but his narrative comments contradicted this. We considered this subject unimproved. Seven of the nine subjects (78%) rated undesired left-hand tension as 0 to 1 at the time of follow-up. These findings suggest that the treatment was efficacious and that there was little or no relapse.

During follow-up, two subjects reported the occurrence of new symptoms in addition to left hand tension. Subject No. 9 later experienced painful neck tension. Subject No. 8, who reported a "relapse," reported muscular tension in her left arm. The other subjects reported no new symptoms. Thus, symptom substitution did not occur.

Table 1

Retrospective self-ratings of left-handed impairment of 3 to 7 months after biofeedback training.

Subject	Number of Treatments	Follow-up (months)	Self Rating of Impairment*		
			Before Treatment	Immediately After Final Treatment	At Time of Follow-up
1	16	4	1-1.5	0.5	0.5-1
2	7	3.5	5	1	1
3	3	4	3	1	0-1
4	3	7	3	1	0-1
5	2	7	3	2	2
6	16	3	3.5	1.5	1
7	6	5	3.5-4	1-2	1
8	6	6	3-4	1	3-4
9	2	5	2	1	1
	Mean=6.8	Mean-=4.9	Median=3	Median=1	Median=1

*In telephone interviews, the subjects were asked to rate on a scale of 0-5 the degree of their disability caused by left-hand tension: 0=no problems and 5=complete incapacity.

The ratings do not tell the whole story. A few quotations from the subjects' comments about their experiences will serve to illustrate the quality of improvement. Subject No. 8 says, "... it makes you relax, because when it beeps you say, 'oh yeah' and then you realize what you're doing." Subject No. 5 noted the tension "went down a little" and described the improvement as "increased awareness of my own control of my body" by learning "what muscles were affected when I did different things ... learning to control it with my mind." Subject No. 6 increased general concentration and described learning specific skills, such as where the thumb should go, bending the wrist more so that the fingers are closer to the strings, not holding the neck of the violin too tightly with the thumb, and pressing lightly with the fingers.

The most frequent reply to the open-ended question about how the training sessions had been helpful concerned learning what to do in order to relax the left hand (five responses). The second most common reply was increased awareness of hand and thumb maneuvers that caused increased muscle tone (four responses). No subject mentioned mental relaxation or decreased anxiety.

Eight of the nine subjects (89%) said they were still using the skills they gained in the training sessions. The subjects agreed that the amount and speed of improvement would have been unlikely through use of the usual violin and viola exercises.

Discussion

These results suggest a beneficial effect of EMG biofeedback training in removing unwanted muscle tension that interferes with skilled performance. In most cases, improvement occurred quickly, in four or five sessions, and it persisted for months. Symptom substitution, defined in the customary way, did not occur. (Two patients were suffering from new symptoms at the time of follow-up and the possibility that biofeedback played a role in causation of new symptoms, perhaps by focusing more attention on physical experiences, cannot be excluded.) Most subjects believed that they benefited by becoming more aware of how to directly decrease muscle tension in the left hand while playing, rather than by a general reduction in anxiety.

This study does not fully convey the benefits of this method. Most players were delighted with having made rapid progress with a problem which they had previously found difficult to solve. Some of the most gratified participants were the more advanced players. In a highly competitive field, where perfection is sought, small improvements can have large effects on a player's career, permitting a professional musician to compete successfully against other advanced players.

This training program differs from biofeedback techniques used in most clinical situations. The goal here was not a decrease of mental tension, performance anxiety, or other psychologic symptoms. Rather, the goal was greater voluntary control over intrinsic muscles of the left hand during performance of a specific skilled task. The method has much in common with other muscle retraining applications of EMG feedback, such as in stroke rehabilitation. One difference in this application is that the neuromuscular system concerned is intact, and, in fact, highly developed. This difference may explain the rapid progress made by the subjects in a few sessions, as well as the ability to retain the skills learned.

A literature review discloses no previous reports on the use of EMG biofeedback in training musical performers. Possibly, acquisition of complex psychomotor skills in other occupations (e.g., engraving, marksmanship, microsurgery) may be impeded by similar excessive muscle tone and may be enhanced by *in vivo* EMG feedback techniques similar to the one employed here.

A few caveats are, however, in order. History is replete with examples of new treatments initially greeted with acclaim that later proved worthless after critical studies. In this study motivated volunteers were used without a placebo control group, and technique assessment was done by interviews conducted under non-blind conditions. Thus, this study must be regarded as no more than suggestive. Improved studies will be required to prove the value of biofeedback in violin and viola pedagogy.

References

Baker, M.P., "Biofeedback in Specific Muscle Retraining," In J. V. Basmajian (Ed.), *Biofeedback-Principles and Practice for Clinicians,* Baltimore: Williams & Wilkins, 1979.

Brudny, J., Karein J., et al., "EMG Feedback Therapy: Review of Treatment of 114 Patients," *Archives of Physical Medicine and Rehabilitation,* 57 (1976):55-61.

Levee, J. R., Cohen M. J. and Rickles, W. H., "Electromyographic Biofeedback for Relief of Tension in the Facial and Throat Muscles of a Woodwind Musician," *Biofeedback and Self- Regulation,* 1 (1976):113-120.

LeVine, W., "Behavioral and biofeedback therapy for a functionally impaired musician," *Biofeedback and Self- Regulation,* 8 (1982):101-107.

THE TREATMENT OF SEVERE MUSCLE
SPASMS WITH BIOFEEDBACK

William R. LeVine
Professor of Psychiatry
University of Kansas School of Medicine

This is a case report of treatment of occupational palsy, also known as craft palsy, in a musician.

The most typical occupational palsy is writers' cramp. It has an interesting history. Imagine yourself back in time before word processors, typewriters, or any kind of mechanical writing contrivance, to the time when all business correspondence, records, and accounts were kept by secretaries who wrote everything out by hand. These people were trained much as a musician is, to write very beautifully, filling whole pages with numbers and letters. At first they used curved feathers, later, pens with steel points. These secretaries had to produce text with no errors, because there was no way to erase. Often they were working against deadlines. The work of a secretary or clerk was a kind of performance.

During the 18th and early 19th Centuries, clerks and secretaries would occasionally develop spasms in their hands. The problem would begin possibly with some uncontrolled trembling or jerking. As they tried to control the trembling, their arms would get tighter and they would get painful cramps. The condition would worsen until they would be unable to write in that beautiful hand. They then became unemployable. It was as great a disaster for those secretaries as it would be for a performing musician today.

We no longer see this problem in secretaries and accountants. We do, however, see it in musicians and others who do work requiring fine dexterity. Let me mention the case of a professional viola player. The onset of her problem began after a change in teachers. (A fair number of cases have been reported from Massachusetts General Hospital under similar circumstances.) As is typical of such cases, once the problem began, it developed a life of its own. The violist tried many treatments, went to teachers and doctors, was hypnotized and underwent varying drug therapies. She began to practice viola in an irrational manner, trying to conquer her problem through will power. Forcing herself to practice ten hours a day, while holding the bow and instrument stiff as a board, did not make things better.

This violist got much better by using temperature biofeedback. I used temperature feedback because warm hands and anxiety are virtually incompatible. It was evident that something had to be done to keep her from practicing when she was anxious. Using the temperature biofeedback machine, she trained herself to keep her hands warm, and then practiced *only* when they were warm. If her hands got cold, she would stop and warm them again before continuing to practice. This treatment worked very well for her. Eight years have passed with no recurrence of the problem.

At the time, I made a video tape for presentation to medical audiences. I've selected a short segment of that tape so that you can see something of how this case was presented and how the treatment proceeded. We'll look at about three or four minutes of this tape. I'll then conclude with two or three brief comments.

(From the video tape) **LeVine:** The treatment consists of three related parts. First, direct instruction to stop irrational practicing. Let's hear her describe the difference between rational and irrational practicing. What is rational practicing?

Patient: Well, it's just taking a piece of music and working out the various musical components. You work on phrasing, the kind of sound you want to produce, the intonation and on any rhythmic problems you might have. You take all these components, acknowledge each one, and work until you put them all together to form a whole. Irrational practicing is worrying totally about how you're doing something physically, and everything else just goes to pot. Not being able to disassociate, which, basically, is something I've done for four years. I'd stay up all night practicing whole notes, trying to figure out how to draw the bow.

LeVine: Irrational practicing, then, increases anxiety and impairs performance. She was instructed not to practice in this manner.

The second part of the treatment requires the patient to develop skills with temperature feedback. We chose the temperature modality because, in this case, cold extremities were a prominent symptom of anxiety. She was asked if she was aware of physical symptoms, such as palpitations or a shortness of breath.

Treatment of Severe Muscle Spasms with Biofeedback

Patient: If I get nervous about something, my temperature will drop and I'll begin to shiver.

LeVine: In the third aspect of the treatment, a plan was developed by which the patient could carry out an *in vivo* biofeedback exercise. That is, she could play the viola while connected to the biofeedback instrument. In developing this exercise, several technical problems had to be solved. If the thermocouple tip is placed on the finger pad, it interferes with holding the bow. We found that placing the thermocouple on the side of the fingers interferes with the fine finger movements needed to balance the bow. It was finally determined that the wire be led between the fingers and fastened, with a minimum of tape, above and below the wrist, elbow, and shoulder, leaving enough slack so that arm movements were not impeded.

Having solved these technical problems, we were able to design an *in vivo* biofeedback exercise to eliminate obsessional practicing. The instructions, as given to the patient, were these: first, do not play the viola until your finger temperature has reached the target (the target is set at a temperature the patient is able to reach with a little effort); second, begin practicing; third, whenever you stop playing for any reason — because of a mistake, for example — check your finger temperature. If it has fallen, do not begin playing again until it has returned to the target temperature; fourth, raise the target temperature one degree every week. (End videotape).

You get the idea. She has to look at the monitoring machine, and raise the temperature of her finger on the bow hand to a certain point. Then she can play. If she starts to get nervous, her hand gets cold. Then she has to stop, and is not to start again until her hand is warm, perhaps for a half hour.

I will conclude with a few comments. You notice that she didn't come to me saying that she had occupational palsy. Her history was a highly disguised one. During this conference the difficulty of communication between physician and musician has been alluded to. I think there is something to the thought that it helps if the doctor has had some musical training and experience. I think it would have been very difficult for me to diagnose her condition if I had not had some musical training. Fortunately, there are many doctors who are also amateur musicians.

Second, this case had a very successful outcome. However, I am not sure that this same technique would work in the next, similar case. Last, I give most of the credit for success to the musician/patient. She endured the suffering, and did all the work needed to make herself better.

Section IV

In Praise of Musical Instruments

INTRODUCTION: IN PRAISE OF
MUSICAL INSTRUMENTS

Helen Myers
Author and consultant
The New Grove Dictionary of Musical Instruments

I come to this conference representing the field of ethnomusicology. We ethnomusicologists have a great many serious questions to pose to the physicians among you about cross-cultural comparisons of the musical experience, of motor behavior in instrument performance and in the dance, as well as the whole question of cognition and perception. I am not going to worry you about any of that this evening. For ethnomusicologists, even the praise of musical instruments is a very serious and somewhat problematic business. Since the first principle of our science is the equality of all music cultures of the world, we also believe in the equality of the instruments played around the world. We tend to feel a proprietary concern for the tens of thousands of shell trumpets, whirling discs, nose flutes, ocarinas, percussion beams, slit-drums, gong-chimes, ribbon reeds, aeolian harps, plosive aerophones, and poly-idiochord musical bows that it is our charge to collect, to examine, and even learn to play. Faced with the impossible task of having to choose something to display for you tonight, I have selected a few favorites, the first among equals of these instruments for me, with which to illustrate my very brief introductory remarks.

Musical instruments are among the most ancient artifacts of humankind. It is very surprising how the peoples of paleolithic times deemed musical instruments such as rattles, scrapers, bull roarers, and bone flutes, among many others, to be necessary equipment. Almost certainly the function of instruments in these early societies was rhythmic, for rhythm is inherent in all body movement, and body movement is inherent in all instrument performance. We may imagine dancers of the Stone Age clapping their hands, slapping their thighs, and stomping their bare feet against the ground. The possibility of sound production was dramatically extended once the dancer fixed rattling devices to his legs and ankles, or shook a rattle of dried seeds or strings of bones and teeth. Stamping the ground could be reinforced by holding a resonant tube made of a length of bamboo in the hand and thumping it on the ground. This simple technique has today reached a remarkable level of sophistication in the Solomon Islands, where girls beat stones of varying sizes with varying lengths of bamboo.

While it is easy to understand the rhythmic function of early instruments, the rise of melodic instrumental performance is much more difficult to explain. Early humans may have seen instruments as a means of extending the possibilities of the human voice. Indeed, many early instruments such as kazoos and megaphones served as voice disguisers or voice modifiers.

The dividing line between singing and playing an instrument is not always clearly drawn, even in modern times. For example, there is music from Rajasthan, a state in the desert area of northwestern India, where a musician plays an instrument called the Narh, an obliquely held flute, while simultaneously singing a drone.

The musical bow is one of the oldest instruments known, dating possibly to 15,000 B.C. Some scholars maintain that the musical bow derived from the hunting bow, since they both have similar construction. Others maintain that the hunting bow derived from the musical bow. Of course, non-musicians might assume that the hunting bow came first, but in fact no conclusive evidence has been found to support either argument. We simply do not know. To play the musical bow convincingly depends not on virtuosity of the fingers, as with nearly all our Western instruments, but rather on virtuosity with the mouth. The player holds the end of the instrument, the bow, in the mouth and taps the bow string with a small stick. Changing the shape of the mouth cavity alters the sound of the instrument, producing a very interesting effect, despite the extremely limited pitch material.

Another mouth instrument is, of course, the tiny jew's harp or jaw's harp. You may be familiar with modern versions of these, The fundamental design of this instrument is very old indeed. It is also a common instrument in most cultures of the world. In many societies the jew's harp is used for courting, quietly conveying tender sounds of endearment that emulate speech to the loved one. One can hear this type of instrument in Hawaii, a bamboo jew's harp called the ne'au kani.

Instruments may be used for other types of signaling. In cultures with tonal languages, particularly those of western Africa, instruments are designed to reproduce the tones of speech, its accents and inflections, thereby to relate precise linguistic messages, hence the famous "talking drums" of Africa. Other African instruments, including xylophones, flutes, and even bells and other idiophones, can also be made to "talk" in this way.

While these instruments are played primarily to imitate human speech, other instruments have given rise to a speech or language of their very own. An example is the tabla of northern India, which is a pair of small drums, one tuned higher than the other. It is surely one of the most remarkable instruments of any culture in the world. The player beats the drums with the fingers, also using the heel of the left hand to vary the tension on the head of the larger drum. Each section of both drumheads produces a different sound when struck. In the classical Indian tradition, the different combinations of finger and hand-strokes, and the positions where the fingers strike the drum heads, all have a particular name. Every student of this instrument must learn to pronounce these names before he is allowed to proceed to play the passage on the drums. In a typical demonstration of tabla playing, the artist first recites the names of the finger movements prior to rendering the passage on the drums.

Just as each culture has its own instruments, each also has its own method of classifying instruments. For example, the ancient Chinese divided musical instruments according to the materials from which they were made: metal, stone, earth, skin, silk, gourd, bamboo, and wood. The ancient Hindus classified instruments by the method of sound production.The first group included cymbals, gongs, bells, and so forth, then drums, strings, and finally winds. The most widely accepted system used by Western scholars was set forth in 1914. It, too, organizes instruments according to the way they produce sounds. Hence, idiophones (self sounders like bells and gongs); membranophones, (vibrating membranes); cordophones (vibrating strings); and aerophones (vibrating columns of air). We have now added a fifth category to accommodate electronophones.

Of the examples I have mentioned, the Solomon Islands stamping tubes and the Hawaiian jew's harp are both idiophones, the tabla is a membranophone, the musical bow is a chordophone, and the Rajasthan flute is an aerophone. Some instruments have, however, successfully eluded classification. The Bengali gopi yantra, for many years classified as a plucked drum, has recently been reclassified as a chordophone. Found in varying sizes, this instrument is a wooden cylinder with a skin membrane and a string which is knotted underneath, extending out from the membrane. It is held up by a split piece of wood which can be flexed to adjust the tension of the string.

The instruments you will hear later tonight are chordophones and aerophones. The guitar is classified as a plucked lute, the violin a bowed lute. The alphorn is classified as a trumpet, as are all Western orchestral brass instruments. These include not only trumpets, but also the French horn, trombone, and tuba, among others. Many non-Western brass instruments are natural trumpets. That is, they have no keys or valves. Trumpets, especially, are found all over the world. A very interesting type is the long trumpet which often is found with people living in mountainous areas. Such an instrument is played in Tibet by Buddhist monks in their monasteries to greet the rising and setting of the sun. This instrument only produces two notes of the natural harmonic series. This limitation of pitch material often leads to orchestras of trumpets in the non-Western world, where trumpets of different sizes play together to produce the melody, each player adding one or two notes at the appropriate time to produce the desired musical effect.

In part, the program this evening, "In Praise of Musical Instruments," praises the inventiveness of humankind who has managed to fashion instruments from every conceivable material, from grass, sticks, shells, and nearly all parts of animals to oil drums, bicycle pumps, automobile tires, and computers. As taste varies from culture to culture, so musical instruments vary. The effectiveness of an instrument must be judged not by Western standards of acoustic perfection or even craftsmanship, but according to the satisfaction it affords its players and listeners.

SCIENCE, ART, AND A BOX WITH THE SOUND YOU DREAM ABOUT

Michael Kasha
Director, Institute of Molecular Biophysics
Florida State University

The responses of scientists, craftsmen, and musicians to my indulgences and adventures in musical instrument design as a working scientist were, in each case, surprising. My scientist friends proved to be the most conservative. "How can you, with your crude physical and mathematical models, dare to intrude into the esthetic domain of musical instruments, perfected by centuries of interaction between the skilled craftsman and the virtuoso performer?"

The craftsman said, "No, Señor, the guitar is not for the mind of the engineer; it is for the fingertips and soul of the craftsman." But the virtuoso musician said, "Please, before I die, help me to hear the sound in my instrument that I hear only in my dreams."

So I was encouraged. Listening to many virtuoso musicians of many instruments respond to my queries, "How would you characterize a beautiful sound on your instrument," and, "Where on your instrument do you find the most deficient sound," I realized that there is no precise musical esthetic vocabulary. Gradually I learned the musical esthetic terms in relation to measurements in acoustics and correlations with the vocabulary of psychoacoustics.

The principal music esthetic terms, with their psychoacoustic counterparts, seem to be:

> **Brilliance**. Also described as round, full, luscious, tonally defined. Translated by the Backhaus criterion in terms of harmonic spectrum (harmonic intensity vs. frequency for a given tone) with a dominant fundamental and successively diminishing overtone intensities. A non-brilliant tone (described in musical esthetic terms as dry, nasal, sharp, penetrating) translates into a harmonic

spectrum in which its fundamental is weak and some higher overtone is strongest.

Brightness. Also described in musical esthetic terms as having presence, being alive, or not being buried within the instrument, is translated as having rapid onset of transient (intensity vs. time) so that the Fourier transform possesses a white noise component. This was demonstrated most aptly by Walter Carlos' synthesizer tone construction in the Moog synthesizer epic Bach transcriptions.

Dynamic range. In musical esthetic terms this element of expression allows for discretion of and control by the artist, and is not left to be an accident of the instrument's imperfection. It translates psychoacoustically as having a power spectrum (integrating intensity vs. instrumental note) over the octave ranges of the instrument in compensating relation to the human hearing spectrum (sensitivity vs. frequency).

Silkiness of tone. In musical esthetics a texture, perhaps a shimmering dynamic character, perhaps a clarity or transparency of tone. This esthetic criterion is in such a subtle range that I have been baffled to find an objective correlation. Perhaps it lies in a most subtle range of the virtuoso musician's execution control, not yet defined by psychoacoustic correlations, and perhaps not inherent in the structure of the instrument.

The next step, that of designing a bridge-soundboard structure for a given string instrument (guitar, violin, viola, cello, harp, piano) has been the principal effort engaging the author's attention.

The brilliance criterion, which translates into a powerful fundamental, is achieved by structuring a frequency-dependent soundboard able to drive the fundamental strongly at each string note. The brightness criterion, which translates into a rapid risetime onset transient, is achieved by the profile adjustment of the coupling bars for control of risetime of the sound produced. The dynamic range, that is, the power spectrum adjustment to the human hearing curve, is achieved in the bridge with a sonic coupling bar structure which is most efficient for each frequency, and especially by adjusting the mechanical impedance of the driving bridge.

Michael Kasha

The procedure used is Model Physics, in which the fundamental laws of physical mechanics are applied to the real instrument, with its craftsman and instrumentalist imposed boundary conditions. Acoustic testing to prove predicted sound quality is then subjected to the ultimate criteria of the virtuoso musician's hands, ears, and esthetic judgment.

References

Kasha, M., "A New Look at the History of the Classic Guitar", *Guitar Review,* 30, Pp. 2-12, 1968.

Perlmeter, A., "Redesigning the Guitar," *Science News,* 98, Pg.180, 1970.

Kasha, M., "Physics and the Perfect Sound," 1974 *Britannica Yearbook of Science and the Future,* Pp. 128-143, Encyclopedia Britannica Inc., Chicago.

Kasha, M. and N., "Applied Mechanics and the Modern String Instrument Classical Guitar," *Journal of Guitar Acoustics,* 6, Pp. 104-121, 1982. (Ed. T.P. White, P.O. Box 128, Grass Lake, MI 49240).

Kasha, M., Schneider, R., and Rodarmer, K., "The Reactions of a Research Scientist, a Master Luthier, and a Performing Artist on Developing a New Guitar," *Journal of Guitar Acoustics,* 6, Pp. 127-130, 1982.

Kasha, M., "A Perspective on the Relation of Science to Esthetics in Musical Instrument Design and Performance," *American Lutherie,* 1987. (Ed., T. Olsen, 8222 S. Park Ave., Tacoma, WA 98408).

COMPOSITION IN THE ELECTRONIC MEDIUM

Milton Babbitt
Professor of Music
Princeton University

I want to thank everyone who made it possible for me to be here because, in this technologic age, it is an uncommon occurrence for a composer to find himself in the professional company of scientists. When an occurrence like this takes place, when we are brought together under highly professional conditions, a composer, at least one of my generation, is bound to recall one of the primary concerns of yesteryear, and that is C.P. Snow's Two Cultures. Not that I wish to revive the fires of that once fiery propagandist relationship. It is rather that I find myself all too often stationed in that no-man's land directly in the line of both fires. But the fact of the matter is, no matter how simplistic was his formulation of the incongruities between and among our fields, the only real argument I still have is with the conservatism of his cardinality, that there are only two cultures.

Because it is a truism that music, music alone, music itself, has never been so pluralistic, has never been so fragmented, fragmented into factionalization, as indeed it is today. This, unlike most truisms, happens to be true. There seem to be as many ways of music making today as there are ways of world-making. The result is that within composition itself we have an enormous fragmentation, which you may regard as stimulating or you may regard as confusing. We live with it; some of us revel in it. Some of us find it a condition that in some ways may be cured by this new synthesis. Some of us, on the other hand, do not see any reason in the world to have a new synthesis. But even by extending the realm of the compositional world, with its fragmentation, to the world of the performer, you extend the fragmentation by a notable factor, particularly when, by virtue of the materials we shall be talking about, the very acts of composition and performance are fused into an insoluble single act.

I do not feel exactly the way W.H. Auden did when he said that when he finds himself in the company of scientists he feels like the shabby mendicant among merchant princes. Nevertheless, I must confess that I often find myself almost begging for understanding, almost begging not to be misunderstood when I begin to talk about the subject of music in mixed professional company. As I said, the Snow formulation, which was a fiery controversy, was conservative in its cardinality. More than that, it dealt not at all with any of *our* concerns. It dealt with literature as one of the arts, not with music or with the interests of most of you scientists.

I cannot overemphasize the fact that we are operating in such a degree of fragmentation that we are so likely to be misunderstood. Hence I want to talk about the very notion of what music we are talking about. When I talk about electronic music to people in other fields, and sometimes in my own field, I find others regard me as either patronizing or paranoid (the paranoia you have probably already begun to suspect). The difficulty comes about when I attempt to characterize this music in terms of the music that my colleagues compose or in terms of that music which motivated the very electronic era, that music which made these electronic artifacts a necessary if not a sufficient condition.

It is a common misunderstanding that there is a music called "electronic"; that its style and idiom, whatever those ill-defined terms signify to you, require a certain disposition on the part of the composer or a set of compositional procedures. Nothing could be further from the truth. The electronic medium is exactly that, a medium, in the same sense that orchestral music refers to music written for a particular medium in which the sounds are produced by instruments being struck, blown, bowed, or plucked. The purely electronic medium happens to produce its materials in a different, technologic way. It is such a vast and flexible medium that it imposes least upon the composer by way of style, idiom, or compositional disposition and procedure.

Another misunderstanding is that this electronic music somehow connotes industrial or economic revolution, a technologic revolution in which the composer is confronted by the machine. We now have the Frankenstein composer sitting at home creating musical monstrosities. This is obviously not the case, in a very deep way. The electronic instrument was not the instigator of the revolution. It was, finally, a revolutionary outcome.

It was perfectly well understood, even before the 1920's (unless you were a great believer in the ghost in the talking machine), that all the information that was incised in the grooves of a phonograph record could not have been put there without the initial acoustic source of a large orchestra, chorus, or other assembly. It was not suggested that anyone incise a phonograph record. Even if that had been technically feasible, I doubt whether anyone would have tried. Although in the 1920's most of the electronic instruments were real time performance devices of rather limited sonic novelty, and no musician was seriously interested in them, there was one medium, the hand written sound track that possessed all of the potential possibilities of the most sophisticated contemporary electronic media. The possibilities were there, the actualities were there, but there was very little attention paid to the work of Feniger in Munich or the Fischinger brothers in Berlin, or others in Russia who continued this work. Musicians felt no need at that particular moment to spend valuable time and energy on the merely possible. There were technical problems created by that necessary conjunction of composer and engineer, because the composers saw no relationship between what this medium might finally offer them and their own compositional needs.

To show rather strikingly why this is the case, I would like to play for you a tape that probably no one here could ever have heard before. But first, an historic anecdote. In 1934-35 the hand written sound track was being developed in Berlin by the Fischinger brothers. When Hitler came to power, Oscar Fischinger left Germany and came to the United States, to Hollywood, where, as many of you may know, he became a very celebrated animator. He never worked on the hand written sound track again, but his brother, who was working in Munich, went to Russia. Russia in those days was doing new things, futuristic things, things that were different and revolutionary. Schalpol, as well as Rimsky-Korsakov, the nephew of the composer, began to work with him on the hand written sound track, developing it to a very high degree of sophistication. With the onset of World War II, they decided to save this particular indication of Russian achievement in a field that practically no other country was working on. So they took every single reproduction, every film of hand written sound track, every print of every film, plus the machinery they used and stored them in the very deepest cellar in Leningrad. What happened then will either restore or destroy your faith in the deity, depending upon how you feel about both the deity and electronic music. The very last bomb of World War II to fall on Leningrad made a direct hit on that cellar. All was destroyed, the entire era of hand written sound track.

When we were forming the Columbia Electronic Music Center, we wished to have an example of hand written sound track. Since my colleague Vladimir Ussachevsky of course speaks Russian, he tried to get any kind of copy that he could. He couldn't find any, not even when he went to Russia. But when Russian composers, including Shostakovitch and other eminent composers, visited us at our studio, Vladimir asked them if they could possibly get an example of this music. They said, "No, you must be mistaken. This was never produced in Russia; there is a mistake. We are not interested in this dehumanized music, and you must be completely mistaken." About six months later a diplomatic pouch arrived at our studio. It was a tape which included, in perfect Oklahoman English, if there is such a thing, a discourse on the history of the hand written sound track in Russia, much of what I have just told you. What our visitors had done, we found out later, was to go out to the Urals somewhere to find an old film of a Jules Verne movie that had a hand written sound track. It was a decaying film, made in 1937, recorded on a tape in Russia. It is purely electronic, made by photographing and by writing on the film track.

The tape also included a long dissertation on the achievement of the Russians in the field of electronics, including all kinds of pieces played on a kind of Hammond organ, which Vladimir had actually seen in the Scriabin Museum in Moscow. They actually claimed to have made the opera, *Carmen*, in which everything had been done by hand written sound track, including the voices and orchestra. This claim is also made in Russian encyclopedias. Whether it is true or not, we may never know. The story about the bomb on Leningrad is, I promise you, true. I would like you now to hear the tape. We re-recorded it on compatible equipment. (Tape plays).

Can you imagine what the reaction of composers was to that sort of thing? By the way, the Fischinger and Feniger boys did other things, like Handel's "Largo" and a sort of palm court music. Composers in general were, of course, totally turned off by the music itself. If they knew Samuel Johnson and heard this music, they probably would say something about dogs walking on their hind legs. If they did not know Samuel Johnson, they would probably say, "Who needs this? If I wanted to write something as simple as that I'd go out and get someone to whistle and play the electronic keyboard." After all, there were Hammond organs even at that time. They could see absolutely no reason to be interested in this music.

After the war, there was no longer any interest in hand written sound tracks. It was too clumsy a medium. The ensuing years gave rise to the tape studio, the RCA synthesizer, and, of course, the computer which now dominates the field. There was somehow the notion that composers turned to the electronic medium because they did not know what to do, because they were grasping for technologic straws. Nothing could have been farther from fact. They knew precisely what they wanted to do, and they knew that the only way to do it precisely was by use of electronic techniques.

It is rather depressing to realize that people still talk about the new sounds that composers are trying to find. Back in 1969, two very distinguished acousticians, Mr. Schroeder and Mr. Barineck, both wrote within a few weeks of each other, one in the *Journal of the American Acoustical Society* and the other in *Physics Today,* that computer electronics were now providing avant garde sounds, whatever they might be. I don't know what an avant garde sound is. And just recently on the TV program, Nova, I saw my old friend, John Pierce, who was one of the genuine pioneers of the computer production of sound, talking about the "new sounds" that were being provided by the computer, in this case for George Lucas.

The fact is that this, too, reflects a very deep misunderstanding. Composers did not turn to these media for a new sound, for ephemeral titillation of the sonic surface. First of all, they were not dissatisfied with the sounds of the symphony orchestra, however dissatisfied they may have been with every other aspect of performance by symphony orchestras. No one knows better than a composer that nothing grows old as quickly as a context-free new sound. If there is one dimension of the music totality, one component which originally led composers to the electronic medium, it was and is the temporal domain.

It is not merely the question that contemporary music had developed complexity, intricacy, and more variety in rhythms. Of course this had happened. Moreover, ensemble rhythms compounded that variety and intricacy. One might think of Stravinsky and other composers. I do not have to emphasize the extent to which 17th, 18th, and 19th Century instruments provide automatic or semiautomatic means of pitch control, but no comparable means of temporal control (which requires a whole different kind of mental imagery). As rhythm became more complex we all began to realize the tremendous discrepancy between what we could hear, what we could structure in the temporal domain, and what could be produced on traditional instruments by accomplished performers. The point is, this new medium of electronics was concerned with changing the hierarchic relationship between order and collection.

Arnold Schoenberg, though not an electronic composer, fundamentally changed hierarchization and demonstrated, with his concern for minimum mutilation of the past, that there was a very close correlation between the temporal domain and the pitch domain. He changed our compositional lives. Those who originally turned, for example, to electronic tape were obviously attracted to the element of control. After all, the tape is not a source of sound; tape is for storage. You can, however, control time as a measurable distance of tape. Here we are talking about rhythm in every sense of the word, every sense of the concept. Not only durational rhythm, but also the time rate of change of register, of timbre, of volume, and of those many musical dimensions which were unforeseen until we tried to find out how we heard and how we could structure the temporal.

It is still common to hear people ask about the "human element." I had hoped we had laid that concern to rest. If it reflects a genuine misapprehension, the answer is a very simple one: never has music been more human. It begins with the human composer who must communicate to electronic instruments every aspect of musical choice to a degree as never before in the past. It could not have been done in the past, and did not have to be dealt with in the past. This, then, is communicated to the new limits of music, not the infinite limits of the electronic, but the much more mysterious and complicated limits of the human perceptual and conceptual mechanisms. This is, of course, the human element. One very significant aspect of all this is that we are not yet in a position to say much about what we know. We still know so little. It is only with the understanding collaboration of scientists and musicians that we can go forward from here.

THE MUSICIAN: ALIVE AND WELL IN THE WORLD OF ELECTRONICS

Robert Moog
Designer and Manufacturer of Electronic Instruments

I'm going to buckshot the whole long and deep history of electronic musical instrument design. I would like to respond to a quote that Milton gave, his quote of Auden, about the shabby mendicant in the presence of technological merchant princes. I've always felt like a harem's eunuch in the presence of musicians. I think most inventors feel this way. Back in the good old days, before electronics, when artisans knew virtually nothing about why things sounded the way they did or why things vibrated the way they did, musical instrument design was an intuitive art. As such, it developed very slowly. Most musical instruments that were played in recorded history underwent thousands and thousands of refinements and were fairly complex structures. The sounds that these instruments produced were complex and interesting to our equally complex ears.

Electronics changed that. Today we know just a little bit about why things sound the way they do and why things vibrate the way they do. What we have now is the technological means for separating and rationalizing three diverse determinants of musical instrument design and musical instrument structure. The first is the sound generator; the second is the interface between the musician and the sound generator; the third is the tactile and visual reality of the instrument that makes the musician feel good when he uses it.

Take something like a trumpet: these three aspects are so intimately intertwined that it's impossible to separate the brass sheen and the way the valves feel from the vibrating column of air. After all, the trumpeter's hand is separated from the vibrating air by 30 thousandths of an inch or so of brass. Some acoustic instruments may also require the musician himself to vibrate, as well as to supply the energy for the vibration. A satisfactory acoustic instrument is really designed as a direct physical extension of the performer.

The electronic medium is different. In a typical electronic musical instrument you can place the circuitry that makes the sound in one part of the room, the part that uses the hands in another part of the room, and neither of them may look anything like a musical instrument.

I'd like to show you some of the early attempts to take these diverse elements and put them together, so you can see how they are separated. (Showing slides) Here you see a piece of the vibration-producing element of an instrument called the Telharmonium, which was built around the turn of the century, before the advent of electronics. You can see the rotating part of an electrical generator that produces two frequencies a factor of two apart. As many of you know, a frequency factor of two produces octaves. So this rotating element produced all notes of a given pitch an octave apart. You can't see the actual rotors because they're inside. This slide shows the transformer in which all the tones or all the vibrations were mixed together. This operation was controlled from a completely separate room by a keyboard. That overhead, horn-shaped device was a turn-of-the-century monitor speaker, from which modern speakers derive.

This instrument is called a Philharmonium. It was installed in Philharmonic Hall in New York City to produce philharmonic music. The inventor was Thadius Cahill, a patent attorney and tinkerer who tinkered on a very grand scale. Cahill, as far as I know, was not responding to a musical need. He was just having fun, which is what I was doing when I began, too. The musical need became evident as musicians tried to use these instruments and either succeeded or failed. As it turns out, the Telharmonium achieved quite a bit of notoriety. In fact, Professor Babbitt's colleague, Otto Leuning, can recall reading about the Telharmonium as a child and being excited about its sonic possibilities. This was back in about 1915 or 1920. The effort to capitalize on the Telharmonium's commercial aspects failed. This instrument was to be music for the masses. People would subscribe to the music and have it brought into their homes through telephone lines, very much like Muzak. But the attempt to make money failed, and according to the story, the Telharmonium was dumped into the East River and has never been found.

In the very early days of electronics when vacuum tube oscillators first were used, people began to experiment not so much with making new sounds as with new ways to control sounds. These were the first knob-controlled instruments. The slide you are looking at shows another development, a piano rad invented by Hugo Gernsback, a publisher. He published Radio Electronics Magazine and a great deal of science fiction. The piano rad has a small piano keyboard which is in the middle of the instrument and one vacuum tube to produce each tone. A key simply turned the vacuum tubes on and off, resulting in a very static sound. It was one of the first keyboard-operated electronic musical instruments. In fact, the piano rad was played on radio until approximately 1928, accompanying violinists, singers, and other soloists.

Another means of sound control is embodied in the Onmartineau, a French development by Maurice Martineau. Not only does this instrument completely separate the method of control from the method of sound production, but the determination of the pitch of a sound is completely separate from the articulation of the sound as well. The sound is articulated by a bar that is under the left thumb of the performer. So, to play a note, first you put your right finger on the key for the pitch and then you bring your left thumb down. It is more than merely starting and ending a note in that you actually shape the sound by how hard you push on the bar. This process was a completely new way to control, shape, and articulate sound. There is no such thing as legato in this machine. Here is a picture of the inventor Maurice Martineau and his sister playing the instrument. The lute-shaped device in the front is actually a speaker. It is an attempt to enrich the very simple electronic wave form by housing the speaker in a cabinet with a thin wood membrane. Strings, which were tuned to the twelve notes of the equally tempered scale, were placed over the membrane so that it resonated very much the same way as a piano does when you play it.

Another attempt at a different way to control sound was the Helorshan. This instrument never became popular because it was very difficult to play. With this instrument you could, for example, control each note of a four-note chord on a separate horizontal bar. It is similar to playing a horizontally placed guitar with the strings about two inches apart. You can imagine how difficult it is to play.

Perhaps the most original development of the 1920s was the Thérémin. Here he is seen giving a demonstration of the instrument he developed, a space-controlled instrument. The wave form that is produced is very simple, not that much different from the Onmartineau. It is the means of control which is completely new. To change the pitch you move your right hand in the space from your shoulder to the antenna. The higher the pitch you want, the closer you bring your hand to the antenna. To articulate, you move your left hand. So the sound variations are controlled directly and continuously by hand motion in the space around the antenna. In the hands of a true artist the instrument can sound very beautiful. Remember, the wave form itself is never changed by the player. The frequency of the wave form and the amplitude of the wave form are the only things controlled. Clara Rockmore mastered this instrument to a very high degree. Her musicianship resulted in a tone, a quality of sound, which came from the way she moved her hands, nothing else. Someone else playing the Thérémin may produce a wail or a shriek, or sound quite different. This variation was well understood by anyone who tried to play the Thérémin and was the least bit analytical. The way a sound moved, therefore, rather than its steady state property, accounted more for its subjective quality. This principle is something that musical instrument designers, in particular electronic musical instrument designers, have directly considered since modern electronics were first used to make musical sounds.

Thérémin also experimented with fingerboard control instruments. These instruments were played like a cello, only instead of using a bow the player would manipulate a lever to articulate the sound. He even tried a dance platform to coordinate dancers' movements with sound. At this point he faced a very fundamental limitation that other multi-media artists have faced. He found that the singers couldn't dance and the dancers couldn't sing. The best that he was able to do was to get Clara Rockmore to play "Ave Maria" just by standing up and sitting down. Notice the originality here. The significant work for performing musicians typically was in the method of control. Many control methods weren't good at all, being either absolutely unplayable or not relevant to what musicians were trying to do.

Here we see an instrument called the Trautonium, a German development. The finger is run along the horizontal part, as you would along a guitar neck. Its biggest advantage was that it had switches which changed the resonant frequency, therefore changing the overtones that were part of the sound. The player could actually change the tone color during performance.

The caption on this slide says, "The piano's most remarkable improvement." What is it? It is the inclusion of electronic organ circuitry inside the piano, and a marketing overstatement. This slide shows a simple diagram of what is inside a Hammond organ. Actually, it is not that much different from a Telharmonium, the first instrument I showed you. Through electronic amplification one could now produce an electronic keyboard instrument that was reliable, didn't sound bad, especially over a radio and records, and could be fit in the same space as a regular piano. This instrument is probably the first commercially successful electronic musical instrument, and is still important for today's pop music sounds.

All of the instruments I have shown you up to now have accommodated performers. Now, let's look at the early efforts to accommodate composers. Composers have been dreaming for years of being able to write something down and have a machine follow it. In this way the composer doesn't have to convey everything to a performer who may or may not be willing to follow the instructions. Among others, Percy Grainger invented a machine called a Free Music machine. It would read a score mechanically, with levers and cams going up and down, following the contours that he would draw. The concept was that the machine would produce sounds which followed the contours that the composer drew on a piece of paper placed on a drum. I do not know if the concept was ever made workable.

This slide shows a much more elaborate composer's machine, the Hennert synthesizer. Hennert was the chief engineer at the Hammond Organ Company. His synthesizer is a device about two feet square that rolled along a long sheet of paper which had notes graphically drawn on it. This synthesizer is not at all unlike the machine that Mr. Babbitt composed on, the RCA synthesizer, with the exception that this one used pencil marks instead of holes. There have been many computer versions of "composers' machines." This one, (referring to slide) located at Bell Laboratories, used a computer memory instead of a piece of paper. The score is realized as a continuous series of variable lines, or contours. Looking at the Groove score (the machine is called a Groove) is to see something quite close to what Percy Grainger had in mind in the early 1930's.

This is Professor Ussachevsky beginning his first experiments to manipulate piano tones with a tape recorder. Sonic contours were created with this machine and this setup. The first tape recorder bought by the Columbia University Music Department was put in the next room so as not to make too much noise. Here we see Ussachevsky and Luening in the Columbia-Princeton electronic music studio about ten years after the preceding picture. They are using a French variable speed tape which is controlled by keys. There is a little one-octave keyboard which allows the composer to record a continuous tone or a series of pitched tones. Today the same operation can be done with much greater ease and speed using computer based instrumentation. At that time, immediately after the second World War, the device gave composers and performers the first actual means for physically manipulating musical sounds. Computer-based instruments now do the same thing with much greater ease. But with the invention of the tape recorder immediately after the Second World War, this was the first time that musicians, composers, or performers could physically manipulate actual sound material. There is a correlation between the physical manipulation of tape and the way musicians would score sound.

This is a Carl Heinz Stockhausen score that has time arranged horizontally and pitch and volume arranged vertically. The contours of the sound are actually drawn. In the 1950's, people thought that this experimental design might make its way into everyone's home, an outrageous idea for that time. Today you can walk into any computer store and buy an accessory to plug into your Apple, IBM, or Radio Shack that does the same thing. With computer peripherals for composing music anyone can compose music right in their own living room.

Next we see one of the very early performance synthesizers, dating from about 1963. This little instrument is one of the first that John Eaton used. It has semi-conducted devices which is why it is so small. It also has a touch-sensitive keyboard. That is, the keys move not only to begin and end the sound, but also to vary the loudness of the sound by pressing harder or softer on the key. Today, a keyboard like this one would be considered incredibly hip. John has concertized widely on this instrument — only a half dozen of these instruments were made. The inventor, Paul Kettoff, an Italian engineer, has more or less retired.

Now, let's talk about the first Moog synthesizer. This slide shows Walter Carlos' studio, where *Switched on Bach* was made. People are aghast when they see all those patch cords. Musicians today, who use instruments similar to Yamaha DX7s, very often have never learned to use patch cords. Working with patch cords is similar to working with a graphic score or a computer keyboard. It requires a new way to think about sounds which, if it is natural to you, can be very creative. At least fifty or sixty records came out in 1969 and 1970 which capitalized on the success of *Switched on Bach*. The conventional wisdom in the musical instrument business then was that the synthesizer was the gimmick of 1969. You bought your synthesizer, you made your record, and then you did something else in 1970.

(Unidentified synthesizer recording is played). The music we just heard was composed by a highly trained New York studio musician who in his earlier days won a thousand dollar prize for composing a string quartet. So this person is not your typical cynical New York musician. The sound he created is typical of most records that came out in the late sixties and early seventies. These recordings forced us as instrument builders to ask ourselves if that particular sound, lacking musicality, was a characteristic of the instrument and Carlos' rendition a fluke, or was it the other way around? Gradually we have realized the importance of the garbage pail. If a composer doesn't use the garbage pail, that is, if he doesn't carefully evaluate his work, it is the composer's fault, not the designer of the technology. As it turns out, the records of 1969 and 1970 should never have made it to the market. The musicians simply did not listen to the instrument. We learned a great deal about the education composers or performers must go through before they fully comprehend and are equipped to exploit a new medium.

This instrument is called the Mini-Moog. It turned out to be one of the more successful stage-oriented electronic keyboard instruments. The primary advantage of this instrument, what musicians found so intriguing, was that it enabled the player to bend pitch up and down and to introduce vibrato and other types of periodic variation. This control alone, once mastered, took a sterile wave form out of the realm of the boring and, in the hands of a talented musician, into the realm of the exciting and expressive.

As you can tell, I am interested in control devices; the interfaces between the musician and the vibrating sound generator. This interface is where most current attention is centered. Musicians are discovering that with electronic circuitry one can make any desired sound, that one can literally replicate the tone of an acoustic piano, a very complex sound. The frontier now is focused on how one chooses to control the sounds generated. Wind pressure and lip motion can be converted into electrical signals which shape sound. We now build synthesizers for musicians who want to control sounds through spatial motion, much as Thérémin did. We now have touch plates which convert the motion of the finger on the plate surface into real time sound. These devices continue to develop rapidly, using the latest technology available. They, like this conference, are to be seen as progress.

The device in this slide converts wind pressure and lip motion into electrical signals which shape sound. This device is just the control part of a Thérémin which we now build for experimental musicians who want to control the sort of sounds you hear from modern day synthesizers through spatial motion. This slide shows a touch plate which converts the motion of your finger on the plate's surface into sound changes, so you can actually draw sound changes in real time with your finger. And here is an experimental keyboard. This keyboard is fairly complex, and we are just beginning to make them for musicians. There is a touch surface where you move your finger on the key's surface to not only turn the sound on and off when you press the key, but also shape three or four different musical variables: tone, color, pitch, wave forms, and so on, through the motion of the key.

It may be surprising today to see how much technology is pouring into these new developments. In fact, they are almost as complex as this conference. Thank you.

THE INSTRUMENT MANUFACTURER
IN THE WORLD OF ELECTRONICS

Karl Bruhn
Senior Vice-President
Yamaha Music Corporation, USA

I'm delighted to be here this evening to talk about the manufacturer's role in the new high-tech world of electronic music. At Yamaha we are very involved and very committed to this expanding segment of the music industry. In fact, we've committed massive amounts of capital and human resources to it. I find it difficult, however, to talk about only the manufacturing aspect, because at Yamaha we are also involved in research and development, music popularization, music education, and market creation. We view all these aspects as interdependent and interrelated.

Before commenting on electronic music, I'd like to discuss the current market situation and the several elements in our society that create a demand for musical instruments. There is the natural love that most people have for music and the desire to create their own music. There is the popular music scene with its artists, records, radio, TV, and concerts. A good example of this particular market is seen in the influence that the Beatles had on guitar sales. But perhaps the most important element that creates a demand for musical instruments is the educational scene, our public and private schools, colleges, and universities. The degree to which our educational system invests in teaching music has both short and long range impact on the demand for musical instruments.

America's educational system is currently having its share of problems. The baby boom is over, there are fewer children in school today than there were a decade ago, budgets have been cut, and many schools have been closed. Activities seen as frills are being cut out of education. In far too many situations music seems to be seen as one of those frills. This strikes me as ironic insofar as our society is based on the ancient Greek concept that music study at an early age is a very important element in the overall education of our citizens. Plato believed that harmony and rhythm found their way into the innermost corner of the soul. It is sad that we've lost track of this; that today music is all too often considered a frill.

While the preceding may sound a bit philosophic, it also has a very pragmatic aspect to it. For example, our research shows that forty or fifty percent of the people who buy organs played in a school band or orchestra. This means that an adult who played in the school band or orchestra is ten times more likely to buy an organ than someone who didn't. This also applies to synthesizers. Generally speaking, someone doesn't just walk into a music store, buy a synthesizer, take it home, and play it. Usually the interest was developed years ago. My point is that the study of music at an early age can create a life long interest in music and, frankly, helps sell musical instruments.

Let me give you some figures. The American Music Conference reports that the United States' music industry is a two billion-dollar industry. This figure breaks down into one billion dollars for manufacturers and one billion dollars for retailers. These figures are the published numbers. But in fact the U.S. music industry is over a three billion dollar industry; a billion for manufacturers, a billion for retailers, and over a billion for music educators. Simply put, the supply side of industry, the retailers and the manufacturers, have had a billion dollar support system. If this support system is suddenly cut by ten, twenty, thirty percent or more, we then have to question what the short and long range impact for the sale of musical instruments and high-tech musical products will be.

While these comments may sound negative to you, there are a number of things going on that make us very excited and optimistic about the future of music, and particularly electronic music. The application of the computer to education, while spotty, has nonetheless been impressive. Today, there are over 300,000 classroom computers available to students in one out of every three public schools. By 1985 that figure is expected to double. Today we see children three or four years old being introduced to computers. Standard instructional programs in most subjects are widely available. The radical changes taking place in education are not, however, generally initiated by teachers or institutions but by the computer industry and, to a lesser degree, by students and their parents. Today, in addition to the considerable influence that commercial firms have upon educational policies, we find that parents are pushing schools to have computer courses in the curriculum because of the fear that their children may be left behind.

What does this mean to the music industry in general, and particularly, what does this mean for that segment called high-tech electronic instruments and music? Let me first comment on what we see from the manufacturer's perspective and then speculate briefly on what might happen in the future.

Generally speaking, music is not the primary reason a school will buy a computer. Music, however, lends itself very well to computer instruction. Some universities have taken the lead in using computers as tools for the teaching of music. Several major school systems have also integrated computers into their music education programs, with others expected soon to follow.

James Rucker, Executive Music Editor for the publishing firm of Silver Burdett, has a few thoughts on computers and music education which I would like to share with you. Jim has found the first steps in teaching music with computers to be quite comfortable for both students and educators. He views the computer as a valuable learning tool for music students, especially as it offers endless possibilities for the study and manipulation of sound. There are many people in our industry who feel that the computer, over the long term, can do more for music education and music popularization than the music industry was ever able to do for itself. That's quite a statement. In fact, there are some in our industry who speculate that before the end of the next decade, we can expect to have one hundred percent of the school population exposed to making music through the use of computers. These statements are only speculations, of course, but obviously a direction has been established, with implementation being just a matter of time.

Education aside, there is much excitement in today's marketplace. For example, the May 28, 1984 issue of *Newsweek* had quite a bit to say about synthesizers, computers, and music. I'd like to read two quotes from that article. It begins, "As synthesizers have grown increasingly computer-like with extensive memory and programmability, home computers have become more musical and, just the way people buy a printer now, they'll buy a keyboard as another computer peripheral. People will be able to create an entire music learning lab in their homes for not much money." The article ends by stating, "A novice will be able to take Beethoven's Fifth, key it onto a diskette, and recreate the sound of an entire orchestra by adding on tracks. In fact, the next Beethoven will probably use a computer and synthesizer himself."

There is a new word that is important to everything we are talking about. It is MIDI, an abbreviation for Musical Instrument Digital Interface. The path of computers and synthesizers crossed about a year ago when synthesizers started coming out with a MIDI port or connection. The MIDI port connection allows one to attach and control several synthesizers from one keyboard. It also allows several keyboards to interface with one computer.

In the past it was only curious musicians who came into music stores to see what new developments were being marketed. Recently, however, a new group of people not currently involved with music have become music store patrons. These are people who own or are interested in computers. Some of them played in school bands or orchestras; most did not. They ordinarily would never visit a music store. It was their interest in computers that brought them into the music store. They are buying instruments and, through newly developed music technologies, they are learning how to create their own music.

The market for all kinds of musical instruments, including newly developed music technologies, is enormous and expanding. It is a natural desire for most people to make their own music. The synthesizer and the computer, together with their newly recognized use in music education, make this a reality for almost everyone, and at an affordable cost.

I have been in the music business most of my life, and have never been more excited about what's happening than right now. I believe in music and the benefits that can come from its study at an early age. Our company is very excited and very optimistic about the newly developed dimensions of the music industry.

Karl Bruhn

Section V

Panel Discussions

MEDICAL CARE OF VOCALISTS

Moderator: Wilbur J. Gould, M.D.
Director, Recording and Research Center
Denver Center for the Performing Arts

Panelists

Florence B. Blager, Ph.D., Associate Professor of Otolaryngology and Psychiatry, University of Colorado Health Sciences Center

Oren L. Brown, Voice faculty, The Juilliard School

Minoru Hirano, M.D., Professor and Head of the Department of Otolaryngology, School of Medicine, Kurame University, Japan

Bruce W. Jafek, M.D., Professor and Chair of the Department of Otolaryngology, Head and Neck Surgery, University of Colorado Health Sciences Center

Lorraine A. Ramig, Ph.D., Assistant Professor of Speech Pathology, University of Colorado at Boulder

Bonnie Raphael, Ph.D., Voice coach, Denver Center of the Performing Arts

Ronald Scherer, Research scientist, Denver Center for the Performing Arts

Ingo R. Titze, Ph.D., Associate Professor, Department of Speech Pathology and Audiology, University of Iowa

Raymond P. Wood, II, M.D., Professor of Otolaryngology, University of Colorado Health Sciences Center

Gould: Each of the panel members has been asked to give a ten minute overview on voice care. Let me begin by sharing some thoughts about voice care which I have developed over my years as a practicing laryngologist. When I started out, about thirty years ago, the main therapy used was to rest the voice for approximately two months. Anyone who has been asked to rest their voice for even a week knows what torture that can be. The actual benefit of this therapy is minimal because the voice achieves maximum rest after a few days. About that time, Dr. Freushel's "chilling" method was introduced. The technique has held up quite well. Dr. Friedrich Brodnitz is well known for his use of this technique and refinement of it. Dr. Robert West, who came from Madison, Wisconsin to settle in New York, startled the medical community by suggesting that speech therapists should know how to use a laryngeal barrier. For this he was severely ostracized. Medically and surgically the rule was, if there was pathology, such as a node or polyp, cut it out. If it was laryngitis, acute or persistent, the treatment was to spray it, either with an irritant such as phenol or with oily droplets. As a matter of fact, Pilling and Company marketed a mixture of the two. I have had the unfortunate experience of seeing a number of singers whose careers were stopped becaue the oily droplets caused lipid pneumonia, resulting in insufficient respiratory exchange to support a singing voice.

Recent changes in laryngology have occurred which are very exciting. They have been the result of teamwork between voice scientists, laryngologists, and therapists. Each one contributes something to the care of the voice. Symposia, such as this, were begun about fourteen years ago by the Voice Foundation, the primary intent being to disseminate information. We all gained from that. Especially, we learned how to speak to each other. The voice scientists and voice teachers, the singer and the actor, all learned a common language.

Voice laboratories are essential to our work. When I started my voice laboratory about fifteen years ago, there were only three recognized laboratories in the entire United States. Now there are thirty-eight. Each of these includes a recognized residency program. In fact, there are over one hundred residency programs nationally. For the future, it has been agreed by the Board of Review for Residency in Ear, Nose, and Throat, that all recognized residency programs shall include a voice laboratory.

The knowledge we gain through these facilities derives from a team effort. I repeat this over and over again. It is not any one discipline that leads the way; it is a multiplicity of disciplines. There are programs, one here in Denver, the other headed by Dr. Titze in Iowa, that make acoustic and aerodynamic evaluations of larynges using the computer. These and other laboratories provide us a network of information and the means to coordinate its dissemination.

So, care is shared. A node now can be treated by a speech therapist or someone trained in voice therapy, prior to considering surgery. That is a big step forward. In the future we will be using photosurgery; we will be able to shorten cords, lengthen them, and alter their position. With the advent of microsurgery, laser surgery, and other techniques that extend our capabilities, there will be an increased need for networks through which ever-expanding knowledge is shared.

Now I would like to ask Ron Scherer to tell us a bit of his viewpoint.

Scherer: I have a few overheads to show. As Dr. Gould has mentioned, we have a voice laboratory here at the Denver Center for the Performing Arts. One of the emphases we have is on the professional voice. This is primarily because we have a resident theater company here at the Center. In addition, we are very interested in Denver-area singers and others who use the voice professionally.

I'd like to speak briefly about research on the professional voice using noninvasive procedures. Such procedures are necessary when dealing with people who use the voice professionally because they tend to avoid procedures that they think may have a negative effect on their skills or health.

We have two basic goals for this type of research. One is to determine the functional behaviors of performance, using noninvasive techniques; the other is to design experiments and to interpret data which, hopefully, will refine phonatory theories and enhance the efficiency of pedagogic and clinical methods.

I would like to review some methods, analyses, and procedures we use in voice research, pointing out those that are more invasive and less invasive. Obviously, we first need a history of the patient, including medical history, training, background, and performance history. It is important to have this information prior to seeing patients for a particular problem. Then there are qualitative observations of the vocal folds and other tissue, the color of tissue, its shape, texture, symmetry or asymmetry, and the gross movements of the structures. These can be obtained by using fiberoptic techniques and indirect laryngoscopy. Indirect laryngoscopy is a technique you may have already experienced at your laryngologist's or otolaryngologist's office. You hold your mouth open and the doctor puts a mirror in your mouth so that he can look at your larynx. This is, of course, a noninvasive technique. A fiberoptic tube can be placed down the patient's throat for the purpose of examining it. The tube does not interfere with speaking, singing, and other normal phonations and it generally viewed as a noninvasive procedure. Qualitative auditory measures and analyses include vocal timbre, loudness, and aspects of pitch and linguistics, including stylistic and interpretive aspects that are usual in the studio.

These, too, are noninvasive. And then, of course, we have tape recorders, paper, pencil, pens, and the like, which are also used.

Earlier we heard talk about neurophysiologic procedures. An example of this would be electromyography of the vocal folds or other muscles which deal with innervation aspects of motor control. These are invasive techniques because electrodes penetrate the skin. However, performers who have undergone this procedure often state that it is a very easy and non-painful experience.

We also do a substantial amount of work in acoustics. We want to measure the spectra, the intensity of sounds people make, frequency components, perturbations such as tremor and jitter, noise components, and so on. We use devices with which you may be familiar such as microphone systems, pressure transducers, signal analyzers, and spectographs.

Another area of great interest to our laboratory, and others around the country, is aerodynamics. This primarily involves the measurement of air flow and air pressure. These measurements are made all over the respiratory system, including the lungs and bronchial system, the trachea, larynx, pharynx, the oral cavity, and in the nose. Air flow and air pressure at these points determine the aerodynamic power that is used to create phonation and speech, as well as allowing us to measure the driving forces that create vibrations in the tissues, especially the vocal folds.

I'd like to show you some devices we use in the laboratory. We use this mask, which is placed over the mouth, like this (demonstration), to measure air flow. With it on, as you can tell, speech is possible. I could sing, if I wanted to. There is a wire mesh by the holes which allows air to pass in and out of the mask. The mesh impedes the air flow so that the air pressure inside the mask is slightly greater than air pressure on the outside. The inside air pressure is recorded by a pressure transducer which, in turn, is connected to the rest of the instrumentation. By measuring the pressure inside the mask, we can determine the air flow coming from the body. One important aspect of this technique is that we can take the flow at the mouth, inverse-filter it, that is, subtract the acoustic influence of the vocal tract, and obtain a measurement of flow right at the glottis. That is an extremely important measure in vocal research. It is a noninvasive technique that really gets to the heart of what we need to know.

Another device we use often in the laboratory is the electroblotograph system. It consists of two plates placed on either side of the front of the neck, right where the vocal folds are. It can be worn very easily. A very small, noninjurious amount of current is passed between the plates, passing through the larynx. When the vocal folds are closed the current has very little impedence to it, going right through the larynx. When the vocal folds are open, the current registers greater impedence by having to go around that opening. The output of this device is, then, greater or lesser, depending on whether the vocal folds, the glottis, or the larynx is open or closed. This, too, is a noninvasive technique, using a device that can be worn and does not hurt. The device tells us, for example, the amount of contact the vocal folds are making, which is very important in developing our theories. We can take such a signal and, by applying parameterization and other modeling techniques, infer the motion of the vocal folds without actually seeing them, that is, noninvasively.

Gould: Thank you Dr. Scherer. Dr. Blager, would you like to speak?

Blager: I would like to share with you a bit of what a speech pathologist does for voice patients. We usually see a patient after a medical problem has developed, such as a vocal nodule, an ulcer, or bowed chords. They are usually referred to us by an otolaryngologist, a pulmonary specialist, or an allergist, someone who has realized there is a sustained problem needing attention. The feeling that most performers have when they come to see a speech pathologist is fear; fear of what the problem may be, or fear of what the treatment may do to the quality of their voice, and the effect this may have on their career; or fear of what might happen if the problem persists, or a general fear of anything that may alter their voice.

Helping a performer gain a sense of hygiene rather than therapy is an extremely important first step. We are usually talking to someone whose physiologic system, whose vocal technique and the demands placed upon that system, has been in balance for many years. What often is seen is that some unusual demands have recently been placed upon it, or that the system has become more vulnerable over time, or both. If a technique has served adequately up to the time of seeing the patient, it is not necessarily true that everything is wrong and must be changed. A person often has had a natural voice, has never studied vocal technique, and is a patient because of burgeoning career demands which outdistance the natural technique, possibly causing nodules or other signs of strain or abuse.

Another type of patient is the one who has an excellent singing technique and a poor speaking technique. This is a very common problem. People often forget how much of their life is filled with verbal communication. For both of these patients it is necessary to lead them to a greater respect for the voice as used in all of its production, both speaking and singing. They particularly need to learn professional speaking techniques.

The first step in treatment is to evaluate the demands on the voice that the patient must meet. Complete rest for someone whose livelihood depends on their voice is often impossible. It may be necessary to bring the patient to a choice between necessary demands on the voice and uses which might be reexamined and/or changed. For example, a performer who is gregarious and sociable, or one who is pressed to build a career or public following, will often do considerable talking before, during, and after a performance. We will encourage the performer to realize that for a while it may be necessary to smile and nod, especially during social communication, to allow the voice to regain a healthy foundation for speaking technique. Using diaphragm breathing, relaxation of the head, neck, and shoulder muscles, use of nasal resonance as opposed to laryngeal forcing, these and other realistic changes in voice use can usually help bring about improvement of voice problems which arise from functional abuse.

These performers usually have a great commitment to make changes in the way they use the voice. Their awareness of their body function is extremely sensitive. They quickly grasp the concepts that are presented to them. While they may do a great deal of questioning, they also develop, with the help of the pathologist, a good concept of vocal hygiene. Teaching, then, may be the most important activity which leads the patient to maintain healthy voice production after the initial problem has been resolved.

Gould: Thank you, Dr. Blager. Now, Dr. Raphael.

Raphael: My job as voice coach for an acting company is to mediate, to help the performer achieve the best compromise between the demands of a particular performance space or characterization. This must also take into account the director's wishes concerning how a role is to be realized. So, my concern is with how to maintain a healthy and durable voice under what can be difficult circumstances. In terms of a day-to-day experience, I work with actors in the development of personalized warm-up regimens to be used during rehearsals and before performances. I also work with some of them on warm-down regimens, particularly after they have used their voice in a strenuous or potentially abusive manner. I help them to learn restorative exercises so that the voice will not become imbalanced. Basically, I teach them vocal hygiene, how to care for the voice, how to work when they are ill, what drugs they should avoid, and how and when to get help when needed.

I am sure everyone seated here can affirm that many actors and singers are terrified of the word "therapist," or "physician." Part of my job is to assist in the demystification of that relationship, letting them know and helping them to understand that these professionals are here to help them. I also work with actors on a process for assessing and adjusting to various acoustic environments. We are very fortunate at the Denver Center for the Performing Arts to have three theaters with excellent acoustics. Despite the number of microphones you see scattered about, this happens to be an excellent acoustic space. My work with actors using this theater relates to the steepness of the house. Here, the actor is tempted to assume a posture, especially a tilted head and neck, that is not well suited for good voice production.

Theater is written about very emotional experiences. The actor must learn to completely release emotions without abusing the voice. Allow me to relate a few examples of the situations we encounter. One of the people I trained in the production of *Sweeney Todd* played the role of a beggar woman. There is a sequence where she has to cough. The city is on fire, and her song is about the city on fire. The director, Hal Prince, wanted her to cough and then sing some of the most difficult music in the show. She was being asked to use her voice under very difficult circumstances. We also did a production of *Cyrano* this year. The entire fourth act takes place during a battle. There is a great amount of musket fire and small explosions. The actors must project and be understood over all that noise. In *Midsummer's Night Dream* by Shakespeare, the actor playing Bottom does several speeches with a huge head of an ass over the entire top part of his body. It is my job to take these untraditional but common demands that are made on the actors, and help them to achieve their fullest artistic potential without abusing the voice.

I also do some screening. If I hear actors with potential problems, I refer them to an otolaryngologist for examination. If I feel they need therapy rather than coaching, I refer them to Dr. Blager.

Lastly, I represent the interests of the actor to the director. If the director makes an unreasonable demand on an actor, as, for example, if there is a scene in which an actor has to scream, and the director runs the scene five or six times in a row, I will draw the potential for vocal abuse to the director's attention. I will be, in a phrase, the bad guy.

Gould: Thank you, Dr. Raphael. Dr. Jafek, would you like to speak next?

Jafek: I would like to represent the otolaryngologist to you, first as a standard, generic otolaryngologist and second as a specialist with some interest in all this.

While living in Philadelphia, I came home one evening and told my wife, "I'm seeing a whole string of patients from a local funny farm." She asked what I meant. I said, "I've got all these hoarse people coming into the office. I reassure them that they don't have cancer, and they're not at all reassured. When I tell them they don't have nodules they're as happy as can be. I simply don't understand." My wife asked, "Where are they coming from?" I said, " I think it is a psychiatric facility called the Curtis Institute." I really did not understand what the problem was. I'm afraid that at that point in my career I represented the standard, generic otolaryngologist.

I'd like to mention one other patient to you. I received a telephone call at 4:30 one afternoon. A hoarse voice on the other end said, "Bruce, I'm hoarse." "I can tell," I responded. He said, "Can you fix it?" "Sure," I said. I told him I'd be happy to see him. "Could you come to the office immediately?" Obviously, he was concerned. "No," he said. "I'm leaving town in a half hour." I said, "Fine. Can you pick up a prescription on the way?" "No," he said. "Well, what do you want me to do?" "Fix it," he said. I told him I'd call something in to the drug store for him to pick up, and that I would see him when he got back. This is a four-pack-a-day smoker who needed to give a speech.

When I first see a patient I need to know, do you want to be "fixed" in four hours, four days, or four weeks. If we have only hours, then there are certain medical management techniques that we can use, like epinephrine to decrease edema, or using high doses of steroids intraveneously to try and decrease inflammation and edema. Here the patient remains capable of performing or doing whatever needs to be done, though not in the style to which they are accustomed; but they are, nevertheless, able to go about and do that which needs doing.

If we have four days, we can be more deliberate in the choice of treatment and medication. If we have four weeks, we can then use the services of professionals like Dr. Blager and Dr. Raphael.

There is a limit to what we can do. We can prescribe some relatively innocuous treatments and we can, as a last resort, recommend surgery. In terms of the innocuous, many voice problems are related to water and strain. One of the unique things about Denver is that performers frequently fly in, perform, and fly out again. If they have a problem, chances are that you see them in the afternoon, knowing they will perform that evening. If you ask them to stop by the office the next day, they say they cannot— they will be in Kansas City. In these circumstances there are some very real limits placed on what we can actually do. Denver is situated in a very dry climate; when people come here they are usually dry. We recommend that on the way to Denver, and while here, they drink all the water they can handle. On the plane coming in they frequently drink an alcoholic beverage, which tends to be a bit diuretic, that is, it dries them out. Water is much to be preferred. Second, we recommend they have a humidifier in their hotel room and dressing room. Third, if you have ever noticed the high decibel levels in an aircraft, you can understand why we discourage excessive talking during a flight. Ordinarily, people try to project their voices over the noise of the engines. Moreover, the air in an aircraft is semi-filtered. We tend to think that air is drawn into the aircraft, circulated throughout the interior, and exhausted through the tail. That is not so. In aircraft, the same old, stale air is recirculated throughout the flight. It thus becomes clear that the dissemination of information is at the same time a mundane and important aspect of our work.

Where the patient's problem appears to be more chronic in nature, we tend to use the services of professionals like Dr. Blager and Dr. Raphael. In fact, we have our patients see them before we contemplate surgery. If the patient remains at a plateau below expectation, we may then contemplate surgery using lasers or more traditional instruments. One of the real advantages of the laser is that it cuts to a certain predetermined depth. It is very controllable, especially when used under the microscope.

I should at this point mention one thing in defense of otolaryngologists. All too often it is heard that a doctor operated on a patient and ruined the patient's voice. I assure you that doctors do not go out and look for patients to operate on. Patients come to doctors with problems. If the voice is ruined, one then needs to remember that before surgery there were some problems which created a situation requiring surgery. Once surgery is completed, the post operative patient cannot simply return to the old habits which led to the problem in the first place. I think it a little unfair to say that surgery ruins voices. I would also be quick to add that surgery should truly be a last resort.

Surgery is not something we want to do for nodules, polyps, and the like. On the other hand, vocal cord palsies are, for example, an entirely different matter. In the case of the usual edema, nodule, or polyp, we first seek to get the patient to a voice coach or therapist. For patients who must, as a last resort, undergo surgery, we cannot assure them that they will recover their good voice. It may well be that we have to accept suboptimal results. It is important that all aspects of the problem and its treatment are explained carefully to the patient prior to operating, if only to place in perspective their possible unrealistic post operative expectations.

Gould: Thank you, Dr. Jafek. Dr. Wood, would you present your point of view?

Wood: One important consideration, which has been emphasized by both Dr. Blager and Dr. Raphael, has been the fact that professional voice users with very subtle problems may come to us from a speech pathologist or a voice coach. Our job as laryngologists is to try to determine, both functionally and morphologically, what is going on in the larynx to cause the problem. In addition to taking the usual history, we must be able, at some point, to visualize the larynx.

It wasn't until the last twenty years or so that real improvements were made over the laryngeal mirror we have used for over one hundred and thirty years. The first marked development was an improved optic system with a right-angle telescope. It was placed in the patient's mouth, much like the mirror, except that it gave better lighting, magnification, and visualization of the larynx. The difficulty with the instrument was that we could not visualize the patients while they were performing. We could visualize them while they were breathing quietly and when they gave us the phonated "ee" we all ask for. Beyond that, however, we could not really determine functionally what was happening with the patient. The telescope had the same limitation as the laryngeal mirror in that a certain number of patients simply will not tolerate an instrument that large in their mouth. Also, there are, from patient to patient, anatomic features of the larynx, such as an overhanging epiglottis, which may completely obstruct our view of the vocal cords. Without a clear view of the vocal cords we cannot say what in the larynx may be contributing to the problem.

Consequently, within the past ten years or so, the fiberoptic flexible scope was developed. It overcame most of our previous difficulties. First, it could be used on almost everyone. There even are scopes small enough to be used with newborn babies. Second, it gets us past most anatomic obstructions, allowing us to see what we need to see. Third, it is not irritating to the nose and pharynx or the hypopharynx and larynx. If need be, it can be used with a topical anesthesia, a very benign procedure. Also, we can photograph and video tape through the scope, while patients carry on their normal phonatory activities. Obviously, we now use this instrument extensively. On days that I see patients, I may examine four, five and more with the scope. Its use is, for all intents and purposes, a common and ordinary examination procedure.

Using the fiberoptic scope passed through the nose, it is even possible, using a topical anesthetic, to look at the vocal cords from the top or the bottom. We now have an instrument which allows us to assess, functionally and morphologically, those alterations in the larynx which up until now were capable of being detected only by the sensitive ears of the more talented voice professionals.

Gould: I had a startling experience last week. I saw for the first time what the vocal folds were like in a trumpet and saxophone player. What startled me was that the vocal folds moved together as they would in speech or singing. One hopes there will be further research in this. I have not yet fully absorbed this, but thought I'd share the information with you.

Dr. Hirano, I believe you wish to discuss pitch and intensity control.

Hirano: I would like to show a summary of the results of our study. (Showing slides). These muscles are the cricothyroid, vocalis, lateral cricoarytenoid, interarytenoid, and posterior cricothyroid. Register is chiefly controlled by the cricothyroid and vocalis muscles. Fundamental freqency is chiefly controlled by the cricothyroid, especially in heavy voice or low register. The cricothyroid is also active in pitch control of the high register. In low registers the vocalis and lateral cricoarytenoid muscles are active in pitch control. The interarytenoid and posterior cricothyroid muscles are active only in extremely high registers.

Intensity is mainly controlled by the respiratory-expiratory pressure. At the same time, especially in a heavy or low register, the vocalis and the lateral cricoarytenoid muscles are active. Generally speaking, you use more respiratory pressure when speaking in a loud voice. In that case, the vocal folds must have a tighter closure to resist, to some extent, the increased respiratory pressure. That closure is primarily accomplished by the vocalis and the lateral cricoarytenoid muscles.

Gould: There is a question which comes to mind. Let us say that the cricothyroid is innervated by the superior laryngeal nerve, and the others by the recurrent nerve. Also, we suppose the superior laryngeal muscle to have a more voluntary aspect to it. What does this mean in regard to your theory?

Hirano: That is a very difficult question to answer. In the medulla oblongata, the brain stem, there is a special nucleus, a mass of neurons, called the nucleus ambiguus. One of my colleagues, Yoshida, determined the location of the motor neurons in the nucleus ambiguus for all five of these muscles. What he found was that the motor neurons for the cricothyroid muscle are in the upper part of the nucleus ambiguus, whereas the motor neurons of the other four muscles are located in the lower portion. The motor neuron of the inferior pharyngeal constrictor is also located in the upper part of the nucleus ambiguus. I don't know how to interpret these findings.

Another thing to be pointed out is that the cricothyroid muscle can only be found in mammals. No other animals have this muscle. Mammals use the vocal folds as a sound generator, something no other animals do. We know that the cricothyroid muscle is very closely related to phonatory function. This may not entirely answer your question. I am just giving some idea of how these things can be interpreted.

Gould: We can now ask for questions from the audience. Maybe I could lead off by asking Dr. Titze one question. I assume that vocal performance depends upon body health and environment. As a scientist and a singer, what suggestions do you have in regard to care of the individual.

Titze: The most important thing I can say here is that, as a singer I have learned to be somewhat introspective about my body. That is, I try to be a bit analytic about how my body feels to me from day to day. I think that some singers are too reckless in assumming their ability to perform will always be there. In taking care of their instrument, they also need to know how to tune in to their body. Speaking as a singer, that may be the easiest way of staying out of trouble.

Audience question: I'm a physician and also a singer. I have often been amazed at the minimal amount of clinical sinusitis, with no post-nasal drip or demonstrated sinus blockage, which could still make a profound change in the vocal quality and capability of a singer. Am I crazy or do you also see that?

Titze: I think we see numerous patients whose complaints of upper respiratory infections of any kind make alterations in their voice. I have found that it is sometimes very difficult for me to track down where in the upper respiratory system the problem is located. In the first place, if you have sinusitis you also, as a rule, have rhinitis. We see a number of patients who want to know if straightening their septum is going to change the resonance of their voice. While I am uncertain as to what change might result from that, it is my presumption that patients with sinusitis, and the almost invariable rhinitis, will certainly have some decrease in resonance and some hyponasality. This probably results more from the rhinitis, that is, swelling of the lining of the mucuos membrane of the nose, than what is going on in the sinus itself.

Brown: Could I add here that there was a question of this nature submitted to the *Bulletin of the National Association of Teachers of Singing* while I was working on the editorial board. We put this question of difference in resonance to Dr. Jeffery Arnold, Dr. Joseph Agura, and two other doctors whose names escape me. At that time they felt that this was negligible as far as the resonance of the voice was concerned.

Same audience questioner: I'm not talking about resonance. I'm talking about a sense of laryngeal edema which is extremely labile. It can quickly change as a result of some apparent sinus oriented physiologic change.

Titze: The one area that must be thought of in that respect would be the nasopharynx. It is very often the offending agent. Often, if this area is cleaned, for example, by a little flush, you can have a remarkable return of the voice, especially where there had been a sense of layer covering. This treatment is non medicinal, but it is a form of medical treatment that works. It is worth examining the nasopharynx by using a scope and looking up each passage. You will probably see pathology there.

Audience speaker: One must understand anatomy and physiology. If you can understand the anatomy and physiology of how the body works, then you can figure out and predict what it is going to do under certain circumstances. The nose and sinuses, for example, produce about a pint to a pint and a half of mucus per day. It is carried by ciliary action to the posterior pharynx and swallowed. From there it goes to the stomach, the great garbage can for sterilization with its acid pH. If there is an infection anywhere along the nose and sinus, you are then exposing that infection to the vocal cords. Mucus is very poorly understood, particularly its rheology characteristics — how sticky or loose it is. It is quite likely that a little bit of coating of your vocal cords may be responsible, in part, for the edematous sensation you experience from the extra mass on the vocal cords. It is not really mass. The extra mucus will, however, negatively effect vocal fine tuning and the demands placed on the voice.

Another thing to reflect on is which aspect of your singing is bothersome. Is it the midrange or is it the high notes? Singers frequently complain about their top notes, that they are unable to get maximum vibration at that point. You probably should not be singing in that range when you have pus or extra thick mucus on the vocal cords. The earlier point made that one can flush, gargle, or rinse is a good one. These temporizing measures can be very helpful.

Gould: Dr. Titze, in his earlier presentation, referred to viscosity. We need to understand in a more scientific manner what effect medications have on viscosity. Speaking about medicines, which drugs do we want to avoid? What do we tell and actor or singer to avoid?

Raphael: Without being an alarmist, I tell them to use as few drugs as possible, including alcohol, tobacco, aspirin, and any drugs of an illicit nature they might be using. I ask that they give their systems as healthy a start as they possibly can. We don't want to exaggerate the negative aspects of aspirin. It is, after all, a very useful drug in many circumstances. If, however, a person is obligated to tremendously heavy voice use, I dissuade my actors from taking a great deal of aspirin.

Unidentified questioner: You mentioned that aspirin has a deleterious effect. In the case of singers who have to take aspirin, do you also suggest a vitamin therapy?

Raphael: I am not a physician, so I do not prescribe. I personally would just as soon the actor take Tylenol or some comparable drug.

Audience question: I am voice chair for the Colorado State Music Teachers Association. I have been concerned with the growing length of programs of all state choirs. My special interest in teaching is the high school solo voice. My main concern is that I feel our music educators and choir directors, many of whom do not understand the voice, tend to push our high school solo voices to a state of fatigue. For example, there were over one thousand singers who competed to be a part of the All-State Choir this past year. The director of the choir proudly stated how much he enjoyed the young people during their seventeen hours of rehearsal. I cringed. I think medical people need to help educate vocal teachers about the dangers of voice overuse, about the dangers of having young voices sing for seventeen hours over four days.

Gould: Your statement is very well taken. As a matter of fact, at the symposium on Care of the Professional Voice this past year, two hours were devoted to that very subject. I would ask Dr. Brown to comment.

Audience question: I am a bit concerned that no one, other than in Raphael's comments about actors, has addressed how much of what goes on in the body affects the throat. We talk about the throat, but we don't talk about the body tension that can partially or completely close it, or make it hoarse.

Gould: Actually, we do consider the postural aspects of vocal production. One must consider all the aspects of body ills that could attend. Dr. Titze alluded to this. Given the time available, we cannot deal with all aspects of voice hygiene. We could discuss metabolic functions, respiratory functions, and other disabilities and systemic illnesses; time, however, restrains us. This is not to minimize the importance of the point you raise. We all know, for example, if a singer sings with a stiff neck there will be poor vocal production.

Titze: Your point is also well taken as it relates to research. We do not have much research on the coordination of different body systems related to phonation. It is a very important question which some researchers are working on. Don't give up hope. Findings might even be reported in a choral journal.

Audience question: Earlier there was some mention of seeing pictures of the vocal folds of wind instrumentalists. Was there any mention of what vowels they were using behind the embouchure?

Gould: They went through a series of vowels. I really have no more experience with this case. As I mentioned, this was just a first viewing. It is, clearly, a wonderful avenue for further research.

Audience question: Have there been any studies in the area of longevity of the professional voice, the professional singer, and the amount of switching between head and chest voice? Is there a correlation between head and chest voice and professional longevity?

Gould: I don't know of any specific studies. Oren?

Brown: I don't know of any studies either. I can only point out that Lena Horne has sung for many years, is still singing, and that in her performances, which are almost daily, she uses her full voice range. In other words, making use of and knowing about the upper part of the voice range is a part of voice health. One of the first great singers I ever heard was Madam Ernestine Schumann Heit, who last performed when she was seventy-five years old. She was known as a very heavy contralto who was capable of singing her upper notes like a soprano.

Gould: As a matter of fact, the whole area of aging of the voice is one that has interested many people. Do you have any comments on that, Dr. Blager?

Blager: Not really. I know that the classic quaver, which seems to be one of the determining qualities of the aging voice, is certainly present in the speaking voice. We have looked upon that as an inevitable. I am interested in an earlier point that perhaps what we think of as vibrato is really a loss of tonicity. Also, there are studies which might be applied to aging as well as to the professional voice, because one could see if there is an oncoming voice change.

Gould: I want to thank you all. You have been a most interesting group.

MUSIC AND MEDICINE

Moderator: Robert Freeman
Director, Eastman School of Music
University of Rochester

Panelists:

Charles O. Brantigan, M.D., Assistant Clinical Professor of Cardiothoracic Surgery, University of Colorado Health Sciences Center, Denver, Colorado

Leonard Essman, M.D., Tour physician and medical consultant for the New York Philharmonic Orchestra; tour physician for the National Symphony Orchestra, Washington, D.C.

Wilbur J. Gould, M.D., Director of the Recording and Research Center, Denver Center for the Performing Arts, Denver, Colorado

Bruce W. Jafek, M.D., Professor and Chair of the Department of Otolaryngology, Head and Neck Surgery, University of Colorado Health Sciences Center, Denver, Colorado

Peter F. Ostwald, M.D., Professor of Psychiatry, University of California, San Francisco, California

Rudolf A. Pyka, M.D., Orthopedic surgeon, Redlands, California

Stuart A. Schneck, M.D., Professor of Neurology, University of Colorado Health Sciences Center, Denver, Colorado

Gerald I. Shapiro, D.M.D., former Associate Chief of Staff, Greenpoint Hospital, Brooklyn, New York

Ivan A. Shulman, M.D., Tour physician and medical consultant for the Los Angeles Philharmonic Orchestra, Los Angeles, California

Frederick Tims, Ph.D., R.M.T., past president of the National Association for Music Therapy, Department of Music, Colorado State University, Fort Collins, Colorado

Freeman: I am honored to be the moderator of this afternoon's panel. In 1984 we are in a situation where our nation, still seen as a relatively young country, has already achieved considerable respect as far as the world of professional music is concerned. We also are seen as being among the world leaders in the field of medicine.

Allow me to speak just about music for a moment. We have some of the world's greatest soloists, born and trained in the United States. We also have people coming to the United States from all over the world, not only Western Europe, but from Asia and South America as well, to study music composition, scholarship, and performance. Musically, we have much to be proud of, including some of the world's greatest orchestras, some of the world's great chamber music societies and groups, wonderful library systems, and an emerging group of very good critics. We also have some problems as well. Among them is the great oversupply of professional musicians and the as yet fairly limited demand for what some people call "serious" music. We have a concomitant phenomenon which is seen in this country's preoccupation with celebrities.

It is unfortunate that many young musicians in this country are trained in a rather narrow way. Many of them are deficient in non-musical, cognitive skills, possibly because musical training so often begins at a time when young people are scarcely in a position to make determination about what they want to do with their lives. Consequently, many professional musicians find themselves at age fifty or sixty frustrated with their lot in the professional world.

Yet another problem is seen in the professional musician's frustration in dealing with the medical community. In my own case, I remember a time during my thirties when I thought myself to be slightly hypertensive. I turned to my private physician, telling him of my problem. He did not see it as a problem. His response was, "There's nothing to worry about. You are a professional musician. Just look at Toscanini, he lived a long time." It would seem that many physicians have a gross misunderstanding regarding the medical needs of professional musicians. Too many musicians take their sore arms, hands, fingers, and wrists to their physician, only to be treated idiosyncratically, as though these ailments were weird or peculiar to that individual. There are, in my judgment, many islands in the field of medicine and too little communication among the islands. This lack of communication extends between physicians and musicians as well.

I would like to thank the organizers of the Denver conference for bringing together the many different professionals who facilitate the biology of music making. I believe that we are on the threshold of a great new era of communication between the worlds of scholarly perception and professional music making, between the musician and the physician. We have things to tell each other, as for example the various topics we will be dealing with today: stage fright, cardiovascular problems, otolaryngologic problems, orthodontic and neurologic problems.

I will end my brief introductory remarks by reading a paragraph from a bibliography developed by Susan Harmon, the reference and circulation librarian at the Library for Medical and Surgical Studies of the State of Maryland. She has put together a comprehensive bibliography of articles that have been written on the subjects I have been talking about. When I first read this article I was struck by the enormity of the field, how far far more extensive it is than one might imagine. If I read just one paragraph (one of many) you will, I am sure, get the idea.

"The diverse occupational diseases reported can be divided into six basic categories: dermatitis, nerve compression syndrome, occupational cramps, intraoral pressure problems, cardiac abnormalities, and miscellaneous. The dermatitis category is exemplified by fiddler's neck, a disease fairly well known among violinists and violists. This causes an acne-like rash on the skin touching the chin rest. Similar diseases affecting other instrumentalists include flutist's chin, clarinetist's cheilitis, cello scrotum, guitar nipple, and trumpeter's lip."

I would ask each speaker to speak about the length of time I have just used, highlighting the problems in his own practice or research and sharing with us a general idea where these may lead us over the next twenty or so years. To begin the panel discussion, allow me to introduce Dr. Bruce Jafek, Chair of the Department of Otolaryngology, University of Colorado Health Sciences Center.

Jafek: I would like to begin by presenting a couple of patients, to try to give you a feel for what physicians can do and some of the research vistas I see, emphasizing some of the points Dr. Freeman has made. The first is a fifty-four year old lawyer who was referred to me by a very conscientious internist who said, "Bruce, this man has hoarseness." I said, "Fine, I'll be happy to see him. How long has he had this?" He said, "Twenty-two years." I examined the patient and, indeed, he was hoarse, the diagnosis being chronic laryngitis. He was unable to follow through with a program of voice rest owing to his regular courtroom obligations. I prescribed some medical management including a saline-urea combination and Benadryl (probably not suitable for a singer) and a suitable detergent agent. It is difficult to get pharmacists to make up this concoction, so I told him where to get it. I also made an appointment with him to see Dr. Florence Blager, a speech pathologist with whom I work very closely. He was to see me again in two weeks. He came back in ten days, so I asked him why he he came back early. "How are you doing?" "Not so good." he replied. "Well, what did Dr. Blager think?" He said, "Oh, I haven't been able to see her yet". "Well," I asked, "What about the medicine?" He said, "You know, I can't find where to get it filled." I asked him if he felt any better. He said he did not.

The second patient was a singer, a very good singer, who had vocal nodules. I recommended that he see Dr. Blager and then come back to me in three weeks. "Have you seen Dr. Blager?" "No." "Well, let's try again. You must see her." He promised to do so. After a period of some weeks he felt that he was making no progress. I, therefore, removed the nodules. Later he comes again to my office. He is very hoarse and cannot talk. It is my fault. He did, after all, undergo the surgery I recommended. So why isn't he better? Can he sing next week? I do not think so, but let's work on it and see what we can do. I made a follow-up appointment with Dr. Blager. We felt that he was probably putting a little excess strain on his voice. He did not keep his appointment with Dr. Blager. One evening he called my home and spoke with my wife, who is a bit smarter at some of these things than I. She asked, "Have you been to see Dr. Blager?" He replied, "No, I just can't reach her." My wife continued, "That's very surprising, because she is very conscientious and very good." Oh," was his only response. The point I am trying to make is that there is a limit to what a physician can do for a patient. The two points I would like to emphasize are communication and education. With regard to education, it is important that the patient try to educate the physician as to the outcomes sought after and that the physician educate the patient regarding the possible outcomes. If a patient comes in with a twenty-two year history, we are not going to give him a little green pill and fix it by tomorrow. It will take a great deal more than that.

Once the physician understands the patient's needs and expectations, communication is then a must. It is important to talk back and forth among other health professionals like the speech therapist, speech pathologist, voice coach, neurologist, and possibly a specialist in hypertension. Only then can the physician home in on the true bases of the problem and evaluate them.

What would I see in the future? An enhanced communication between the patient, the physician, other health professionals, and the scientist. The basic scientist can be isolated in a laboratory doing many interesting and exotic things that, unless seen in action under working circumstances, may not be too important to the physician. The physician and scientist are of little use to the patient unless they both are able to make their efforts workable and functional in everyday application. We all need to communicate, to educate each other.

A quote from a book I recently read states, "With regard to chronic laryngitis, if voice rest is not curative, then the patient may be encouraged to take up another occupation." What other occupation might Michael Jackson take up? I think we need to keep that in mind as we deal with our patients. Singers sing. That is their occupation. A career change may not be desired. At the very least, it certainly is fraught with difficulty and impracticality. Let me then conclude with a plea. Don't be unrealistic in your expectations from physicians. Communicate with the physician. Educate him or her as to what your expectations are. Understand that there are times when the physician does not cure, that often the voice pathologist or the voice therapist cures the problem by reeducating the patient. What we need is physicians and patients communicating with and educating each other.

Freeman: Thank you, Dr. Jafek. Two remarks, briefly, in response. First, I fully agree that it is important for those of us responsible for the education and training of professional artists to provide for them the possibility of other kinds of employment and other kinds of professional interests. Second, speaking as a patient who is surrounded by physicians, I think it is very important for physicians to realize that patients wish to be communicated with far more than time often allows. In my own personal experience I've had physicians say, "Well, your affliction is A-B-C. Take these pills and see me in three weeks." I think, the patient wants an understandable description of what A-B-C is, the different phenomena associated with it, whether or not it is threatening, and if so, how, and the things to watch out for. I don't believe that view is idiosyncratic or personal.

Peter Ostwald is a violinist and professor of psychiatry. He is also an author of several books. Currently he is engaged in the writing of a series of biographic studies of musicians with medical problems. His book, *Schumann: The Inner Voices of a Musical Genius* will be appearing this fall. Dr. Ostwald.

Ostwald: I thought I'd share with you some of the experiences that we have had in San Francisco in developing a specialized treatment program for musicians. I want to discuss this in terms of two basic requirements for such a program; first, the need for experts from the medical community, and second, the need for acceptance by the musical community. In terms of medical experts, I think it is essential that a physician who is well trained in music, and preferably himself a performing musician, be available for the initial contact with the patient. In our clinic, this so called triage function is taken care of by me or by my associate, Dr. Engelman, a rheumatologist and violinist. We always encourage the patient to bring along his instrument, to play it and, if possible, demonstrate the problem. We feel that our first job is to help the patient feel accepted. The next job is to decide on the proper strategy for diagnostic workup and treatment.

The complaints our patients have are always very real; it requires a great deal of courage for them to admit that they are suffering. Being told not to worry, or that it is all in the head, can be just as traumatic as being referred to a doctor who exaggerates the problem. We have an excellent internist who is also a pianist. He accepts musicians for the basic physical examination and laboratory studies that many of our patients require. We also have experts available as diagnostic consultants for more specialized work and for definitive treatment. We have an excellent orthopedic surgeon who, although not a musician, has a background in sports medicine, a broad cultural perspective, and a deep appreciation for the arts. We have a neurologist who has devoted the greater part of his career to the problems of artistic and creative patients. The director of our Center for Deafness and Hearing Disorders has access to all the best audiologic assessment techniques. We have a child psychiatrist who specializes in the treatment of gifted adolescents. We also have a number of experts in physiotherapy, family therapy, and psychotherapy who are interested in working with musicians, as well as an otolaryngologist who is especially interested in the voices of singers. I am presently looking for institutional support from the University of California with the hope that we might also add experts in biofeedback and other specialities to the team.

Now let me say a few words about the music establishment. The Bay Area has a rapidly expanding musical community, with top flight symphony orchestras in Oakland, San Jose, and San Francisco. We have an opera company with its own orchestra, a ballet orchestra, and numerous chamber ensembles. It is through personal contact with players and conductors that we are building a network of musician referrals. We are also very fortunate to have in San Francisco a conservatory of music whose administrators have long been interested in what we are doing.

It may not be premature to make some recommendations on the basis of our experience. First, we think it is a mistake to lump together all musician patients. We have found distinct differences in the treatment needs of several groups. There are the professional orchestra musicians who work long hours and have relatively little opportunity for personal advancement. Fatigue, depression, chronic physical disorders, and other long term occupational diseases are common in this group. Then there are students, particularly those who are referred from the conservatory and other music schools. They are much more likely to suffer from acute disorders related to conflicts about goals, parent authority, personal and sexual identity, competitiveness, attachment to teachers, and alcohol and drug abuse. We also have a group of patients who are composers. They have been some of the most challenging and rewarding patients we have treated. Never in my experience has true creativity been reduced as the result of medical treatment. The old adage that you have to be sick to be a genius is simply not true. It is a myth based upon some very peculiar theories of disease stemming from the 19th Century.

Finally, there is a very small group of VIP patients, or superstars, who require professional help of a very special kind. Here it is equally important to to use tact and understanding, since the fact of patienthood may have to be concealed from the public. I must confess to you that in the interest of saving reputations as well as lives, we have occasionally had to be somewhat manipulative, as, for example, in admitting a patient to the Intensive Care Unit under an assumed name.

Let me conclude by saying that, for me, music is a language of the emotions. Musicians, sick or well, need a great deal of emotional support. No matter what their complaints may be, whether they derive from physical, psychologic, or social disorders, the problem itself will produce mental anguish. This can lead to bodily symptoms, to doubts about one's competence and ability to perform, and even to the idea of quitting or of committing suicide. Performance anxiety itself, in our opinion, is not pathologic. We think it may indicate a desirable level of emotional arousal leading to greater achievement and success. What *is* pathologic is fear, despair, rage, or other emotional overreactions that make a physical or mental disorder worse. Here we require diagnostic expertise and definitive treatment. This may include medication, hospitalization, or surgical intervention. Emotional support is always necessary, not only for the musician patient, but also for those closest to him or her, for members of the family, for friends, for students and for teachers. For this reason I would strongly recommend a team approach, with the inclusion of mental health experts.

Freeman: I am not sure that I agree that music is a language of emotions. That, however, is a subject for a different conference. I thank you for all your other remarks.

Next we will hear from Dr. Rudolf Pyka. He received his medical degree from the University of Würzburg after completing a course of study at his home town conservatory of music in Poland. He currently is a fellow of the American Academy of Orthopedic Surgeons and the American College of Surgeons. Doctor Pyka.

Pyka: I specialize in general orthopedics, handling a great deal of trauma, doing hand surgery, and reconstructive work. In other words, my concern is with the final executive machinery that most musicians use. I do believe that the initiation of everything begins in the brain. But a million things happen when I do simple, ordinary tasks as, for example, when I lift something. Here we are talking about coordination, the proper orchestration of muscle movements. Each muscle must contract at the proper time, relax at the proper time, and then, when necessary, come into play again. As we know from electromyography, these things happen several times every second. If, for example, a pianist executes a leap with the left or right hand, the movement is initiated by a muscle contraction which yields the movement, followed by another muscle contraction which stops the movement. The same thing happens when you walk. You first accelerate the leg, then decelerate it. Coordination thus means using the proper muscles with the proper strength at the proper time.

An expert is one who puts the least effort into the system, one who cheats by productively using gravity, inertia, and so on. An expert uses less effort than an amateur, and does not fatigue as an amateur very often does. The first sign that something may be wrong can be the feeling of fatigue, maybe pain, and a general dissatisfaction with one's performance. What a patient feels — a pianist, for example — is much more accurate than any of our available instruments can show. A patient at this stage should probably have an initial evaluation to rule out any organic abnormalities. Then the patient should be brought to the attention of a teacher like Dorothy Taubman, where retraining to remedy the faults that brought on the problem can be undergone. For most pianists this is sufficient to realize a cure.

If the problem persists, we are then in a phase where anatomic lesions must be considered. The general terms of arthritis, tendinitis, and bursitis do not at all satisfy me. One should be much more specific and say what exactly one means by that. If you do not know what you are treating, your treatment will fail unless, of course, you are dealing with a self-limited condition which goes away through the kindness of nature. One needs to know whether the problem is in a tendon, a joint, a nerve, a ligament, or whether the bone is to blame.

There are some simple guidelines one can follow without incurring a large diagnostic bill. For example, if one moves a joint passively and it hurts, the problem is probably in the joint. If the joint is squeezed together and there is pain, the trouble is probably in one of the gliding surfaces. If you pull the joint in an abnormal direction and it hurts, the problem is probably associated with ligaments. If there is pain when the muscle is stretched, the problem is probably in the muscle. These are ways by which one can grossly determine more or less what is going on.

What are the entities in the human hand that can develop problems, where an anatomic lesion may develop? We see tendon compartments which are too tight as a result of swollen tendons. We also see nerve entrapments, crepitating tenovaginitis, peculiar lesions along the flexor carpi ulnaris and the flexor carpi radialis, impingement syndromes where the wrist or finger hurts only in certain positions, and cartilage erosion. There is not much one can do about the last.

As far as treatment is concerned, the physician must be very careful. Medical methods are designed for the average population. The musicians are entirely different in that they are high performance athletes. Loss of some motion in a joint may mean very little to the average population, but to a musician it may be the difference between professional life and death. I have encountered in this audience a lady who has a fused distal and middle joint of the left index finger and fused distal joints in both thumbs, and still she plays the piano. This raises the question, just what standard of wellness do we need for performing music? We do not know the answer. What are the results of injuries in musicians? What happens if a musician breaks his wrist, and how is his capability affected once the break is healed? How do they do when they break a finger or cut a tendon? These kinds of data are simply not available.

On the other hand, a patient should not be treated if there are no symptoms. This is not as silly as it sounds, because there are many people literally crying, "Doctor, make me better, make me more beautiful, and so forth." Surgery should be be considered only with great caution. Every cut or incision heals with scarring. This may not be a problem in most cases, but when the hand of a musician is scarred it may mean loss of critical motion. Before a surgical procedure is done, the physician must sit down with the patient and carefully explain what the procedure entails and what results may be gained over the short and long term. Then it must be decided which is the lesser evil, leaving things alone or intervening. One can arrive at such a decision only by openly and honestly discussing the situation with the patient. Only in this way can the patient make an informed choice.

Once again, our methods are designed for treating the average population. There is very little information about the treatment of high performance individuals. Books are beginning to appear about the treatment of ballet dancers which suggest their treatment is different from the ordinary. In the future these matters will have to be worked out. We are here to start on this.

Freeman: Thank you Dr. Pyka.

Dr. Stuart Schneck, our next speaker, is professor of neurology at the University of Colorado Health Sciences Center. He is interested in the medical problems of musicians, particularly with relation to the function of the hand, arm, and shoulder, and has started a clinic at the University Hospital for musicians with problems in these areas. Dr. Schneck.

Schneck: My interest in the medical problems of musicians goes back to 1969 when I was consulted by two professionals, one a violinist and the other a violist. Both complained of difficulty using their left hand to produce a vibrato. I could find nothing wrong with their hands, arms, or necks, and could not offer a diagnosis at that time. Soon after this I saw a concert pianist with an even more curious complaint. For about five years she had experienced increasing difficulty with the use of her right hand at the keyboard. The difficulty started with pain in the extensor aspect of the forearm which culminated in an almost instantaneous collapse of her third, fourth, and fifth fingers, making her appear as if she were trying to play on her knuckles. In addition, the hand would involuntarily turn over. All this happened almost immediately after her right hand touched the keyboard. This is a motor control problem called musician's cramp.

Since then, here in Colorado, and during some time I spent at Massachusetts General Hospital and the Mayo Clinic, I have seen an increasing number of musician patients. Together with a rheumatologist, Dr. Walter Briney, and an electromyographer, Dr. Michael Cherrington, we have begun a clinic at the University Hospital for musicians with upper extremity problems, this patterned after one at Massachusetts General. The patients come to us with a variety of stories. From a medical point of view they say they have pain, tightness, stiffness, fatigue, weakness, numbness or tingling. Their musical complaints include a loss of control, decreased facility in rapid passages, decreased endurance, decreased speed, or diminished strength. Pianists complain primarily about their right hand, string players about the left. Both groups usually have many symptoms referrable to the forearm, particularly on the extensor surface. Many of these patients have decided for themselves or have been told by others that all they need to do is increase their practice time. Some have also tried to change their technique or repertoire. Sadly, a number of patients, because of the magnitude of their disablity, have had to stop playing, such as the concert pianist I mentioned earlier. Many have had operations for alleged thoracic outlet syndrome, for carpal tunnels, or both. Clinics of our kind are often the last stop before they actually give up their career.

What are the diagnoses we make? We agree with others that most problems fall into the category of disorders of tendon, synovium, or joint, as you heard Dr. Pyka mention. Thus far we have not been able to solve many motor control problems. In Dr. Hochberg's large series from Massachusetts General, about twenty-five percent of the patients consulting him and his colleagues had control problems, although fortunately few had it as a major complaint. We also see thoracic outlet syndromes and, on occasion, carpal tunnel syndromes and entrapments of other nerves such as the ulnar nerve. Neurologic diseases and primary psychiatric diseases are very uncommon, though every physician who deals with this group of patients recognizes that anxiety and depression inevitably accompany their medical problems.

I want to speak briefly about the problem from three aspects: the patient, the doctor, and the teacher. The patients are terrified of anything that will decrease their musical ability or shorten their career. Professional musicians are particularly reluctant to let anyone know of their problem. They feel in jeopardy from management and ambitious colleagues. Somehow or other, just as in sports, the attitude of playing with pain has erroneously taken root. I consider that there is nothing worse than this. There is an enormous amount of self-diagnosis and self-treatment. Acute problems are often ignored while one home remedy after another is undergone, leading these problems to become chronic and pathologic. The diagnostician is frequently the person in the next chair, dispensing advice which is not always very helpful. It amazes me to see how ready people are to undergo operations in this situation. It is not uncommon for us to see two or three scars on a professional musician. They grasp at straws and, as Dr. Jafek said, look for a quick fix to problems which have taken years to develop. I am not being critical of these people, but merely recognizing the tremendous anxiety they have.

The doctors have problems as well. Many are unfamiliar with the mechanics of playing and the demands of the instrument or repertoire. Doctors are usually very, very busy. Also, there is an enormous communication problem between a physician who does not speak the language of music and a musician who does not speak the language of medicine. Last summer, at the Aspen Music Conference on the Medical Problems of Musicians, Dr. Hochberg and Gary Graffman spoke about this and said it literally took them months to understand each other. The practice of music medicine is uneconomic. We may see one or two patients in an entire morning. Frequently the problems are not in our specific field, which is why you heard Dr. Ostwald and others talk about the team approach. I work with people whose skills are very different from mine, consulting with otolaryngologists, orthopedists, and others. It is a sad fact that some long-standing problems currently remain untreatable. This gives rise to patients who are willing to undergo magical or bizarre treatments. Physicians may not necessarily be aware of nontraditional treatments such as the Alexander method, myotherapy, biofeedback, and others.

Teachers also have a problem. Most do not understand the mechanical principles of movement. Teachers are frequently unaware that they are dealing with a medical problem, thinking that greater practice and diligence will solve the problem. It is also a sad fact that many teachers teach as surgeons teach, by fear and terror (with apologies to my surgical colleagues). One last concern I have is that organized music — that is, musicians' unions and symphony orchestras — needs to recognize these as occupational injuries. There needs to be appropriate insurance coverage, appropriate compensation methods, and there should be job protection so that a performing musician is not afraid to admit to a medical problem.

Freeman: Thank you, Dr. Schneck.

Dr. Charles Brantigan is a graduate of Cornell University and Johns Hopkins University School of Medicine. He is presently Assistant Clinical Professor of Cardiothoracic Surgery at the University of Colorado Health Sciences Center in Denver. An accomplished tubist, he has a special interest in performance stress, and has published several scientific papers on the use of anti-anxiety drugs in music performance. Dr. Brantigan.

Brantigan: The work that my brother, Tom, and I have done has been in the area of stage fright as it affects the professional musician. I would like first to define for you what we consider stage fright to be, then to give you some idea of what we have done about the problem, concluding with some very personal ideas about what is in the future, especially what the research possibilities are in dealing with this particular problem.

Let me begin by saying that stage fright is a form of anxiety. I must hasten to add, as I am sure my psychiatric colleagues will agree, not all anxiety is bad. Some anxiety is good, even protective, and should not be tampered with. If, for example, you are a mediocre violinist who today will sightread a musical composition in front of a very knowledgeable audience, you are going to be apprehensive and anxious. The anxiety you feel is a protective mechanism that your brain imposes. It is good and should not be tampered with. If, on the other hand, you are a polished performer getting up to perform in front of this audience, you will feel a certain excitement. That is also a form of anxiety. It adds a certain sheen and brilliance to the performance and therefore should not be tampered with either.

In contrast to that are the pathologic forms of anxiety. These can either take the form of psychologically based terror or of disabling symptoms. For example, your heart may pound in your chest, which can be a distraction. It can also race to such an extent that your cardiac output goes down, leading to a severe disability. The physical manifestations of stage fright, when they reach the point of disability, are often nothing more than the fight or flight reaction that many doctors study in elementary physiology. The fight or flight reaction is what you incur when meeting a grizzly bear in the park, when adrenalin pours into your system preparing you to fight or run like hell. That is an appropriate reaction when chased by a bear, but not appropriate when performing music where fine motor skill is required.

This sympathetic nervous system response, this fight or flight reaction, can be blocked by a very specific class of drugs known as beta-blockers. That is where we have centered our research. What we have found is that these physical manifestations can be very specifically blocked by beta-blocking drugs without having any central nervous system effects that we can identify. These drugs are not tranquilizers. Rather, they attack a portion of the sympathetic nervous system with almost surgical precision, blocking just the biochemical cause of the reaction. All of our studies, and those of Dr. Ian James of Great Britain, have been double blind control studies where neither the investigator nor the performer knows who has received an active compound or a sugar pill. In all studies that have been carried out under these circumstances, experienced music critics have judged that the active ingredient causes an improvement in the subject's musical performance.

That is where we are today. As far as the future is concerned, there are two areas of research which are in great need of development. One is the attempt to use these drugs as an adjunct to a retraining program for musicians based on psychologic techniques. My personal view is that that is where the future lies. Pill-popping to give a musical performance is not a satisfactory solution, for a wide variety of reasons. The second important area for research is to identify what, if any, differences there are among people who experience stage fright and those who do not. This may have biochemical implications.

Two ideas that come to mind immediately are, first, the possibility that people with stage fright have a higher incidence of beta receptors, so that a smaller amount of adrenalin has a greater effect in causing stage fright. Or, as another example, we have identified antibodies against beta receptors in some asthma patients. One would expect that these antibodies would function the same way as do beta-blocking drugs. Perhaps some of the people who are faced with a high degree of somatic anxiety are actually biochemically different than those who have no anxiety at all. Perhaps the ones who have no anxiety at all are the abnormal ones; perhaps they have antibodies against beta receptors.

I think the entire area of stage fright is exciting because we have identified part of the biochemistry and physiology that causes it. I think there are exciting possibilities in the future as we investigate it further and as we add new psychologic techniques to drug therapy.

Freeman: Thank you, Dr. Brantigan.

Dr. Leonard Essman is a graduate of the George Washington Medical School. He practices internal medicine in metropolitan New York and serves as tour physician and medical consultant to the New York Philharmonic Orchestra and the National Symphony Orchestra in Washington, D.C.

Essman: My background as a physician is not the point of my discussion, because when I go on tour with these fine musicians I act in the capacity of a general practitioner. What I would like to do is describe what has happened on three of the four tours I have taken, two with the New York Philharmonic and one with the National Symphony. The trips are not all fun and games. The key words are waiting and going. It is waiting for buses, trains, and planes, invariably late, and going to strange places with a strange language, strange food, strange customs, and sleeping or not sleeping in strange beds. As the tour goes on, fatigue builds up and the hours of sleep loss pile up. In the face of all this, to practice, rehearse, and play requires a high level of professionalism. The large majority of orchestra members, despite frequent personality quirks, are real professionals who have my sincere respect.

Now what I am going to do, as rapidly as possible, is describe the tours, city by city. I have, out of my own curiosity, hundreds of pages of notes covering personal, social, and medical incidents. First, let's note some numbers. In the 1980 New York Philharmonic European tour there were nineteen concerts and six rehearsals in thirteen cities in twenty-eight days. This is a built-in stress and fatigue situation, almost as if it had been designed for an experimental study. Here are some of my observations from New York to Edinburgh. The orchestra is dull, suffering from jetlag. In Lucerne we climbed Mt. Pilatus. I have a picture of Henry Fogel, the orchestra manager, feeding a pigeon and the pigeon is facing away. I used the photograph as a metaphor for orchestral management. In Salzburg I made my first deal with the orchestra: I won't tell them musician jokes if they won't tell me doctor jokes. Oslo and Stockholm were lovely. In Oslo a musician on anticoagulant therapy, Coumadin, developed hematomas (these are black and blue lesions due to bleeding under the skin) — *my* observation, *his* confession. You see, musicians tend to conceal their health problems and self-medicate. Fear should be discussed. With blood tests in Oslo, and later in Bonn, the Coumadin problem is brought under control. After Oslo, West Berlin, where for personal reasons the orchestra musicians wanted to sound especially good, the concert was absolutely amazing. The hands of one player are a mess from banging them against the walls of his room because, among other things, he feels he is not playing well. He is afraid, therefore, that he may not remain with the orchesatra. Incidently, he still is with the orchestra. He has had past psychiatric care, though he has hidden the fact. It takes five harrowing days to convince him that he is not letting the orchestra down by going home. In Bonn, one of three pregnant string players develops vaginal spotting and cramps. There is a question of a threatened abortion, and she is sent home. The first day in Vienna I have my one and only experience with a malingerer. On the second day an orchestra member falls, sustaining a gaping laceration over the right supraorbital area. Three sutures are needed and applied. On the third day Zubin throws a party. I drink too much new wine and become a patient. On the fourth day a very interesting thing occurred. A composer whose music is being played by the orchestra comes to me with conjunctivitis. He stays for an hour and a half; he talks, I listen. The essence of what he has to say is about his anxiety that his music, which he has worked so hard to write, will not be interpreted properly by the orchestra. Then Brussels and Paris. In Paris a freak accident occurs when a violinist ruptures the distal head of the biceps of his right arm. The muscle is completely avulsed from its insertion. He is flown home on the Concorde for orthopedic care. Incidently, the orthopedist at that time had the choice of either reattaching the muscle to the bone or letting it alone. Reattaching it meant that the violinist would remain in a splint for six weeks. Since he was in his sixties, the orthopedist decided not to operate, thinking that he would have more function with his disability than if the joint tightened, as it might after six weeks in a splint. The orthopedists we use are the so-called non-operating ones. Finally, in London, I removed the Vienna sutures with good cosmetic result, much to my surprise, because after four corneal transplants my sight is not that good, and I am not a surgeon. That night, in the absence of royalty, I sneaked into the Royal Box to listen to the concert. At the end of the concert, Zubin, pointing to the box, dedicates an encore to the young lady seated next to me. It is Jacqueline du Pre, in a wheelchair. She has been diagnosed with multiple sclerosis, which is very sad.

I will skip the Mexican tour and go on to the 1982 South American tour; seven cities, sixteen concerts, and five rehearsals in three weeks. In Caracas a lady guest is mugged. In Rio de Janiero two oboists are knocked out by diarrhea; it was the cold asparagus soup. Our English horn plays the oboe. In São Paulo twelve musicians are mugged, one seriously. A violinist writhes with severe pain. She is taken to an orthopedic clinic where a very sophisticated orthopedist, speaking only Portuguese, does a lovely job. In Montevideo and Buenos Aires there is no significant, reportable incident. The first day in Santiago a splint is removed and the wrist functions fine. In the afternoon, a musician develops an acute renal stone and is hospitalized. Fortunately, the stone is passed the next day, and he continues the tour. We finally reach Quito, where everyone gets sick. The city is 13,500 feet above sea level. There is oxygen which the stage hands have brought along, and there is also oxygen in the theater. The hall is a converted movie theater with acoustics that are very flat and dry. The locals forget to build a shell, which makes the acoustics only that much worse. Our concertmaster plays a violin concerto. He has diarrhea, is short of breath, and has a runny nose and cough. Still, he plays beautifully.

Lastly I'll briefly discuss the National Symphony 1984 South American tour; three cities, seven concerts, three rehearsals in eleven days. Only three muggings occur in Sao Paulo this time. In Montevideo one violinist is sent home with thrombophlebitis, a condition which he has hidden from me for days. Also, an alcoholic decompensates, requiring supportive therapy. In Buenos Aires all goes well. The acoustics in the Teatro de Cologn are superb, and the orchestra plays at its best. Finally we have a farewell party at the American embassy.

Some short observations. Orchestral musicians are not an especially happy lot. I would guess that the string players are the unhappiest. A form of depersonalization takes place. Their contract stipulates that everyone dress alike. They play music frequently not of their choosing or interpretation. Mostly they sit in their chairs, at attention, prepared to enter on cue, on pitch, and on time. They are, as they say, prisoners of the downbeat. As one player put it, "I come to the hall to play their music, then I go home and play my own."

Freeman: Homer and his odyssey had nothing on Leonard Essman.

Wilbur Gould is a renowned otolaryngologist practicing in New York. He has long experience in the treatment of vocal problems of actors, singers, and public speakers, and has authored many papers on the subject of clinical voice and respiratory function. He is a founding organizer of the Juilliard symposia on Care of the Professional Voice, now in its twelfth year, the director of the Recording and Research Center of the Denver Center for the Performing Arts, founder and chairman of the board of the Voice Foundation, and director of the Vocal Dynamics Laboratory at Lennox Hill Hospital in New York City.

Gould: I am delighted by what so many speakers have already said, that a combined approach to care of patients, a team approach, is needed. It is not an individual matter. It is not only a laryngologist looking at the vocal cords saying, "Um, it looks like X." It is the entire Gestalt of the matter which one must refer to, but I'll not belabor that any longer.

I became interested in voice some twenty-five or thirty years ago. I soon learned that the most difficult thing for me was to understand the human voice. It is one thing to say that you will treat the physical factors related to it, but quite another to try to understand why this or that happened to it. I felt that it was quite impossible to take care of people unless I had such an understanding. This led to the establishment of a laboratory based on a cooperative team of specialists at Lennox-Hill Hospital in New York. This laboratory, as well as our group here at the Denver Center for the Performing Arts and the Voice Foundation at Juilliard, is a cooperative effort, a team operation.

At the Denver Center we have a rather unique situation in that we have developed a voice research laboratory which was set up with the help of Dr. Jafek, Dr. Wood, and Dr. Blager. It has proven to be an enormous asset in helping us to understand what happens to a professional as he or she goes through various aspects of their vocal work. The laboratory includes an excellent recording area. Here we put vocalists through actual workaday circumstances, allowing us to study, for example, vocal fatigue. This type of study requires a team of professionals including, among others, a voice therapist, an acoustic scientist, a laryngologist, and psychologist. We want to know why a performer has a painful throat after performing. We want to know why some performers get tired to the point of not being able to complete an effort. We want to know why a singer gets a backache after prolonged singing. These are difficult questions which we hope to be able to answer.

Another project of ours is the enhancement of the professional voice. We know that selected aspects of recording production yield better vocal results than others. In the recording area our staff includes a recording engineer, a psycholinguist, and a psychoacoustician. We do not mind using audio technology in a way which makes a mediocre singer sound like Caruso.

We are also interested in medications regarding the larynx. One significant problem is the mucus that builds up and adheres to the vocal folds, a particular nuisance for a professional performer. There are medicines by the dozen to relieve this problem, organidins, entaxins, and potassium products. They are all mucolytic agents, but not very efficient. We are now doing studies on the surface mechanics of the vocal folds. This type of work requires a very advanced scientific methodology.

Another interest of ours is the study of what happens to the voice when beta-blockers are used. Here our focus is on the analysis of acoustic data. That is, we try to understand what happens to the quality of the voice by using objective measurements. On a problem such as this we would like very much to work with other experts, such as Dr. Brantigan, for example.

The major thing we do, then, is attempt to bring quality information to the professional voice user. We have set up a program called Glimpes, a name that derives from glottal imaging, as opposed to the more common spelling. This program is a net work of laboratories around the United States that have the capability of analyzing particular types of data. A laboratory which, for example, is not fully equipped, might send their data to another facility for analysis and interpretation. This network also serves as a repository for particular types of information.

Clearly, we can not take care of people properly without a better understanding of the problems involved. It is our goal to be able to develop some of that kind of information.

Freeman: Thank you very much, Dr. Gould. Those of you who have not yet seen that facilities of which Dr. Gould spoke are earnestly entreated to visit them. The facilities are most impressive.

Gerald Shapiro received his doctorate from Tufts University College of Dentistry. He has practiced dentistry for forty-five years, with special interest in oral surgery and periodontics. He is a former Associate Chief of Staff at Greenpoint Hospital in Brooklyn, and is a fellow of the International College of Anesthesia. Dr. Shapiro has lectured throughout the United States, and in China has organized dental teaching tours involving five dental schools of the People's Republic.

Shapiro: All musicians, not just singers and wind players, must protect their oral health to function as good musicians. Breathing and swallowing are important in the playing of wind instruments. These functions are influenced by the manner in which the lower jaw is braced during the approximately six hundred to two thousand times a day we swallow. Malocclusion or the absence of teeth influence the tongue, the proper use of which is so important to the subtle nuances of air flow control. Prospects for ultimate victory over cavities, leading to the retaining of natural dentition, is now possible with flouride therapy, pit and fissure sealants, home care, and even immunization with vaccines. Much attention is now on periodontal disease, where we see progress. True, in later life teeth may drift, or even be lost. We can, however, control the drifting and replace the teeth without impinging on the arch form or the freeway space, that two to three millimeter opening between the upper and lower teeth which is necessary room for the tongue, and needed to play or sing fine music. Portere of London says it best: "Other than wind instrument players, it would be difficult to find such a large number of potential patients who put their mouth, lips, jaws, teeth, tongues, and faces to a use which is so different from the normal functions of eating, speaking, and expression."

Some things that may happen in eating and speaking may not matter very much. But it matters very much indeed what sound a musician produces. Even total loss of teeth, formerly the death knell for the professional wind player, need not now cause panic. Complete denture replacements can be made, which in most cases, will function perfectly well. Where not adequate, special performance dentures to be used only during performance can be fabricated, ensuring confidence in the wearer.

Here I should mention the latest technique of ridge augmentation by hypoxy appetites, bone grafting, and metal implants. A metal post implant procedure in the proper and carefully selected patient allows for the replacement denture to be snapped into place and firmly secured. The American Dental Association has lately changed its characterization of this procedure from experimental to safe and effective.

In the violin and viola player we see symptoms of temporomandibular joint dysfunction that far exceed a random sampling of the general population. This condition produces pain and tenderness in front of the ear, headache, noise or clicking on opening or closing the mouth, and limited or irregular jaw movements. Latest studies support the notion that tension and stress are the primary causes. The treatment varies from radical surgical and prosthetic procedures, which are seldom necessary, to the more passive relief of stress and tension. Most treatments are multidisciplinary, with bite guards and relaxation splints having been found useful.

Freeman: Thank you very much, Dr. Shapiro.

Ivan Shulman, a fellow of the American College of Surgery, is the son of a musician. He has been the tour physician for the Los Angeles Philharmonic since 1981, having traveled with that orchestra to Mexico, Japan, Korea, and Europe. During these trips he has occasionally been called upon to play extra oboe with the orchestra. It is from this unique perspective that he has developed his interest and expertise in the medical problems of performing artists. A long time student at Aspen, Dr. Shulman participated in the first Conference on the Medical Problems of Musicians held there last summer. He is currently the president of the Los Angeles Doctors Symphony Orchestra.

Shulman: One of the pleasures for me in attending this conference was to meet Leonard Essman and to compare notes on our various experiences as tour physicians for major symphony orchestras. I think it is an unusual experience for us to be with each other today, both musicians and physicians, to have the experience of being with those who are interested in the medical problems of musicians. When working in this area, you can feel like an island in the sea, completely isolated. You may not know what other people are doing. One of the great benefits of a conference like this is to be able to share the knowledge and experiences that people on this panel and in the audience bring.

In a sense, I am speaking to the converted. The people here today are sincerely interested in the problems of musicians. Those of you who are musicians are obviously interested in being able to communicate better to physicians about the problems we both face. I have a real concern about the ability of musicians to find qualified physicians and other medical personnel in the community who are interested and able to care for the problems of musicians.

We all know that the many thousands of music students nationally are not going to be able to make a living as professional musicians. Perhaps some of them might be redirected into the medical field. We would do well to welcome them. I know several people, both here in the audience and elsewhere, who have made that kind of transition, and have made terrific doctors.

Musicians, too, need to understand better the difficulties that are related to the treatment of their problems. Dr. Brantigan's point about taking beta-blockers is well taken. Musicians must not be trapped into seeking only the quick fix. They need to pursue the matter of anxiety in a logical and comprehensive way, and not be satisfied with pill-popping as the ultimate solution. Physicians need to follow through in this process of education. Musicians must learn to understand that medicine contains large grey areas, that it is full of tentative and uncertain responses. This requires tolerance, both by the patient and the physician.

I would suggest to medical school educators and administrators that they try to identify students, interns, and residents in their programs who have musical interests. They should seek to encourage those people to continue their interests throughout their training. I think it very, very important that they be encouraged to perform, to attend concerts, and to generally be active participants in music. It may take some personal adjustment for the medical educator and administrator to do this; however, as one who has been there, I think it is fair to say that in the long term the results will be very satisfying and productive.

Freeman: Thank you, Dr. Shulman. It has always seemed to me that the efficacy of our primary and secondary music school programs could be measured by the degree to which people who play the oboe or violin in their teens continue to support various musical enterprises, purchase recordings or attend concerts, or support the National Endowment throughout their life. If that does not happen, the fault then lies at our door as music educators and directors of music schools. I would also like to say, especially to my fellow music school directors across the country, that anything they can do to encourage students with the view that you have put forward, that it is possible to live happily in a professional area without a career in music, would help us very much.

Frederick Tims received his bachelor degree at Hendricks College in Arizona and his doctorate in music education at the University of Kansas. He is currently the Coordinator of Music Therapy programs at Colorado State University. A member of the advisory council of the Association of Professional

Music Therapists in Great Britain, Dr. Tims is the immediate past president of the National Association for Music Therapy.

Tims: As we have all been stimulated by this conference during the past few days, a thought occurred to me. What if a newspaper reporter entered the conference and listened to the proceedings? Might we not read in tomorrow's paper that making music is very bad for one's health, and perhaps an activity which humans should avoid. While we all understand this perception and are very concerned with the problems of musicians, I would like to take a slightly different approach, looking at some aspects of music making that are actually quite good for one's health. If we take the view that illness is probably caused by a lack of integration, as do classic Chinese medicine and Hippocratic medicine, we then see illness as a consequence of imbalance and disharmony. The converse is that wellness is achieved when we are in synchrony with ourselves physically, mentally, and spiritually, as well as being in rhythm with our surrounding world.

I want to present to you an example of music doing just this, music at once illustrating disharmony in someone's life and also the integration which comes with healing and wellness. You will see a tape of a twenty-one year old patient in a German hospital with a diagnosis of multiple sclerosis. At times the symptoms were in remission, at other times she had powerful symptoms requiring hospitalization. (Tape plays). Here you see her where symptoms of the disease are predominant. This is her first experience with music therapy, the first time we have ever met. She has absolutely no musical training. I sit down at the piano and explain to her that there are various instruments around the room, and say only, "Let's make music." Here are the results of that. I want you to listen for the disharmony and then finally some of the integration.

After this session the patient, who had not slept for four days, slept for eleven hours straight and, I think, the healing process began. At the next session we explored the difference between her quiet side in music and the side you heard on the tape. She said she had never realized this before. After the third and final session she announced that she was packing her bags and leaving the hospital. An anecdotal story which perhaps shows some of the power in music for wellness.

Freeman: Thank you very much, Dr. Tims.

We have some specific comments and questions from the audience. I'd like to invite Dr. Kasha to make some brief comments about vitamin B$_6$ deficiency. Dr. Kasha.

Kasha: Last summer a dramatic announcement was made of a new, high toxicity of vitamin B6. It was found that athletes and others were zonking themselves with 2,000-6,000 milligrams per day. The only penalty was numbness of the hands and extremities. I am surprised the penalty was so light. Warnings were published in the *New England Journal of Medicine* and word was spread through the Albert Einstein School of Medicine that it was dangerous to take vitamin B6 is such quantities. They also warned that all use of vitamin B6 should be restrained as a dietary supplement. That warning has been widely disseminated through the news media, newspapers, neurologic journals, medical journals, and even chemical journals. The danger is this: the Federal Food and Drug Administration (FDA) recommended allowance of vitamin B6 is 2 mg. per day. Most vitamin B6 complex formulations abide by this guideline. Most people taking a vitamin supplement think they are getting adequate amounts of the vitamin. As it turns out, B6 is one vitamin the body does not store. The actual body needs are more than previously thought necessary, especially for people over the age of thirty.

Carl Volker's group at the Institute of Biomedical Research in Austin, Texas has been looking at this problem for some ten years. They have published twenty-five research papers, most of them in the *Proceedings of the National Academy of Sciences*. These very competent biophysical and biomedical studies include double blind experiments and large samplings of people of all ages. Their findings are quite remarkable. Ninety-five percent of all their subjects were found to be deficient in vitamin B6; sixty- five percent were subclinically ill with stiffnesses of all kinds, including neuroarthritic maladies in up to thirty percent of the pathologic cases, carpal tunnel syndrome, neuropathies, and so forth.

The researchers found that this deficiency can be diagnosed using a blood test, and that this technique is highly reliable. Moreover, they found that for subclinical manifestations, 50 mg. per day completely removed the symptoms in approximately twelve weeks. A slightly longer period of time was required for carpal tunnel syndrome. This is a very noteworthy advance in medical knowledge. It means that musicians, and all people whose skills depend on very precise use of their upper extremities, can find relief from many forms of stiffness. It also points out that most of the population is taking subuseful amounts. I think it would be extremely interesting to take a sampling of piano students, test their dexterity, find out what their B6 level is, and after some twelve, twenty-four, and fifty-two weeks of treatment measure their piano technique improvement.

Freeman: Dr. Schneck has a response.

Schneck: It is difficult to believe that ninety-five per cent of the human population has been, for generations and generations, deficient in vitamin B6. I am familiar with the work you cited, and have treated patients with carpal tunnel syndrome with 100-200 mg. of vitamin B6 per day as recommended for twelve weeks, and have had absolute failure.

Essman: I would like to speak to a different aspect of this discussion. There is a segment of musicians, and also younger people, who feel that if something is good for you, more is better. I admitted a female marathon runner, about twenty years old, with nausea, vomiting, diarrhea, and some fortunately transient liver disease, who was taking eighteen megavitamin pills per day in preparation for her race. Fortunately, deprived of the extra vitamins, her problems totally cleared in two weeks.

This pertains not only to vitamins, but in some respects to the taking of propranolol. There are patients who ought not take these drugs. Nevertheless, too many musicians and music students, and too many medical students, do not consult with their physician about them. Asthmatics and people with rapid heart action should not take propranolol. It and similar drugs are not a panacea. We should not leave this conference thinking otherwise, be it about propranolol, or any other medication that becomes a fad, its benefits notwithstanding. We need to face the fact that musicians self-medicate because they are afraid to admit their illness, afraid to lose their jobs. The management of orchestras should be more sensitive to these problems, and encourage musicians to admit to their illnesses. This needs to be emphasized.

Freeman: I think Dr. Brantigan has a response about propranolol.

Brantigan: I'd like to emphasize some of the points Dr. Essman has made, and perhaps clarify some of the points I have already made. Propranolol, or Inderal, one of the beta-blocking drugs, has become one of the most widely abused substances among musicians in the United States. Unfortunately, much of that abuse is due to the misapplication of the research that has been done by my brother and myself, and the work of Dr. James in London. I think it is important to realize that it is not a panacea. The idea of taking a pill just so you can get up on stage to do your job is incredible. Such an anxiety is something that is best addressed by using longstanding psychiatric or psychologic techniques to solve the basic problem. The solution to your or the world's problems does not come out of a bottle. Beta-blocking drugs are potent drugs with strong cardiovascular effects. They should not be used without supervision. I cannot emphasize that point enough. In all our publications on the subject, both in lay journals and medical journals we have emphasized that point. The value of beta-blocking drugs is to intervene in an isolated crisis of severe stress. Perhaps its most useful application is as an adjunct to a more definitive treatment using some other techniques to eliminate the basic and fundamental problem. I think Dr. Essman and I are in agreement on that.

Freeman: And certainly under a physician's supervision.

Brantigan: Absolutely. This business of passing drugs from musician to musician, particularly drugs as potent as beta-blockers, is to be condemned. Some serious problems are going to come from that.

Essman: It should be mentioned that any physician who uses it is using a drug not approved by the FDA, and is therefore subject to great liability in case of a problem.

Brantigan: I'm certainly not a lawyer, but I would question the business of liability. Many drugs in this country are used for purposes not approved by the FDA. Certainly there is a wide body of experimental evidence, which has been confirmed by several different investigators, supporting the use of this drug in these circumstances.

Essman: Could someone talk about drug interactions, like the use of Inderal and marijuana and other substances that are frequently abused?

Shulman: I'd like briefly to address this. We know that drugs are being used in the Los Angeles Philharmonic. I know of no hard drug usage, but certainly beta-blockers are commonly used, Afrin is abused, and marijuana is used on tour and at home. I think the most important thing to keep in mind is that we are not going to modify these behaviors unless they are addressed in a major way with, as Dr. Brantigan suggests, psychotherapeutic intervention.

Brantigan: I'd like to go one step further. When our work was first published, there was considerable skepticism among members of the medical profession concerning the propriety of using such drugs for what, to physicians, was a trivial problem. To a physician, stage fright is a minor discomfort. To a performing artist it may be a severe disability. If a physician is going to treat a musician, or any patient for that matter, he must figure out just what the problem is with that patient, and how that problem relates to the patient's life style. Just because stage fright is seen as a minor disability to the physician does not mean that the disability is in fact minor. Musicians have specific problems, and need understanding doctors to elucidate for them what to do about them. There needs to be the open communication that Dr. Jafek spoke about.

Freeman: An additional word for the physicians is that some of the most famous concert artists, who have some of the highest fees, and who perform regularly in front of audiences all over the world, suffer most severely from the syndrome that we are speaking of.

I'd like now to move to a brief wrap-up by asking the question, is this conference based on an idea we should develop? Would you like to have further meetings in the future? What kinds of suggestions do you have for the 1980's and 1990's?

Brantigan: I think we are on the verge of something that is very exciting. Those of us who practice both music and medicine may have some understanding of the problems which beset professional musicians. Even so, we lack full understanding. I think there is a great role for cooperation in the future, and certainly some very exciting areas of potential research.

Shulman: I mentioned earlier this week that the Greeks had one god, Apollo, for music and medicine. I think that musicians and physicians have a great deal in common, and that is it good to talk about these matters.

Tims: As a musician, I would like to reinforce that comment.

Essman: In brief, I would like to see the diseases of musicians identified, codified, and indemnified, either under Workman's Compensation or other financial arrangements, so that the musician need not be frightened or financially concerned about seeking medical attention.

Gould: I think this conference carries on a tradition of improving relations between the patient and the physician. I think the Aspen conference has been beautifully demonstrative of this as well. We are seeing a trend toward better understanding of the problems of musicians.

RESEARCH GOALS AND METHODOLOGY
IN MUSIC PERFORMANCE

Moderator: George P. Moore
Professor of Biomedical Engineering
University of Southern California

Panelists

Robert Efron, M.D., Professor of Neurology, University of California at Davis School of Medicine, Davis, California

Tedd Judd, Ph.D., Neuropsychologist, Psychiatry and Behavioral Medicine, Pacific Medical Center, Seattle, Washington

Ronald Scherer, Ph.D., Research Scientist, Recording and Research Center, Denver Center for the Performing Arts, Denver, Colorado

Donald Shetler, Ph.D., Director of Graduate Research Studies in Music Education, Eastman School of Music, Rochester, New York

Christoph Wagner, M.D., Professor of Physiology of Music, Institut für Experimentelle Musikpadogogik, Hochschule für Musik und Theater, Hannover, West Germany

Moore: I'll say at the outset that it is probably impossible for us to reach any clear consensus about research goals and methodology if only because we represent so many different constituencies. We represent performers, teachers, therapists, medical people, basic scientists, quacks, and chronic malingerers. And that just describes the panel! Recognizing this lack of consensus, both in terms of esthetics and basic science, it will be our hope to share with you the reasons for it.

The first speaker is Ronald Scherer, a research scientist at the Recording and Research Center, Denver Center for the Performing Arts.

Scherer: Many of you may not be familiar with the goals and methods of research which apply to the professional voice. I would like to review some of these. I will point out that there are many parallels and overlaps between professional voice research and research in other artistic endeavors. The main objective in professional voice research, as in other areas discussed during this conference, is to understand, in utilitarian terms, how beauty and skill of performance is produced, perceived, and taught. In a sense, we seek to analyze artistry in order to enhance it. As has been said here many times, this research is not done except by teamwork. There is some solo research. Most research, however, is done in collaboration among voice scientists, voice teachers, voice coaches, speech pathologists, laryngologists, physiologists, engineers, and many more, depending on the focus and scope of the project.

It is important to point out that for over ten years voice professionals have been coming together to share their problems and concerns. This has been done under the auspices of the Voice Foundation in New York, headed by Dr. Wilbur Gould. People who attend continue to discover ways to share ideas and views, to share vocabulary and methods, and to learn from each other. This interaction removes barriers and increases the efficiency with which they care for their students and clients.

I'd like to indicate some of the goals that we have in the laboratory. One is to determine the relationships among the functional voice, the health of the voice, and the pedagogy of voice. In our area they are all interdependent; you cannot study one without studying the other. We wish to differentiate among the different levels of performance proficiency. This is a very important topic in our own lab. We also differentiate between proficiency, normal voice function, and pathologic function. Many of us believe that you cannot really look at one aspect of voice without having an appreciation for and a perspective about the entire spectrum of vocal function, including pathologic function.

Another goal we have is to devise efficient pedagogic and therapeutic techniques for diagnostics and monitoring. We see these as enhancing, not replacing, studio teaching techniques. We hope to develop comprehensive mathematic computer models of phonatory function based on accurate physical and physiologic theories and data. A problem which we hope to overcome is the clarification of pedagogic terms that have been in use for decades and centuries. Terms, such as breath support, need an operational definition, as does the whole idea of vocal registers (everyone uses register terms). Other terms we are interested in include ring of the voice, mass, tone focus, and placement. The many charms used to good advantage in the studio are not well understood, nor do they have common meaning from studio to studio.

The aspects of professional voice function we study include the neurophysiologic aspects of muscle control function, varying aspects of aerodynamics and biomechanics; acoustic and auditory processes; psychologic and perceptual phenomena; and perhaps more in our area, histrionics. We deal with a body that moves through physical space, and therefore are concerned with questions about the interdependencies of acting and singing.

I won't go into a great deal of methodology here. I would, however, like to mention that we use both humans and animals in our research. Human subjects are, of course, extremely important. But one cannot easily study subsystems in humans because the variables can't be controlled. As you might imagine, these variables are many. We use models of the human vocal system, including live animals such as dogs, monkeys, and bovines. From the animals we use excised larynges to study specific laryngeal phonatory mechanisms.

We also have inanimate models of the human vocal system. These models can have moving parts, like collapsible tubes to mimic the vocal folds. The models can be stationary, as with plexiglass models, to permit study of pressures and flow through systems that look like the airway. We have electrical, mathematic, and especially computer models of phonatory function. Computer models also allow for independent tests of isolated parts as well as facilitating the incorporation of inferences into hypotheses and the alteration of existing theory.

I would like to impress on everyone that singing and other professional voice usage is a very broad area of study, possibly broader than most people would have thought. It entails the entire body. The techniques that we use, the concerns that we have, parallel the study of the body in relation to all the instruments musicians play.

Moore: Our second speaker is Donald Shetler, Director of Graduate Research in Music Education at the Eastman School of Music.

Shetler: Most of our work as teachers, or teachers of teachers, therapists, and researchers in the area of music teaching and learning is done in an academic setting, a somewhat protected environment. Studies are often done as a master's thesis or doctoral dissertation to fulfill the degree requirements in music therapy, music education, or performance. Since the late 1960's, researchers have initiated studies of pedagogy and performance problems that cross the lines separating the traditional disciplines of psychology, neurophysiology, and other related fields. We've developed a serious interest in the central nervous system, psychoacoustics, and the topology and physiology of the ear.

In our current approach we are exploring the complex interactions that occur in learning: perception, concept integration, psychomotor development, and affective or esthetic devlopment are major interests. Since 1975, hemispheric laterality has attracted a good deal of attention.

Allow me to cite a few studies that represent baby steps moving in the direction that others here have suggested. Jane Van Middlesworth, in 1975, working with Dr. Albert Craig of the University of Rochester Medical School, studied breathing by the wind instrument player. In a parametric study she found no difference in the vital lung capacities of wind and nonwind players. She could find no basis for the claim that physical exercise can increase lung capacity in wind players. Though the average male wind player had greater lung capacity than the average female wind player, there appears to be no relation to breath requirements for playing the instrument. This contradicts the reasoning of some teachers who discourage women from pursuing careers as wind instrument players on the basis of their lesser lung capacities.

David Fray, in his DMA dissertation, reviewed the literature on the physiology of string playing. His study is reviewed in *The American String Teacher*, but as far as I know has not been published in a journal of physiology. David found several studies from the United States and Europe that dealt with electromyography, vibrato (especially cello vibrato), and planned breathing, including string players. Some of you may know of Gerhard Mantell's principles of cello technique, published in German in 1972. Irving Phillips, a Ph.D. candidate in music education at Eastman, is studying the phenomenon of handedness as a variable in the development of music performance skills. He is consulting with Alfred Bolan and Sheldon Wagner, both clinical psychologists at the University of Rochester.

Timothy Seiss recently studied performance anxiety, specifically analyzing the results of a series of desensitization sessions on anxiety reduction in trombonists; this appears to be a very sound study.

My own studies of gifted children have led to a longitudinal case study of youngsters who are exposed to their first musical stimulation in utero, beginning near the end of the mother's first trimester of pregnancy. This work is, if you'll pardon the expression, in its infancy. Consultations with several fine medical colleagues at the Center for Brain Research in Cognitive Studies are proving most helpful.

Finally, I believe that experimental studies and longitudinal protocols involving musicians and medical professionals hold enormous promise. If music is a living art, and if your life and mine are more complete because of our musical experiences, this type of work, and the work started here at this conference, is of immense importance to us all.

Moore: Our last preliminary speaker is Tedd Judd, a neuropsychologist in the Department of Psychiatry and Behavioral Medicine at the Pacific Medical Center in Seattle, WA.

Judd: I would be very disappointed if the musicians and music educators left here saying to themselves, "Gee, those scientists have a lot to offer us, research that they can do for us." I'd be disappointed because I think one of the things this conference can do is to help musicians and music educators to start thinking scientifically, and possibly to start doing research. By this I don't necessarily mean that they find themselves a laboratory and computer and begin to turn out sophisticated studies. What I mean is that they ask questions and decide if those questions are answerable — to challenge the assumptions supporting what is being done and to find ways of testing those assumptions.

An example of what I'm talking about is Dr. Babbitt, who, working as a composer, has raised important questions about perceptual phenomena. He has not run fifty subjects through tests in order to publish the results in a journal. Dr. Babbitt goes to the computer and says, "I think I'll try to make a sound that sounds like this." A sound comes out, but it is not what he expected. Instead of feeling frustrated at having to modify his input and repeat his effort, he says, "What does that mean about the way we hear things?" From this he learns something. We can see in Babbitt's work the truth of Newton's principle that chance favors the prepared mind. This way of thinking can be an example for us all.

I urge musicans to think about their assumptions, to challenge those assumptions, to look systematically for answers to them. This does not require a great deal of research money. It does not necessarily take computers. If you wait for scientists to do the work, you may have a long wait.

Questions and Answers

Moore: I want to get some preliminary expression from the panel, so I'm going to ask this: suppose there is $100,000 out there waiting to be awarded for research. Bob Efron, what would you do?

Efron: I'd be terrified. Let me tell you why. Don Shetler was just talking about cross-fertilization. The whole essence of this conference is in the tradition of interdisciplinary stimulation and fertilization. I would just caution people thinking about such experiments to keep in mind that animal breeders have found that sometimes cross-fertilization yields cross *sterilization*; you can get a hybrid that is unable to breed.

I think that anyone giving $100,000 will want to see something. It seems to me that we should really be asking the question, "What is it that is important for musicians to find out about? What do they want to know more about?" I put it to you, are we really interested in the detailed biomechanics of the nervous action potentials while bowing a cello? Is this what this audience really wants to know? Would you put $100,000 into that? *Some* may want to; I'm not sure *I* would want to. In fact, I have problems with virtually every discipline represented here. I was introduced as an iconoclast. Maybe I'll act on that false identification by saying to whomever offers the $100,000, "Listen, maybe we ought to go back to the drawing board and think through the question of what we really most want to know about music." Do we really want to know mostly about about music performance, creativity, esthetics; what makes a beautiful sound? Do we want to get down to the reductionist's basis of what neurons are doing in the brain at different times? I'm not sure I know what the priorities are for people in music. I consider myself an interloper in their world and would, therefore, be very hesitant to recommend what to do with the $100,000. In essence, I'm passing on this point.

Moore: Don, what is your reply?

Shetler: We started this dialogue this morning at breakfast. It may or may not be much fun for you in the audience to listen to its continuation. The issue I raised of interdisciplinary work — cross-fertilization, if you will — was not intended to produce a nonreproducing animal. The position I expressed was that it would not have been possible for many fine musicians, doing short studies as part of their academic work, to do the studies *at all* absent assistance, understanding, guidance, and productive questioning from people in the biomedical sciences and, in some cases, the hard sciences. As an academic person I find that the constant buzz in my brain of questions without answers is a challenge. It is the challenge of learning for the sake of learning. If I am turned on, my students also may be turned on. I try to encourage people to regard failure as a productive act. Musicians are always terrified of failure. Researchers live with it, constantly. There is such as thing as successful failure, where the problem unsolved leads to another problem which may be solvable. We know so little about our art.

Moore: Dr. Wagner.

Wagner: I think $100,000 is a great deal of money. As to its use, I'm reminded of Aultmann's books, Trenden's too, published a half-century ago and now forgotten. I think there is too much that is forgotten. I would suggest that some institution continue this dialogue through the development of a journal. I am afraid that after a conference like this, everyone returns to their job and communication is shut off. Perhaps we could use this money to continue the dialogue. Especially the dialogue between musicians and scientists.

Unidentified speaker: The first thing I'd do would be to set up a board to administer the money. I wouldn't trust myself with that much money. In my application to the board, I would look to setting up a study which involves looking at a group of people. This group would include exceptionally talented people from a variety of musical backgrounds, including varying types of performers, composers, conductors, sound engineers, and others involved in the process of making music happen. I would also include people with particular kinds of brain damage, idiots savants, deaf musicians, and prodigies. The $100,000 could be used to develop the methodology for doing such a study. The study would not only look at musical abilities, but at other abilities as well. It would seek to obtain a thorough cognitive and psychologic profile and, ideally, be longitudinal. In other words, we'd start with the young and follow them through their development.

Unidentified speaker: Well, it is a difficult question. A number of things run through my mind. In the context of this conference, I think I might invest a small amout of the $100,000 into doing the following: I would choose three very bright, creative, college level music students who are interested in music performance, music science, and who have a flair for research. I would use the remainder of the $100,000 to cover the travel expenses for about twenty of the brightest, most creative people in the world, perhaps in the music world, who would train these students. They would teach them, raise their curiosity, encourage their questioning about all matters micro and macro, develop their fullest potential. With such an investment I would hope to come out with three more people who, in turn, would plant more seeds such as we are talking about at this conference.

Unidentified speaker: I'd like to answer the question and simultaneously respond to something that Ted (Judd) said, and to an earlier remark by Bob (Efron). When Bob talked about the danger of an interaction that would produce a paralysis, I think he made made an excellent point. In general, music theorists have not been given sufficient credit by the scientific community. Music theorists *do* think scientifically. I would encourage collaboration, for example, between music theorists and cognitive psychologists. I think these people share common insights.

Furthermore, I think there is a real problem about what constitutes an appropriate way to study musical perception. For example, there are studies which demonstrate that we are indeed sensitive to certain tonal rules. What do these studies really show? Do they show anything other than that we have learned certain rules and that we can repeat them back. Do they really demonstrate something universal about our capacity to process musical information? I think we need to be very careful interpreting experiments that purport to demonstrate how humans process musical information. Music theorists and composers are reluctant to accept ideas simply on the basis of traditional thinking, and their input would appear to be invaluable. They are more likely to encourage caution, replication, and experimental redesign when asking questions about innate human capacity for music.

Moore: What strikes me is that no one on the panel has indicated a clear future direction. I think this is not only an expression of the different constituencies that we represent, but also of the fact that we are talking about research in subjects that are very difficult and very embryonic. They are embryonic for the very reason that they are so difficult. We are talking about questions that are difficult to formulate within any of the parent disciplines on which these interdisciplinary studies are based. In part, I am surprised that from everything that has gone on in this conference, there is no clear cut consensus or any particularly informed optimism about how rapidly this field might progress. Therefore, we might be wise to use the $100,000 for training or, perhaps, give it back while we reconsider.

Efron: That would be an incredible strategy because you would become known as the only honest man in the world. If an idea ever did come, you would probably get a great deal more than $100,000.

Unidentified speaker: One of the issues raised this morning was the sometimes artificial chasm that exists between basic research and the kinds of research that tend to be characteristic of teacher training and educational research. The latter tends to be applied research. Maybe one of the panel members would like to speak to this. There is probably a good deal of necessary thinking about the role of basic research among people who are working on applied problems, and about applied research among those who deal with fundamental questions. It seems that some crossing of these paths should be possible.

Moore: I'm sure members of the audience have things to say which might be related to this issue. Maybe you would like to tell us what you think are the areas of research that need attention. Or maybe you would like to tell us about research you heard about that you didn't like, and what you thought might have been wrong with it.

Efron: Could I do that? I'm going to reopen just a bit of this morning's conversation. It began with a joke you have all heard many times before, one that has to be retold. It's the story of a drunk who has dropped his wallet and is hunting for it in the gutter. A man comes along and asks, "Can I help you?" "Yes," says the drunk, "I've dropped my wallet and am looking for it." The man says, "Where do you think you dropped it?" "Over there," says the drunk. "But why, then, are you looking for it over here?" "Because the light is better over here." This is a terribly old and worn joke; its applicability is as follows. One of the terrible risks in science is that the scientist becomes the most crass opportunist in the world. He discovers a technique and, having the tool, wants to use it to work on a problem. He has discovered the light, but the light is only shining over the area to which his tools apply. He starts working there. The question is, is that spot where the problem is? This morning we wondered how much of the research described during these past few days was research being conducted because people had the tools to work under a particular light; whether, that is, they were ignoring the real questions. Should we be looking at temporal pattern analysis in the nervous system or should we be trying to understand principles of esthetics? The danger I see in a great deal of basic research is not its lack of general relevance, but whether it is relevant to key issues in music. Is it relevant to ask why music is important to human beings? Is it relevant to ask why music should be taught to children? My own sense is that all of us, and I'm just as guilty as the next, are really describing what we found under our particular light. We may have lost track of what the real and most important issues should be. I may be wrong.

Moore: The accusation was, as unleashed this morning, directed at me. I happily plead guilty to the accusation. I'll tell you the reasons why. First of all, unlike the subject in the joke, we don't have a wallet that we are looking for. We don't know exactly what we are looking for. We are in a very murky area, where goals need to be defined. It isn't as if we are turning our backs on agreed upon goals and issues. We don't know what they are. Sometimes they are formulated in the most global and generally acceptable terms, like, for example: "Let's study the esthetics of music." That turns out to be, for all practical purposes, an unapproachable research goal. On the other hand, if you look under the light, whatever that is for you, and you know that there are wallets everywhere, because you are looking at absolutely virgin territory, then there isn't any place you can look and not make an exciting discovery.

Efron: But George, that is the Griffin shoe polish proposal. It's my favorite example. If you want to get a grant in neurobiology, you propose to inject brown Griffin shoe polish into the spinal fluid of animals and see what happens. The grounds for doing this experiment are: first, it never has been done before — you might find something interesting; second, you might find some chemical in Griffin shoe polish that might solve the problem of multiple sclerosis. You turn us loose, like the famous monkeys, and just maybe we'll type up some Shakespeare. As a strategy it seems highly dubious.

Unidentified speaker: One of the things that comes to mind is that perhaps this conference could try to define the goals that are within reasonable reach and that are meaningful to the people here, muscians and physicians.

Unidentified speaker: That's for next year.

Unidentified speaker: It never hurts to put the question into focus, even a year ahead of time. One might be able to sharpen the focus during the intervening twelve months. It is becoming apparent that basic science and psychology would have a great deal to offer to the art of teaching a musical instrument. You saw what could be done by understanding muscle physiology in performing on the cello. I think that kind of information would greatly facilitate cello instruction. In the clinical areas, we can learn how better to deal with anxiety and the pain experienced by music performers. I think that certain subsets of these could be defined. Then there are the broader issues of memory organization, perceptual understanding, and recognition. These are probably years away from having an impact on what is being taught to musicians.

Judd: During this entire conference I, as an amateur musician and clinical psychologist, have been thinking about how these two interests might interface. One of the questions I've heard asked at this conference is, what is music? It was interesting to me that no one raised this question until the conference was well under way. We need to define what music is. Also, we assume that music is somehow helpful, of benefit to humans, but we don't understand how. These are crucial questions. Another question to which I've heard no answer is, how can music be taught most effectively? There are considerations from my profession which relate to this question. For example, theories of communication, learning theories, theories of self-esteem, and the impact of needs assessment upon pedagogy.

One of the things I've been thinking about is a descriptive type of study that would query a large variety of people about some of the questions we've raised. The study would examine their responses for patterns. Out of that, perhaps, we might be able to tie some things together in a more integrated fashion.

Moore: There are many disciplines involved in this meeting. One that is not represented is the history of science. There might be some lessons to be learned from our historian friends, especially with respect to the emergence of a new discipline. I went through this in the field of biophysics when, about twenty five years ago, there were serious questions being raised as to whether the field actually existed, whether it should exist, and whether people should come together as biophysicists. Enough people were interested. They got together and decided they wanted to continue to meet. It seems to me that in this group meeting here in Denver, the motivation to create a discipline is not quite mature, although it is growing. You have to take this matter of an emerging discipline as an article of faith. If you say that there will be a new field which is at the interface of music and esthetics on the one hand and science on the other, with fairly well defined questions, I'm convinced that that discipline will emerge. When will we have these well defined questions? That I can't say. If we could somehow use that $100,000 to keep sufficient activity going as we move toward a point of clarifying the field, what its major questions are, then that would be, in my opinion, money well spent.

Unidentified speaker: Let me respond to that; it is such an important issue. To respond directly to the matter of the history of science, the issue that we are now addressing, I want you to think about the role that Galen, the Greek physician, played as perhaps the first music therapist. Both medical and musical considerations were involved in his work. Rosalie Pratt, at Brigham Young University in Provo, is working on a major paper with her son, a medical doctor, on the history of music in education. This paper should be out next year or the year following. Frederick Tims, a music therapist, and others in the field have found an entirely pragmatic and practical way to apply the knowledge we have about various systemic considerations of human behavior, including the application of music as curative or healing technique. It may be that the path we are seeking has already been blazed by the music therapists. There is, of course, some very spongy, exotic, and questionable thinking going on about music, music therapy, and human behavior. If we could just squash some of that, extinguish it, we might have made some head-way.

There are two or three other areas that have been touched on. Efron touched on them when he asked the global questions, "Why do we need music? Why is music a human consideration? What is music?" These are the questions which cause one to lose sleep at night. What about the crucial question of motivation? Why is it that a severely impaired person, blind, deaf, orthopedically ruined, can yet produce musical beauty? How does this happen? If you really want to get slippery, look at the issue of creativity and imagination. We also need to look at the sociologic considerations which derive from the few trying to preserve an elite art in the face of a popular culture that does not accept it. We need people who will pick up the torch. I'm delighted to see some of them at this meeting and on this panel.

Rudolf A. Pyka, M.D.: I think more research should be done in the biomechanical field. Look at the research going on in sports medicine. They are spending millions of dollars to find out how someone can jump one inch higher. So what? They spend millions of dollars to find out if a person can run .01 seconds faster. So what? It would be very interesting to use their methods on instrumentalists. I know from my experience in orthopedics that a great deal of everyday knowledge was gained from these studies; how we walk, how we stand, muscle function, and so on. I would wish we could apply this technology to the upper extremities, something which has not yet been done.

Moore: We also shared that view, so we looked at the sports medicine literature. We found that it is a popular myth, this belief that athletic movement could be analyzed in order to improve performance. It is a widely held belief that is, in fact, not true. There are simply no findings we can borrow from. We don't know how we stand, how we walk, and we certainly are in no position to tell someone how to broad jump. This is something that has been sold to the public as an achievement of sports medicine.

Unidentified speaker: Things have gotten better in the last fifty years, even without coaches.

Moore: I think coaches are indispensable to the improvement of performance. I said that computer analyses in biomechanics are not a principle component in the improvement of performance. It is a myth. Do we think that all we have to do is appropriate those biomechanic advances and apply them to the upper extremities of musicians? To do that is to buy into a fantasy, a myth. It is no more true than saying we understand the basic neurology or basic neurophysiology of *any* skilled movement, let alone the skilled movements of musicians.

Unidentified speaker: I agree totally, but we have to start somewhere.

Moore: Let's start with a confession. We in the basic sciences are at ground zero.

Unidentified speaker: All right. Let's start with something very practical. Just issue a statement identifying nonmusical exercises which help musicians keep their upper extremities in shape.

Efron: I am really quite amazed. There may be a sampling error here. I seem to detect that the majority of speakers from the audience want applied, "how to" engineering applications of science to their field. I'm quite startled. I thought you would not be interested in mechanical and reductionistic things, that you'd be interested in higher matters. What you seem to be saying, if true, is that you are most interested in how better to bow a string instrument; that you are interested in "how to" manuals. Can I get some better sense if that's what you are saying?

Unidentified speaker: I don't happen to agree with the idea that the study of our vocal folds is going to make us better singers. We need to know much more about physiology, about the likenesses of all the performing activities, whether they be in sports or the arts. How does this apply to the sciences? I think we can get somewhere because, for example, a dancer in second position plié has the same type of body stance in the torso that a good singer has just before singing. I think we can profitably look into things like this.

Unidentified speaker: What I'm interested in is not how to become a better musician or how to become a better person in medicine, but rather how to become a better person through music, through medicine. We need people who can ask the right questions. We need people who take a global view. We need the philosopher who begins to ask questions about the human predicament. We need to address the larger issues, to see our view of research in a larger context. We need people who can bring people together. The philosopher is that person. As someone once put it, the philosopher is the janitor of all the sciences. My plea is that we bring together theologians, philosophers, and others able to take a global view, to ask the question, how does this affect the world, how does this affect people? Then we can get at the problems which are most important in music.

Unidentified speaker: I think we really only have two basic research goals. One is to understand the human response to music. The other is to understand how humans produce music. Out of this can grow application. For those of us who are trying to be responsible music therapists, music educators, and music pedagogues, we ask for interdisciplinary help. Scientists need to look at our research to learn about some of the things we are trying to do. There are several of us who have traveled to Austria, three or four times, for the sole purpose of interdisciplinary discussions. We've come here for interdisciplinary discussions. We need to continue this type of dialogue because we know that if there are any answers, it will have to come through this type of exchange. These are very complex problems, with no easy answers.

Unidentified speaker: I want to join in this cry against reductionism. There are a few things we need to keep in mind. One is that we don't really need a lot of solutions to symptoms that affect only a very few. We still have the Horowitzs, the Sterns and the Rubinsteins. Our music schools do an outstanding job of developing good musicians. A second thing to remember is to guard against getting carried away with this whole issue. The Russian Kirov Ballet accepts only those children having certain physical proportions at age ten. Such restrictions preclude them from ever producing something like the Dance Company of Harlem, which accepts people of all types and sizes. By studying things too closely, we can give birth to the mule, to the sterilization spoken about earlier. We should not get too single-minded in our thinking.

Unidentified speaker: I'd like to add something on a much more simplistic and practical level, even, perhaps, on a selfish level. I'm a junior high school band director. I would very much like to be able to verbalize to the average taxpayer the benefits of music in a child's life. Not with a heavy emphasis on academic matters, but as a part of the human experience. Lorin Hollander gave a wonderful talk. It was very dynamic, he had a wonderful delivery and a great deal to say. It was, nonetheless, an emotional plea. When I speak to an engineer, I cannot speak in terms of the intangible. I would very much like to have something definite and tangible to say, and I'm looking to the scientists for help. PET scans seem to be edging us toward the time when we will be able to say, in a clinical sense, that this or that is what music really is and what it does for people. This is why humankind has music.

Unidentified speaker: I'd like to speak as a practicing pianist and, for most of my life, a practicing teacher. I'm asking whether it isn't possible to start, not from the bottom up, by putting together a multitude of small facts, but rather from the top down. That is one reason I'm so interested in brain research. I'm asking if it is possible to observe an instrumentalist over thousands of hours of practice, and to make a composite of all the things practiced, such as quality of sound, phrasing, rhythm, timing, sequencing, breathing, and so on, with the end in mind to develop a model of auditory imaging; something that gives us an image of all the actions that have been practiced related to a musical image of a piece to be performed.

Efron: I would venture to say, and I probably would not be contradicted by anyone in the house, that your question will not be answered in the next five hundred years.

Unidentified speaker: I would like to say something about creativity. I work in science, and am on the National Science Board. We spend enormous amounts of money on scientific research. We are presently preoccupied with pouring money into science education for students. As was stated earlier this week, there are twenty reports about deficiencies in the science education of American students. The most impressive words that I heard this week were at the end of Lorin Hollander's speech, when he stated, I think correctly, that art and music are the only test for creativity in children. In science, it takes many years of rigorous training before a scientist ever has the chance to be creative. A small fraction of scientists are truly creative. Whereas in the arts, which, I think are not so rigorously defined, we have a chance for creative expression at the earliest stages. I think that is where the great value to society is in art and music education.

Unidentified speaker: I'd like to comment on that. This is such a tender and touching issue for me. I hope that the educators here have read Elliot Eisner's book, *Cognition and Curriculum*, because it deals with the issue just raised. If we, as arts educators or esthetic educators, are to make a difference, we are going to have to put in some time on the task. Scientists are going to have to understand that that doesn't just happen, magically, in the school day. The people who are promoting computer literacy and science literacy have to realize the value of arts education. Arts education is fundamental to developing a creative view of the world, as well as to cognitive processing at the highest levels. We need some time in the school day schedule to teach this.

Unidentified speaker: I am a symphony musician. When I think of a physician, I think of someone who is going to make me feel better, or cure me of something. We have many problems among the players in symphonies. We go deaf from what we do. Our hands hurt. Brass players have hernias and bleeding hemorrhoids. There are all kinds of things we need answers to.

Before you run out and spend that $100,000, please give us a thought. We, too, need your help.

Efron: I was not making any moralistic judgments. I was merely saying that I was surprised because I came here thinking that the audience would be less application oriented than seems to be the case. I'm pro-medicine and pro-engineering. I grew up as a doctor. I gave it up in the Pleistocene or Cretaceous Period, but I am pro-medicine and I am also anti-hemorrhoids; I think they should be wiped out; I think we should mount a national campaign against them. I'm not belittling, in any sense whatsoever, the practical. All I was communicating was my own surprise at the strength of interest in this audience for practical matters. Perhaps I should not have been surprised. I do read the newspapers. I am aware of occupational diseases. These are very important and should not be belittled. They should be addressed.

The question was put to this panel, by the chairman, of what to do with $100,000 for an R&D effort. If I accept your terms, which I do, then I really have the same problem all over again. What is the critical issue? Should it be the hemorrhoids or the carpal tunnel syndrome? Not being a professional musician, I would like guidance in the matter of priorities.

In my own laboratory, as a result of the very theoretic work we are doing, it dimly crossed our minds, about three years after we had developed a fairly fullblown theory, that our findings might be applied to deafness. It might be applied to a conceptually new and different kind of hearing aid. It may turn out that we are wrong and full of nonsense. I was, nevertheless, embarrassed that there was a three year latency before the issue of practicality was considered.

Moore: I think it would be fair to say, then, that there are some relatively simple questions which are of interest to the audience. We can probably get some answers to them in the near future. There are also much more difficult questions which will take a great deal longer to work out. Then there are some very difficult global issues which seem to be of interest to more and more people. As we get closer to the universal questions of interest, I think we need to recognize that no philosopher will provide the answer, nor will any medical person provide the answer. If the ultimate question is, what is music?, we know that to be a question that will be asked forever, for which there never will be a final answer.

Epilogue 84/Prologue 87

Reflections on the 1984 Conference

APPLICATIONS OF RESEARCH TO PEDAGOGY

Elizabeth Jones
National Director of Instruction
Music Education Division
Yamaha Music Corporation, USA

I would like to begin by sharing with you my feelings about this conference. It has been a banquet of bewilderment, of a kind of enlightened bewilderment. Lewis Thomas has something to say about bewilderment. Let me recall some lines from his book, *Late Night Thoughts on Listening to Mahler's Ninth Symphony*. He writes, "Bewilderment is a view of the world shared by both scientists and humanists. Everyone knows this, but it is not much talked about. Bewilderment is kept hidden in the darkest closets of all our institutions of higher learning. Repressed, whenever it comes out into public view, sometimes glimpsed staring from attic windows, like a mad cousin of learning. It is the best kept family secret of 20th Century sciences and 20th Century arts and letters as well."

I like that statement very much. I was born and raised in a time and place of attics, spending many bewildering moments there. In addition, I've been a lifelong wanderer in a creative bewilderness, making my way, following my curiosities and those of others. The trail has led me to this conference, where I sit with many other self-confessed, mad cousins of learning.

When addressing the C.P. Snow two-culture controversy, Thomas writes, "Science and the humanities are all of a piece. One and the same kind of work for the human brain, done by launching guesses and finding evidence to back the guesses." That, it strikes me, is why we are here.

On to my thoughts on the biology of music making. These thoughts will be from the point of view of a somewhat zealous missionary. My business card reads, "National Director of Instruction for Yamaha Educational System." It does not capture the fervor and urgency I feel about my mission.

I find myself in a most unlikely setting to carry out my mission, an international business corporation named Nippon-Gakki, which in Japanese means music instrument company. This is a company which for twenty to thirty years has given over substantial amounts of money to find out how children learn music, and to discover how best to teach it to them. It is our hope that as children grow into adulthood, making music will be a natural function of living, that they will communicate through music activity of some type throughout life.

At this remarkable meeting of the mad cousins of learning, much time has been given to the damaging effects we now know can result from any number of physical, psychologic, mental, or social overuses and abuses in connection with musical performance. As a performer, I know the importance of remediating these problems. Remedies are badly needed, and in many cases long overdue. I am equally concerned with the prevention of such problems. We need to assure our gifted musicians that they will be able to have long and productive careers. It is they, after all, who bring us so closely in touch with our humanness.

It would be of great interest to me, as an educator involved in the field of early childhood, to know how much of the injury, illness, and anxiety experienced by performers might have been prevented if only the learning of music had flowed through natural processes beginning in early childhood. In all the music conferences I attend, going back to beginnings means going back to the child's first music lesson. No matter how much we learn about the advanced performer, if we don't also know how to excite and develop musical behaviors in our young, we may find ourselves with no future audiences for music.

If *only* those children capable of becoming Olympic athletes were allowed to run, swim, and turn somersaults, the world would surely come to a standstill. Clearly, no one would be equipped by experience to appreciate the superior skills of a champion. Exclusivity, where the many buy tickets to sit and hear the few do music, is wrong. I'm not proposing the discontinuance of concert giving. What I am suggesting can, in fact, broaden and enrich this aspect of music making. We need to be reminded that there is a whole world of music making beyond the spotlight and stage.

The crux of what I wish to express is my sense that the process of active participation in music should connect people to each other and themselves. Lorin Hollander's plea for research related to the intuitive aspects of music, the importance of music as a foundation of learning, his description of the harm done by the criticisms of others, their mindless judgments, and his admonitions about damaging rather than nurturing creativity, all reflect my own thoughts and, indeed, my all-too-poignant experiences in these matters.

To me, the biology of music making means giving outward musical expression to inner biologic processes. Each new life, when set in motion, is ready, within its own neurologic structure, to give evidence of the music of its own life. That is the kind of beginning I spoke about a moment ago.

Frank Wilson has said that we possess anatomic and physiologic attributes which constitute a musical birthright. For deep and lasting imprinting, it is easiest and most natural to claim that birthright early in life, learning the musical language right along with the spoken language. Young children should have the opportunity to hear and see music performed before they read and perform it, just as the spoken language is heard and spoken before it is read and written. Infants and children are endowed by nature with superb sensory capabilities which allow them to do this. They also possess an inner drive to learn. They have an unsurpassed ability to imitate. This formative period, from birth to about age six or seven, gives us several years to guide gently our children's development of their innate music capabilities.

By innate capabilities I mean such deeply rooted, unseen, and up to now, almost unmeasurable skills as aural receptivity, pattern storage, phrase sense, emotional and physical response, pitch discrimination and accuracy, feeling for intervals, word imagery, muscle memory, and a sense of harmony, among others. By the time children are well enough developed to begin the process of mastering a musical instrument, they ought to have sufficient musical preparation to allow them to concentrate on the technical and expressive capacities of that instrument.

The system I work with provides a gentle and sociable family initiation into the inner rewards of music. What we have learned through the Japanese experience and through our experiences at the research and development centers in La Miranda and Irvine, California, is that children of preschool age are gifted in the receptive skills of music. They quickly store up countless musical patterns, if given them in a manner which is sufficiently musical and appropriate to their development. The fine motor skills associated with technical skills at the keyboard are, however, much less well developed.

One of our objectives, as teachers of the primary music course, is to learn from our students and their/our music. In a sense, everyday is an experiment for us. How does one handle the asymmetry between physical and cognitive development, where muscle control lags behind receptive skills? The answer appears to lie in keeping the musical ear satisfied and improving, while providing proper training and allowing enough time for the muscles of the hand, fingers, and eyes to develop at their normal, slower pace.

From this you can correctly surmise that our course is not an instrument course. It is a fundamental music skills course. Essentially, what we do is guide the children to use and become familiar with their own strengths, their innate capabilities, especially their ability to hear and to imitate. We use the voice to train their slowly maturing music skills. We help them make musical connections, a process that depends on the successful convergence of several conditions. First, as a social condition, the learning must take place in a group. Moreover, the group must include the parents. The group develops into a music ensemble, and therein lies a power too complex to discuss at this time. Second, this may surprise some of you, we use fixed "do, re, mi" solfege and the keyboard as learning tools. We use electronic keyboards because of the ease of pressing on the keys and their ability to stay in tune. Finally, and this is a very difficult area, we require adult understanding of how children learn.

Let me mention that we have launched a system-wide project which addresses three major shortcomings adults have with understanding how children learn. First, they lack a basic insight into the differences between their own learning, which is based on logic, and that of the child, which is biologic. Second, adults show a lack of understanding about sensory motor development, particularly as related to music skills. Third, most adults do not understand the power that words have to either frustrate or facilitate body coordination in music. As a part of our effort to raise the level of understanding among parents, we have developed some rules for parents. These rules, in the form of three R's, apply to all parents while the classes are underway. First, respect the way the child is biologically compelled to learn. Second, respond to music for yourself, not for the child. Third, restrict adult chatter. The importance of these rules is, I believe, self evident.

I'm going to summarize, very quickly now, with a song. I cheated a bit by prerecording it last week. It was inspired by two lines from a poem by e.e. cummings having to do with attention to our inner perceptions:

> eye of my eyes open
> ear of my ears awake

I've used children in this song as a metaphor for human sensibility in its freshest form of biologic renewal. I'm also singing to the children within ourselves, because that is the only way we can activate our sensibilities on behalf of our children.

> Faces, faces, small and hopeful, every day of our lives.
> Trusting eyes aglow with wonder,
> Looking at us, waiting for us to see them, see them.
> Voices, voices, clear and joyful
> Every day of our lives.
> Ringing of voices alive with music,
> Joining with us, wanting for us to hear them, hear them.
> It takes such sensitivity to truly hear and truly see
> The magic messages for us
> On children's faces, in children's voices.
> Children, children, bright with promise
> Every day of our lives,
> Light us with your fires for learning,
> Teach us to teach you,
> Help us to reach you.